D0711261

NON SANZ DROICT.

William Shakespeare

The Tragedy of
OTHELLO
The Moor of Venice

Edited by Alvin Kernan

The Signet Classic Shakespeare
GENERAL EDITOR: SYLVAN BARNET

PUBLISHED BY THE NEW AMERICAN LIBRARY

COPYRIGHT © 1963 BY ALVIN KERNAN
COPYRIGHT © 1963 BY SYLVAN BARNET
ALL RIGHTS RESERVED

First Printing, May, 1963
Second Printing (Canada), May, 1963
Third Printing, November, 1964

SIGNET TRADEMARK REG. U.S. PAT. OFF. AND FOREIGN COUNTRIES
REGISTERED TRADEMARK—MARCA REGISTRADA
HECHO EN CHICAGO, U.S.A.

SIGNET CLASSICS *are published by*
The New American Library of World Literature, Inc.
501 Madison Avenue, New York, New York 10022

PRINTED IN THE UNITED STATES OF AMERICA

Contents

Shakespeare: Prefatory Remarks

Between the record of his baptism in Stratford on 26 April 1564 and the record of his burial in Stratford on 25 April 1616, some forty documents name Shakespeare, and many others name his parents, his children, and his grandchildren. More facts are known about William Shakespeare than about any other playwright of the period except Ben Jonson. The facts should, however, be distinguished from the legends. The latter, inevitably more engaging and better known, tell us that the Stratford boy killed a calf in high style, poached deer and rabbits, and was forced to flee to London, where he held horses outside a playhouse. These traditions are only traditions; they may be true, but no evidence supports them, and it is well to stick to the facts.

Mary Arden, the dramatist's mother, was the daughter of a substantial landowner; about 1557 she married John Shakespeare, who was a glovemaker and trader in various farm commodities. In 1557 John Shakespeare was a member of the Council (the governing body of Stratford), in 1558 a constable of the borough, in 1561 one of the two town chamberlains, in 1565 an alderman (entitling him to the appelation "Mr."), in 1568 high bailiff—the town's highest political office, equivalent to mayor. After 1577, for an unknown reason he drops out of local politics. The birthday of William Shakespeare, the eldest son of this locally prominent man, is unrecorded; but the Stratford parish register records that the infant was baptized on 26 April 1564. (It is quite possible that he was born on 23 April, but this date has probably been assigned by tradition because it is the date on which, fifty-two years later, he died.) The attendance records of the Stratford grammar school of the period are not extant, but it is reasonable to assume that the son of a local official attended the school and received substantial training in Latin. The masters of the school from Shakespeare's seventh to fifteenth years held Oxford degrees; the Elizabethan curriculum excluded mathematics and the natural sciences but taught a good deal of Latin rhetoric, logic, and literature. On 27 November 1582 a marriage license was issued to Shakespeare and Anne Hathaway, eight years his senior. The couple had a child in May, 1583. Perhaps the marriage was necessary, but perhaps the couple had earlier engaged in a formal "troth-plight," which would render their children legitimate even if no further ceremony were performed. In 1585 Anne Hathaway bore Shakespeare twins.

That Shakespeare was born is excellent; that he married and had children is pleasant; but that we know nothing about his departure from Stratford to London, or about the beginning of his theatrical career, is lamentable and must be admitted. We would gladly sacrifice details about his children's baptism for details about his earliest days on the stage. Perhaps the poaching episode is true (but it is first reported almost a century after Shakespeare's death), or perhaps he first left Stratford to be a schoolteacher, as another tradition holds; perhaps he was moved by

> Such wind as scatters young men through the world,
> To seek their fortunes further than at home
> Where small experience grows.

In 1592, thanks to the cantankerousness of Robert Greene, a rival playwright and a pamphleteer, we have our first reference, a snarling one, to Shakespeare as an actor and playwright. Greene warns those of his own educated friends who wrote for the theater against an actor who has presumed to turn playwright:

There is an upstart crow, beautified with our feathers, that with his *tiger's heart wrapped in a player's hide* supposes he is as well able to bombast out a blank verse as the best of you, and being an absolute Johannes-factotum is in his own conceit the only Shake-scene in a country.

The reference to the player, as well as the allusion to Aesop's crow (who strutted in borrowed plumage, as an actor struts in fine words not his own), makes it clear that by this date Shakespeare had both acted and written. That Shakespeare is meant is indicated not only by "Shake-scene" but by the parody of a line from one of Shakespeare's plays, *3 Henry VI:* "O, tiger's heart wrapped in a woman's hide." If Shakespeare in 1592 was prominent enough to be attacked by an envious dramatist, he probably had served an apprenticeship in the theater for at least a few years.

In any case, by 1592 Shakespeare had acted and written, and there are a number of subsequent references to him as an actor: documents indicate that in 1598 he is a "principal comedian," in 1603 a "principal tragedian," in 1608 he is one of the "men players." The profession of actor was not for a gentleman, and it occasionally drew the scorn of university men who resented writing speeches for persons less educated than themselves, but it was re-spectable enough: players, if prosperous, were in effect members of the bourgeoisie, and there is nothing to suggest that Stratford considered William Shakespeare less than a solid citizen. When, in 1596, the Shakespeares were granted a coat of arms, the grant was made to Shake-speare's father, but probably William Shakespeare (who next year bought the second-largest house in town) had arranged the matter on his own behalf. In subsequent transactions he is occasionally styled a gentleman.

Although in 1593 and 1594 Shakespeare published two narrative poems dedicated to the Earl of Southampton, *Venus and Adonis* and *The Rape of Lucrece,* and may well have written most or all of his sonnets in the middle nineties, Shakespeare's literary activity seems to have been almost entirely devoted to the theater. (It may be significant that the two narrative poems were written in years when the plague closed the theaters for several months.) In 1594 he was a charter member of a theatrical company called the Chamberlain's Men (which in 1603 changed its name to the King's Men); until he retired to Stratford (about 1611, apparently), he was with this remarkably stable company. From 1599 this company acted primarily at the Globe Theatre, in which Shakespeare held a one-tenth interest. Other Elizabethan dramatists are known to have acted, but no other is known also to have been entitled to a share in the profits of the playhouse.

Shakespeare's first eight published plays did not have his name on them, but this is not remarkable; the most popular play of the sixteenth century, Thomas Kyd's *The Spanish Tragedy,* went through many editions without naming Kyd, and Kyd's authorship is known only because a book on the profession of acting happens to quote (and attribute to Kyd) some lines on the interest of Roman emperors in the drama. What is remarkable is that after 1598 Shakespeare's name commonly appears on printed plays—some of which are not his. Another indication of his popularity comes from Francis Meres, author of *Palladis Tamia: Wit's Treasury* (1598): in this anthology of snippets accompanied by an essay on literature, many playwrights are mentioned, but Shakespeare's name occurs more often than any other, and Shakespeare is the only playwright whose plays are listed.

From his acting, playwriting, and share in a theater, Shakespeare seems to have made considerable money. He put it to work, making substantial investments in Stratford real estate. When he made his will (less than a month before he died), he sought to leave his property intact to his descendants. Of small bequests to relatives and to friends (including three actors, Richard Burbage, John Heminges, and Henry Condell), that to his wife of the second-best bed has provoked the most comment; perhaps it was the bed the couple had slept in, the best being reserved for visitors. In any case, had Shakespeare not excepted it, the bed would have gone (with the rest of his household possessions) to his daughter and her husband. On 25 April 1616 he was buried within the chancel of the church at Stratford. An unattractive monument to his memory, placed on a wall near the grave, says he died on 23 April. Over the grave itself are the lines, perhaps by Shakespeare, that (more than his literary fame) have kept his bones undisturbed in the crowded burial ground where old bones were often dislodged to make way for new:

> Good friend, for Jesus' sake forbear
> To dig the dust enclosèd here.
> Blessed by the man that spares these stones
> And cursed be he that moves my bones.

Thirty-seven plays, as well as some nondramatic poems, are held to constitute the Shakespeare canon. The dates of composition of most of the works are highly uncertain, but there is often evidence of a *terminus a quo* (starting point) and/or a *terminus ad quem* (terminal point) that provides a framework for intelligent guessing. For example, *Richard II* cannot be earlier than 1595, the publication date of some material to which it is indebted; *The Merchant of Venice* cannot be later than 1598, the year Francis Meres mentioned it. Sometimes arguments for a date hang on an alleged topical allusion, such as the lines about the unseasonable weather in *A Midsummer Night's Dream,* II.i.81–87, but such an allusion (if indeed it is an allusion) can be variously interpreted, and in any case there is always the possibility that a topical allusion was inserted during a revision, years after the composition of a play. Dates are often attributed on the basis of style, and although conjectures about style usually rest on other conjectures, sooner or later one must rely on one's literary sense. There is no real proof, for example, that *Othello* is not as early as *Romeo and Juliet,* but one feels *Othello* is later, and because the first record of its performance is 1604, one is glad enough to set its composition at that date and not push it back into Shakespeare's early years. The following chronology, then, is as much indebted to informed guesswork and sensitivity as it is to fact. The dates, necessarily imprecise, indicate something like a scholarly consensus.

PLAYS

1588–93	*The Comedy of Errors*
1588–94	*Love's Labor's Lost*
1590–91	*2 Henry VI*
1590–91	*3 Henry VI*
1591–92	*1 Henry VI*
1592–93	*Richard III*
1592–94	*Titus Andronicus*
1593–94	*The Taming of the Shrew*
1593–95	*The Two Gentlemen of Verona*
1594–96	*Romeo and Juliet*
1595	*Richard II*
1594–96	*A Midsummer Night's Dream*
1596–97	*King John*
1596–97	*The Merchant of Venice*
1597	*1 Henry IV*
1597–98	*2 Henry IV*
1598–1600	*Much Ado About Nothing*
1598–99	*Henry V*
1599	*Julius Caesar*
1599–1600	*As You Like It*
1599–1600	*Twelfth Night*
1600–01	*Hamlet*
1597–1601	*The Merry Wives of Windsor*
1601–02	*Troilus and Cressida*
1602–04	*All's Well That Ends Well*
1603–04	*Othello*
1604	*Measure for Measure*
1605–06	*King Lear*
1605–06	*Macbeth*
1606–07	*Antony and Cleopatra*
1605–08	*Timon of Athens*
1607–09	*Coriolanus*
1608–09	*Pericles*

1609–10	*Cymbeline*
1610–11	*The Winter's Tale*
1611–12	*The Tempest*
1612–13	*Henry VIII*

POEMS

1592	*Venus and Adonis*
1593–94	*The Rape of Lucrece*
1593–1600	*Sonnets*
1600–01	*The Phoenix and Turtle*

Shakespeare's Theater

In Shakespeare's infancy, Elizabethan actors performed wherever they could—in great halls, at court, in the courtyards of inns. The innyards must have made rather unsatisfactory theaters: on some days they were unavailable because carters bringing goods to London used them as depots; when available, they had to be rented from the innkeeper; perhaps most important, London inns were subject to the Common Council of London, which was not well disposed toward theatricals. In 1574 the Common Council required that plays and playing places in London be licensed. It asserted that

> sundry great disorders and inconveniences have been found to ensue to this city by the inordinate haunting of great multitudes of people, specially youth, to plays, interludes, and shows, namely occasion of frays and quarrels, evil practices of incontinency in great inns having chambers and secret places adjoining to their open stages and galleries,

and ordered that innkeepers who wished licenses to hold performances put up a bond and make contributions to the poor.

The requirement that plays and innyard theaters be licensed, along with the other drawbacks of playing at inns, probably drove James Burbage (a carpenter-turned-actor) to rent in 1576 a plot of land northeast of the city walls and to build here—on property outside the jurisdiction of the city—England's first permanent construction designed for plays. He called it simply the Theatre. About all that is known of its construction is that it was wood. It soon had imitators, the most famous being the Globe (1599), built across the Thames (again outside the city's jurisdiction), out of timbers of the Theatre, which had been dismantled when Burbage's lease ran out.

There are three important sources of information about the structure of Elizabethan playhouses—drawings, a contract, and stage directions in plays. Of drawings, only the so-called De Witt drawing (*c.* 1596) of the Swan—really a friend's copy of De Witt's drawing—is of much significance. It shows a building of three tiers, with a stage jutting from a wall into the yard or center of the building. The tiers are roofed, and part of the stage is covered by a roof that projects from the rear and is supported at its front on two posts, but the groundlings, who paid a penny to stand in front of the stage, were exposed to the sky. (Performances in such a playhouse were held only in the daytime; artificial illumination was not used.) At the rear of the stage are two doors; above the stage is a gallery. The second major source of information, the contract for the Fortune, specifies that although the Globe is to be the model, the Fortune is to be square, eighty feet outside and fifty-five inside. The stage is to be forty-three feet broad, and is to extend into the middle of the yard (i.e., it is twenty-seven and a half feet deep). For patrons willing to pay more than the general admission charged of the groundlings, there were to be three galleries provided with seats. From the third chief source, stage directions, one learns that entrance to the stage was by doors, presumably spaced widely apart at the rear ("Enter one citizen at one door, and another at the other"), and that in addition to the platform stage there was occasionally some sort of curtained booth or alcove allowing for "discovery" scenes, and some sort of playing space "aloft" or "above" to represent (for example) the top of a city's walls or a room above the street. Doubtless each theater had its own peculiarities, but perhaps we can talk about a "typical" Elizabethan theater if we realize that no theater need exactly have fit the description, just as no father is the typical father with 3.7 children. This hypothetical theater is wooden, round or polygonal (in *Henry V* Shakespeare calls it a "wooden *O*"), capable of holding some eight hundred spectators standing in the yard around the projecting elevated stage and some fifteen hundred additional spectators seated in the three roofed galleries. The stage, protected by a "shadow" or "heavens" or roof, is entered by two doors; behind the doors is the "tiring house" (attiring house, i.e., dressing room), and above the doors is some sort of gallery that may sometimes hold spectators but that can be used (for example) as the bedroom from which Romeo—according to a stage direction in one text—"goeth down." Some evidence suggests that a throne can be lowered onto the platform stage, perhaps from the "shadow"; certainly characters can descend from the stage through a trap or traps into the cellar or "hell." Sometimes this space beneath the platform accommodates a sound-effects man or musician (in *Antony and Cleopatra* "music of the hautboys is under the stage") or an actor (in *Hamlet* the "Ghost cries under the stage"). Most characters simply walk on and off, but because there is no curtain in front of the platform, corpses will have to be carried off (Hamlet must lug Polonius' guts into the neighbor room) or will have to fall at the rear, where the curtain on the alcove or booth can be drawn to conceal them.

Such may have been the so-called "public theater." Another kind of theater, called the "private theater" because its much greater admission charge limited its audience to the wealthy or the prodigal, must be briefly mentioned. The private theater was basically a large room, entirely roofed, and therefore artificially illuminated, with a stage at one end. In 1576 one such theater was established in Blackfriars, a Dominican priory in London that had been suppressed in 1538 and confiscated by the Crown and thus was not under the city's jurisdiction. All the actors in the Blackfriars theater were boys about eight to thirteen years old (in the public theaters similar boys played female parts, but a boy Lady Macbeth played to a man Macbeth). This private theater had a precarious existence, and ceased operations in 1584. In 1596 James Burbage, who had already made theatrical history by building the Theatre, began to construct a second Blackfriars theater. He died in 1597, and for several years this second Blackfriars theater was used by a troupe of boys, but in 1608 two of Burbage's sons and five other actors (including Shakespeare) became joint operators of the theater, using it in the winter when the open-air Globe was unsuitable. Perhaps such a smaller theater, roofed, artificially illuminated, and with a tradition of a courtly audience, exerted an influence on Shakespeare's late plays.

Performances in the private theaters may well have had intermissions during which music was played, but in the public theaters the action was probably uninterrupted, flowing from scene to scene almost without a break. Actors would enter, speak, exit, and others would immediately enter and establish (if necessary) the new locale by a few properties and by words and gestures. Here are some samples of Shakespeare's scene painting:

> This is Illyria, lady.
>
> Well, this is the Forest of Arden.
>
> This castle hath a pleasant seat; the air
> Nimbly and sweetly recommends itself
> Unto our gentle senses.

On the other hand, it is a mistake to conceive of the Elizabethan stage as bare. Although Shakespeare's Chorus in *Henry V* calls the stage an "unworthy scaffold" and urges the spectators to "eke out our performance with your mind," there was considerable spectacle. The last act of *Macbeth*, for example, has five stage directions calling for "drum and colors," and another sort of appeal to the eye is indicated by the stage direction "Enter Macduff, with Macbeth's head." Some scenery and properties may have been substantial; doubtless a throne was used, and in one play of the period we encounter this direction: "Hector takes up a great piece of rock and casts at Ajax, who tears up a young tree by the roots and assails Hector." The matter is of some importance, and will be glanced at again in the next section.

The Texts of Shakespeare

Though eighteen of his plays were published during his lifetime, Shakespeare seems never to have supervised their publication. There is nothing unusual here; when a playwright sold a play to a theatrical company, he surrendered his ownership of it. Normally a company would not publish the play, because to publish it meant to allow competitors to acquire the piece. Some plays, however, did get published: apparently treacherous actors sometimes pieced together a play for a publisher, sometimes a company in need of money sold a play, and sometimes a company allowed a play to be published that no longer drew audiences. That Shakespeare did not concern himself with publication, then, is scarcely remarkable; of his contemporaries only Ben Jonson carefully supervised the publication of his own plays. In 1623, seven years after Shakespeare's death, John Heminges and Henry Condell (two senior members of Shakespeare's company, who had performed with him for about twenty years) collected his plays—published and unpublished—into a large volume, commonly called the First Folio. (A folio is a volume consisting of sheets that have been folded once, each sheet thus making two leaves, or four pages. The eighteen plays published during Shakespeare's lifetime had been issued one play per volume in small books called quartos. Each sheet in a quarto has been folded twice, making four leaves, or eight pages.) The First Folio contains thirty-six plays; a thirty-seventh, *Pericles*, though not in the Folio is regarded as canonical. Heminges and Condell suggest in an address "To the great variety of readers" that the republished plays are presented in better form than in the quartos: "Before you were abused with diverse stolen and surreptitious copies, maimed and deformed by the frauds and stealths of injurious impostors that exposed them; even those, are now offered to your view cured and perfect of their limbs, and all the rest absolute in their numbers, as he [i.e., Shakespeare] conceived them."

Whoever was assigned to prepare the texts for publication in the First Folio seems to have taken his job seriously and yet not to have performed it with uniform care. The sources of the texts seem to have been, in general, good unpublished copies or the best published copies. The first play in the collection, *The Tempest,* is divided into acts and scenes, has unusually full stage directions and descriptions of spectacle, and concludes with a list of the characters, but the editor was not able (or willing) to present all of the succeeding texts so fully dressed. Later texts occasionally show signs of carelessness: in one scene of *Much Ado About Nothing* the names of actors, instead of characters, appear as speech prefixes, as they had in the quarto, which the Folio reprints; proofreading throughout the Folio is spotty and apparently was done without reference to the printer's copy; the pagination of *Hamlet* jumps from 156 to 257.

A modern editor of Shakespeare must first select his copy; no problem if the play exists only in the Folio, but a considerable problem if the relationship between a quarto and the Folio—or an early quarto and a later one —is unclear. When an editor has chosen what seems to him to be the most authoritative text or texts for his copy, he has not done with making decisions. First of all, he must reckon with Elizabethan spelling. If he is not producing a facsimile, he probably modernizes it, but ought he to preserve the old form of words that apparently were pronounced quite unlike their modern forms—"lanthorn," "alablaster"? If he preserves these forms, is he really preserving Shakespeare's forms or perhaps those of a compositor in the printing house? What is one to do when one finds "lanthorn" and "lantern" in adjacent lines? (The editors of this series in general, but not invariably, assume that words should be spelled in their modern forms.) Elizabethan punctuation, too, presents problems. For example, in the First Folio, the only text for the play, Macbeth rejects his wife's idea that he can wash the blood from his hand:

> no: this my Hand will rather
> The multitudinous Seas incarnardine,
> Making the Greene one, Red.

Obviously an editor will remove the superfluous capitals, and he will probably alter the spelling to "incarnadine," but will he leave the comma before "red," letting Macbeth speak of the sea as "the green one," or will he (like most modern editors) remove the comma and thus have Macbeth say that his hand will make the ocean *uniformly* red?

An editor will sometimes have to change more than spelling or punctuation. Macbeth says to his wife:

> I dare do all that may become a man,
> Who dares no more, is none.

For two centuries editors have agreed that the second line is unsatisfactory, and have emended "no" to "do": "Who dares do more is none." But when in the same play Ross says that fearful persons

> floate vpon a wilde and violent Sea
> Each way, and moue,

need "move" be emended to "none," as it often is, on the hunch that the compositor misread the manuscript? The editors of the Signet Classic Shakespeare have restrained themselves from making abundant emendations. In their minds they hear Dr. Johnson on the dangers of emending: "I have adopted the Roman sentiment, that it is more honorable to save a citizen than to kill an enemy." Some departures (in addition to spelling, punctuation, and lineation) from the copy text have of course been made, but the original readings are listed in a note following the play, so that the reader can evaluate them for himself.

The editors of the Signet Classic Shakespeare, following tradition, have added line numbers and in many cases act and scene divisions as well as indications of locale at the beginning of scenes. The Folio divided most of the plays into acts and some into scenes. Early eighteenth-century editors increased the divisions. These divisions, which provide a convenient way of referring to passages in the plays, have been retained, but when not in the text chosen as the basis for the Signet Classic text they are enclosed in square brackets [ ] to indicate that they are editorial additions. Similarly, although no play of Shakespeare's published during his lifetime was equipped with indications of locale at the heads of scene divisions, locales have here been added in square brackets for the convenience of the reader, who lacks the information afforded to spectators by costumes, properties, and gestures. The spectator can tell at a glance he is in the throne room, but without an editorial indication the reader may be puzzled for a while. It should be mentioned, incidentally, that there are a few authentic stage directions—perhaps Shakespeare's, perhaps a prompter's—that suggest locales: for example, "Enter Brutus in his orchard," and "They go up into the Senate house." It is hoped that the bracketed additions provide the reader with the sort of help provided in these two authentic directions, but it is equally hoped that the reader will remember that the stage was not loaded with scenery.

No editor during the course of his work can fail to recollect some words Heminges and Condell prefixed to the Folio:

It had been a thing, we confess, worthy to have been wished, that the author himself had lived to have set forth and overseen his own writings. But since it hath been ordained otherwise, and he by death departed from that right, we pray you do not envy his friends the office of their care and pain to have collected and published them.

Nor can an editor, after he has done his best, forget Heminges' and Condell's final words: "And so we leave you to other of his friends, whom if you need can be your guides. If you need them not, you can lead yourselves, and others. And such readers we wish him."

SYLVAN BARNET
Tufts University

Introduction

When Shakespeare wrote *Othello,* about 1604, his knowledge of human nature and his ability to dramatize it in language and action were at their height. The play offers, even in its minor characters, a number of unusually full and profound studies of humanity: Brabantio, the sophisticated, civilized Venetian senator, unable to comprehend that his delicate daughter could love and marry a Moor, speaking excitedly of black magic and spells to account for what his mind cannot understand; Cassio, the gentleman-soldier, polished in manners and gracious in bearing, wildly drunk and revealing a deeply rooted pride in his ramblings about senior officers being saved before their juniors; Emilia, the sensible and conventional waiting woman, making small talk about love and suddenly remarking that though she believes adultery to be wrong, still if the price were high enough she would sell—and so, she believes, would most women. The vision of human nature which the play offers is one of ancient terrors and primal drives—fear of the unknown, pride, greed, lust—underlying smooth, civilized surfaces—the noble senator, the competent and well-mannered lieutenant, the conventional gentlewoman.

The contrast between surface manner and inner nature is even more pronounced in two of the major characters. "Honest Iago" conceals beneath his exterior of the plain soldier and blunt, practical man of the world a diabolism so intense as to defy rational explanation—it must be taken like lust or pride as simply a given part of human nature, an anti-life spirit which seeks the destruction of everything outside the self. Othello appears in the opening acts as the very personification of self-control, of the man with so secure a sense of his own worth that nothing can ruffle the consequent calmness of mind and manner. But the man who has roamed the wild and savage world unmoved by its terrors, who has not changed countenance when the cannon killed his brother standing beside him, this man is still capable of believing his wife a whore on the slightest of evidence and committing murders to revenge himself. In Desdemona alone do the heart and the hand go together: she is what she seems to be. Ironically, she alone is accused of pretending to be what she is not. Her very openness and honesty make her suspect in a world where few men are what they appear, and her chastity is inevitably brought into question in a world where every other major character is in some degree touched with sexual corruption.

Most criticism of *Othello* has concerned itself with exploring the depths of these characters and tracing the intricate, mysterious operations of their minds. I should like, however, to leave this work to the individual reader and to the critical essays printed at the back of this volume in order to discuss, briefly, what might be called the "gross mechanics" of the play, the larger patterns in which events and characters are arranged. These patterns are the context within which the individual characters are defined, just as the pattern of a sentence is the context which defines the exact meaning of the individual words within it.

Othello is probably the most neatly, the most formally constructed of Shakespeare's plays. Every character is, for example, balanced by another similar or contrasting character. Desdemona is balanced by her opposite, Iago; love and concern for others at one end of the scale, hatred and concern for self at the other. The true and loyal soldier Cassio balances the false and traitorous soldier Iago. These balances and contrasts throw into relief the essential qualities of the characters. Desdemona's love, for example, shows up a good deal more clearly in contrast to Iago's hate, and vice versa. The values of contrast are increased and the full range of human nature displayed by extending these simple contrasts into developing series. The essential purity of Desdemona stands in contrast to the more "practical" view of chastity held by Emilia, and her view in turn is illuminated by the workaday view of sensuality held by the courtesan Bianca, who treats love, ordinarily, as a commodity. Or, to take another example, Iago's success in fooling Othello is but the culmination of a series of such betrayals that includes the duping of Roderigo, Brabantio, and Cassio. Each duping is the explanatory image of the other, for in every case Iago's method and end are the same: he plays on and teases to life some hitherto controlled and concealed dark passion in his victim. In each case he seeks in some way the same end, the symbolic murder of Desdemona, the destruction in some form of the life principle of which she is the major embodiment.

These various contrasts and parallelisms ultimately blend into a larger, more general pattern that is the central movement of the play. We can begin to see this pattern in the "symbolic geography" of the play. Every play, or work of art, creates its own particular image of space and time, its own symbolic world. The outer limits of the world of *Othello* are defined by the Turks—the infidels, the unbelievers, the "general enemy" as the play calls them— who, just over the horizon, sail back and forth trying to confuse and trick the Christians in order to invade their dominions and destroy them. Out beyond the horizon, reported but unseen, are also those "anters vast and deserts idle" of which Othello speaks. Out there is a land of "rough quarries, rocks, and hills whose heads touch heaven" inhabited by "cannibals that each other eat" and monstrous forms of men "whose heads grow beneath their shoulders." On the edges of this land is the raging ocean with its "high seas, and howling winds," its "guttered rocks and congregated sands" hidden beneath the waters to "enclog the guiltless keel."

Within the circle formed by barbarism, monstrosity, sterility, and the brute power of nature lie the two Christian strongholds of Venice and Cyprus. Renaissance Venice was known for its wealth acquired by trade, its political cunning, and its courtesans; but Shakespeare, while reminding us of the tradition of the "supersubtle Venetian," makes Venice over into a form of *The City*, the ageless image of government, of reason, of law, and of social concord. Here, when Brabantio's strong passions and irrational fears threaten to create riot and injustice, his grievances are examined by a court of law, judged by reason, and the verdict enforced by civic power. Here, the clear mind of the Senate probes the actions of the Turks, penetrates through their pretenses to their true purposes, makes sense of the frantic and fearful contradictory messages which pour in from the fleet, and arranges the necessary defense. Act I, Scene iii—the Senate scene—focuses on the magnificent speeches of Othello and Desdemona as they declare their love and explain it, but the lovers are surrounded, guarded, by the assembled, ranked governors of Venice, who control passions that otherwise would have led to a bloody street brawl and bring justice out of what otherwise would have been riot. The solemn presence and ordering power of the Senate would be most powerfully realized in a stage production, where the senators would appear in their rich robes, with all their symbols of office, seated in ranks around several excited individuals expressing such primal passions as pride of race, fear of dark powers, and violent love. In a play where so much of the language is magnificent, rich, and of heroic proportions, simpler statements come to seem more forceful; and the meaning of *The City* is perhaps nowhere more completely realized than in Brabantio's brief, secure answer to the first fearful cries of theft and talk of copulating animals that Iago and Roderigo send up from the darkness below his window:

> What tell'st thou me of robbing? This is Venice;
> My house is not a grange.   (I.i.102–03)

Here then are the major reference points on a map of the world of *Othello*: out at the far edge are the Turks, barbarism, disorder, and amoral destructive powers; closer and more familiar is Venice, *The City*, order, law, and reason. Cyprus, standing on the frontier between barbarism and *The City,* is not the secure fortress of civilization that Venice is. It is rather an outpost, weakly defended and far out in the raging ocean, close to the "general enemy" and the immediate object of his attack. It is a "town of war yet wild" where the "people's hearts [are] brimful of fear." Here passions are more explosive and closer to the surface than in Venice, and here, instead of the ancient order and established government of *The City,* there is only one man to control violence and defend civilization—the Moor Othello, himself of savage origins and a converted Christian.

The movement of the play is from Venice to Cyprus, from *The City* to the outpost, from organized society to a condition much closer to raw nature, and from collective life to the life of the solitary individual. This movement is a characteristic pattern in Shakespeare's plays, both comedies and tragedies: in *A Midsummer Night's Dream* the lovers and players go from the civilized, daylight world of Athens to the irrational, magical wood outside Athens and the primal powers of life represented by the elves and fairies; Lear moves from his palace and secure identity to the savage world of the heath where all values and all identities come into question; and everyone in *The Tempest* is shipwrecked at some time on Prospero's magic island, where life seen from a new perspective assumes strange and fantastic shapes. At the other end of this journey there is always some kind of return to *The City,* to the palace, and to old relationships, but the nature of this return differs widely in Shakespeare's plays. In *Othello* the movement at the end of the play is back toward Venice, the Turk defeated; but Desdemona, Othello, Emilia, and Roderigo do not return. Their deaths are the price paid for the return.

This passage from Venice to Cyprus to fight the Turk and encounter the forces of barbarism is the geographical form of an action that occurs on the social and psychological levels as well. That is, there are social and mental conditions that correspond to Venice and Cyprus, and there are forces at work in society and in man that correspond to the Turks, the raging seas, and "cannibals that each other eat."

The exposure to danger, the breakdown and the ultimate reestablishment of society—the parallel on the social level to the action on the geographical level—is quickly traced. We have already noted that the Venetian Senate embodies order, reason, justice, and concord, the binding forces that hold *The City* together. In Venice the ancient laws and the established customs of society work to control violent men and violent passions to ensure the safety and well-being of the individual and the group. But there are anarchic forces at work in the city, which threaten traditional social forms and relationships, and all these forces center in Iago. His discontent with his own rank and his determination to displace Cassio endanger the orderly military hierarchy in which the junior serves his senior. He endangers marriage, the traditional form for ordering male and female relationships, by his own unfounded suspicions of his wife and by his efforts to destroy Othello's marriage by fanning to life the darker, anarchic passions of Brabantio and Roderigo. He tries to subvert the operation of law and justice by first stirring up Brabantio to gather his followers and seek revenge in the streets; and then when the two warlike forces are met, Iago begins a quarrel with Roderigo in hopes of starting a brawl. The nature of the antisocial forces that Iago represents are focused in the imagery of his advice to Roderigo on how to call out to her father the news of Desdemona's marriage. Call, he says,

> with like timorous [frightening] accent and dire yell
> As when, by night and negligence, the fire
> Is spied in populous cities.   (I.i.72–74)

Fire, panic, darkness, neglect of duty—these are the natural and human forces that destroy great cities and turn their citizens to mobs.

In Venice, Iago's attempts to create civic chaos are frustrated by Othello's calm management of himself and the orderly legal proceedings of the Senate. In Cyprus, however, society is less secure—even as the island is more exposed to the Turks—and Othello alone is responsible for finding truth and maintaining order. Here Iago's poison begins to work, and he succeeds at once in manufacturing the riot that he failed to create in Venice. Seen on stage, the fight on the watch between Cassio and Montano is chaos come again: two drunken officers, charged with the defense of the town, trying to kill each other like savage animals, a bedlam of voices and shouts, broken, disordered furniture, and above all this the discordant clamor of the "dreadful" alarm bell—used to signal attacks and fire. This success is but the prologue for other more serious disruptions of society and of the various human relationships that it fosters. The General is set against his officer, husband against wife, Christian against Christian, servant against master. Justice becomes a travesty of itself as Othello—using legal terms such as "It is the *cause*"—assumes the offices of accuser, judge, jury, and executioner of his wife. Manners disappear as the Moor strikes his wife publicly and treats her maid as a procuress. The brightly lighted Senate chamber is now replaced with a dark Cyprus street where Venetians cut one another down and men are murdered from behind. This anarchy finally gives way in the last scene, when Desdemona's faith is proven, to a restoration of order and an execution of justice on the two major criminals.

What we have followed so far is a movement expressed in geographical and social symbols from Venice to a Cyprus exposed to attack, from *The City* to barbarism, from Christendom to the domain of the Turks, from order to riot, from justice to wild revenge and murder, from truth to falsehood. It now remains to see just what this movement means on the level of the individual in the heart and mind of man. Of the three major characters, Desdemona, Othello, and Iago, the first and the last do not change their natures or their attitudes toward life during the course of the play. These two are polar opposites, the antitheses of each other. To speak in the most general terms, Desdemona expresses in her language and actions an innocent, unselfish love and concern for others. Othello catches her very essence when he speaks of her miraculous love, which transcended their differences in age, color, beauty, and culture:

> She loved me for the dangers I had passed,
> And I loved her that she did pity them. (I.iii.166–67)

This love in its various forms finds expression not only in her absolute commitment of herself to Othello, but in her gentleness, her kindness to others, her innocent trust in all men, her pleas for Cassio's restoration to Othello's favor; and it endures even past death at her husband's hands, for she comes back to life for a moment to answer Emilia's question, "who hath done this deed?" with the unbelievable words,

> Nobody—I myself. Farewell.
> Commend me to my kind lord. O, farewell!
> (V.ii.123–24)

Iago is her opposite in every way. Where she is open and guileless, he is never what he seems to be; where she thinks the best of everyone, he thinks the worst, usually turning to imagery of animals and physical functions to express his low opinion of human nature; where she seeks to serve and love others, he uses others to further his own dark aims and satisfy his hatred of mankind; where she is emotional and idealistic, he is icily logical and cynical. Desdemona and Iago are much more complicated than this, but perhaps enough has been said to suggest the nature of these two moral poles of the play. One is a life force that strives for order, community, growth, and light. The other is an anti-life force that seeks anarchy, death, and darkness. One is the foundation of all that men have built in the world, including *The City;* the other leads back toward ancient chaos and barbarism.

Othello, like most men, is a combination of the forces of love and hate, which are isolated in impossibly pure states in Desdemona and Iago. His psychic voyage from

Venice to Cyprus is a passage of the soul and the will from the values of one of these characters to those of the other. This passage is charted by his acceptance and rejection of one or the other. He begins by refusing to have Iago as his lieutenant, choosing the more "theoretical" though less experienced Cassio. He marries Desdemona. Though he is not aware that he does so, he expresses the full meaning of this choice when he speaks of her in such suggestive terms as "my soul's joy" and refers to her even as he is about to kill her, as "Promethean heat," the vital fire that gives life to the world. Similarly, he comes to know that all that is valuable in life depends on her love, and in the magnificent speech beginning, "O now, forever/ Farewell the tranquil mind" (III.iii.344–45), he details the emptiness of all human activity if Desdemona be proved false. But Iago, taking advantage of latent "Iagolike" feelings and thoughts in Othello, persuades him that Desdemona is only common clay. Othello then gives himself over to Iago at the end of III.iii, where they kneel together to plan the revenge, and Othello says, "Now art thou my lieutenant." To which Iago responds with blood-chilling simplicity, "I am your own forever." The full meaning of this choice is expressed, again unconsciously, by Othello when he says of Desdemona,

> Perdition catch my soul
> But I do love thee! and when I love thee not,
> Chaos is come again. (III.iii.90–92)

The murder of Desdemona acts out the final destruction in Othello himself of all the ordering powers of love, of trust, of the bond between human beings.

Desdemona and Iago then represent two states of mind, two understandings of life, and Othello's movement from one to the other is the movement on the level of character and psychology from Venice to Cyprus, from *The City* to anarchy. His return to *The City* and the defeat of the Turk is effected, at the expense of his own life, when he learns *what* he has killed and executes himself as the

only fitting judgment on his act. His willingness to speak
of what he has done—in contrast to Iago's sullen silence—
is a willingness to recognize the meaning of Desdemona's
faith and chastity, to acknowledge that innocence and
love do exist, and that therefore *The City* can stand,
though his life is required to validate the truth and justice
on which it is built.

Othello offers a variety of interrelated symbols that
locate and define in historical, natural, social, moral, and
human terms those qualities of being and universal forces
that are forever at war in the universe and between
which tragic man is always in movement. On one side
there are Turks, cannibals, barbarism, monstrous de-
formities of nature, the brute force of the sea, riot, mobs,
darkness, Iago, hatred, lust, concern for the self only,
and cynicism. On the other side there are Venice, *The
City,* law, senates, amity, hierarchy, Desdemona, love,
concern for others, and innocent trust. As the characters
of the play act and speak, they bring together, by means
of parallelism and metaphor, the various forms of the
different ways of life. There is, for example, a meaningful
similarity in the underhanded way Iago works and the
ruse by which the Turks try to fool the Venetians into
thinking they are bound for Rhodes when their object is
Cyprus. Or, there is again a flash of identification when
we hear that the reefs and shoals that threaten ships are
"ensteeped," that is, hidden under the surface of the
sea, as Iago is hidden under the surface of his "honesty."
But Shakespeare binds the various levels of being more
closely together by the use of imagery that compares things
on one level of action with things on another. For example,
when Iago swears that his low judgment of all female
virtue "is true, or else I am a Turk" (II.i.113), logic
demands, since one woman, Desdemona, *is* true and
chaste, that we account him "a Turk." He is thus identi-
fied with the unbelievers, the Ottoman Turks, and that
Asiatic power, which for centuries threatened Christendom, is shown to have its social and psychological equivalent in Iago's particular attitude toward life. Similarly,

when Othello sees the drunken brawl on the watchtower, he exclaims,

Are we turned Turks, and to ourselves do that
Which heaven hath forbid the Ottomites? (II.iii.169–70)

At the very time when the historical enemy has been defeated, his fleet providentially routed by the great storm, his characteristics—drunken loss of control, brawling over honor, disorder—begin to conquer the island only so recently and fortuitously saved. The conquest continues, and the defender of the island, Othello, convinced of Desdemona's guilt, compares his determination to revenge himself to "the Pontic Sea, / Whose icy current and compulsive course / Nev'r keeps retiring ebb" (III.iii.450–52). The comparison tells us that in his rage and hatred he has become one with the savage seas and the brute, amoral powers of nature that are displayed in the storm scene at the beginning of Act II. But most important is Othello's identification of himself at the end of the play as the "base Judean" who "threw a pearl away richer than all his tribe." The more familiar Quarto reading is "base Indian," but both words point toward the barbarian who fails to recognize value and beauty when he possesses it—the primitive savage who picks up a pearl and throws it away not knowing its worth; or the Jews (Judas may be specifically meant) who denied and crucified another great figure of love, thinking they were dealing with only a troublesome rabble-rouser. A few lines further on Othello proceeds to the final and absolute identification of himself with the infidel. He speaks of a "malignant and a turbaned Turk" who "beat a Venetian and traduced the state," and he then acknowledges that he is that Turk by stabbing himself, even as he once stabbed the other unbeliever. So he ends as both the Turk and the destroyer of the Turk, the infidel and the defender of the faith.

When Iago's schemes are at last exposed, Othello, finding it impossible for a moment to believe that a *man* could have contrived such evil, stares at Iago's feet and then says sadly, "but that's a fable." What he hopes to find when he looks down are the cloven hoofs of the devil, and had they been there he would have been an actor in a morality play, tempted beyond his strength, like many a man before him, by a supernatural power outside himself. In some ways I have schematized *Othello* as just such a morality play, offering an allegorical journey between heaven and hell on a stage filled with purely symbolic figures. This is the kind of abstraction of art toward which criticism inevitably moves, and in this case the allegorical framework is very solidly there. But *Othello* does not see the cloven hoofs when he looks down; he sees a pair of human feet at the end of a very human body; and he is forced to realize that far from living in some simplified, "fabulous" world where evil is a metaphysical power raiding human life from without, he dwells where evil is somehow inextricably woven with good into man himself. On his stage the good angel does not return to heaven when defeated, but is murdered, and her body remains on the bed, "cold, cold." He lives where good intentions, past services, psychic weaknesses, and an inability to see through evil cannot excuse an act, as they might in some simpler world where more perfect justice existed. In short, Othello is forced to recognize that he lives in a tragic world, and he pays the price for having been great enough to inhabit it.

Here is the essence of Shakespeare's art, an ability to create immediate, full, and total life as men actually live and experience it; and yet at the same time to arrange this reality so that it gives substance to and derives shape from a formal vision of all life that comprehends and reaches back from man and nature through society and history to cosmic powers that operate through all time and space. His plays are both allegorical and realistic at once; his characters both recognizable men and at the same time devils, demigods, and forces in nature. I have discussed only the more allegorical elements in *Othello,* the skeleton of ideas and formal patterns within which the characters must necessarily be understood. But it is equally true that the exact qualities of the abstract moral values and ideas, their full reality, exist only in the characters. It is necessary to know that Desdemona represents one particular human value, love or charity, in order to avoid making such mistakes as searching for some tragic flaw in her which would justify her death. But at the same time, if we would know what love and charity *are* in all their fullness, then our definition can only be the actions, the language, the emotions of the character Desdemona. She is Shakespeare's word for love. If we wish to know not just the obvious fact that men choose evil over good, but *why* they do so, then we must look both analytically and feelingly at all the evidence that the world offers for believing that Desdemona is false and at all the biases in Othello's mind that predispose him to believe such evidence. Othello's passage from Venice to Cyprus, from absolute love for Desdemona to extinguishing the light in her bedchamber, and to the execution of himself, these are Shakespeare's words for tragic man.

ALVIN KERNAN
Yale University

The Tragedy of
OTHELLO

The Moor of Venice

The Names of the Actors

Othello, the Moor
Brabantio, father to Desdemona
Cassio, an honorable lieutenant
Iago, a villain
Roderigo, a gulled gentleman
Duke of Venice
Senators
Montano, Governor of Cyprus
Gentlemen of Cyprus
Lodovico and Gratiano, two noble Venetians
Sailors
Clown
Desdemona, wife to Othello
Emilia, wife to Iago
Bianca, a courtesan
[Messenger, Herald, Officers, Gentlemen,
    Musicians, Attendants
        Scene: Venice and Cyprus]

The Tragedy of Othello

ACT I

Scene I. [*Venice. A street.*]

Enter Roderigo and Iago.

Roderigo. Tush! Never tell me? I take it much un-
   kindly
That thou, Iago, who hast had my purse
As if the strings were thine, shouldst know of this.

Iago. 'Sblood,° ¹ but you'll not hear me! If ever I did
   dream
Of such a matter, abhor me.

Roderigo.   Thou told'st me   *5*
Thou didst hold him in thy hate.

Iago.   Despise me
If I do not. Three great ones of the city,
In personal suit to make me his lieutenant,
Off-capped° to him; and, by the faith of man,
I know my price; I am worth no worse a place.   *10*
But he, as loving his own pride and purposes,
Evades them with a bombast circumstance,°

---

¹ The degree sign (°) indicates a footnote, which is keyed to the text by
the line number. Text references are printed in *italic* type; the annota-
tion follows in roman type. I.i.⁴ *'Sblood* by God's blood ⁹ *Off-capped*
doffed their caps—as a mark of respect ¹² *bombast circumstance*
stuffed, roundabout speech

Horribly stuffed with epithets of war;
Nonsuits° my mediators. For, "Certes," says he,
"I have already chose my officer." And what was
15   he?
Forsooth, a great arithmetician,°
One Michael Cassio, a Florentine,
(A fellow almost damned in a fair wife)°
That never set a squadron in the field,
20   Nor the division of a battle knows
More than a spinster; unless the bookish theoric,
Wherein the tonguèd° consuls can propose
As masterly as he. Mere prattle without practice
Is all his soldiership. But he, sir, had th' election;
25   And I, of whom his eyes had seen the proof
At Rhodes, at Cyprus, and on other grounds
Christian and heathen, must be belee'd and calmed
By debitor and creditor. This counter-caster,°
He, in good time, must his lieutenant be,
And I—God bless the mark!—his Moorship's an-
30   cient.°

Roderigo. By heaven, I rather would have been his
    hangman.

Iago. Why, there's no remedy. 'Tis the curse of service:
Preferment goes by letter and affection,°
And not by old gradation,° where each second
35   Stood heir to th' first. Now, sir, be judge yourself,
Whether I in any just term am affined°
To love the Moor.

Roderigo.   I would not follow him then.

---

[14] *Nonsuits* rejects [16] *arithmetician* theorist (rather than practical)
[18] *A . . . wife* (a much-disputed passage, which is probably best taken as
a general sneer at Cassio as a dandy and a ladies' man. But in the story
from which Shakespeare took his plot the counterpart of Cassio is
married, and it may be that at the beginning of the play Shakespeare
had decided to keep him married but later changed his mind)
[22] *tonguèd* eloquent [28] *counter-caster* i.e., a bookkeeper who *casts*
(reckons up) figures on a *counter* (abacus) [30] *ancient* standard-bearer;
an underofficer [33] *letter and affection* recommendations (from men
of power) and personal preference [34] *old gradation* seniority
[36] *affined* bound

Iago. O, sir, content you.
 I follow him to serve my turn upon him.
 We cannot all be masters, nor all masters   40
 Cannot be truly followed. You shall mark
 Many a duteous and knee-crooking° knave
 That, doting on his own obsequious bondage,
 Wears out his time, much like his master's ass,
 For naught but provender; and when he's old,
  cashiered.   45
 Whip me such honest knaves! Others there are
 Who, trimmed in forms and visages of duty,
 Keep yet their hearts attending on themselves,
 And, throwing but shows of service on their lords,
 Do well thrive by them, and when they have lined
  their coats,   50
 Do themselves homage. These fellows have some
  soul;
 And such a one do I profess myself. For, sir,
 It is as sure as you are Roderigo,
 Were I the Moor, I would not be Iago.
 In following him, I follow but myself.   55
 Heaven is my judge, not I for love and duty,
 But seeming so, for my peculiar° end;
 For when my outward action doth demonstrate
 The native° act and figure of my heart
 In complement extern,° 'tis not long after   60
 But I will wear my heart upon my sleeve
 For daws to peck at; I am not what I am.

Roderigo. What a full fortune does the thick-lips owe°
 If he can carry't thus!

Iago.   Call up her father,
 Rouse him. Make after him, poison his delight,   65
 Proclaim him in the streets, incense her kinsmen,
 And though he in a fertile climate dwell,
 Plague him with flies; though that his joy be joy,

---

⁴² *knee-crooking* bowing   ⁵⁷ *peculiar* personal   ⁵⁹ *native* natural, innate
⁶⁰ *complement extern* outward appearances   ⁶³ *owe* own

Yet throw such chances of vexation on't
70 As it may lose some color.

Roderigo. Here is her father's house. I'll call aloud.

Iago. Do, with like timorous° accent and dire yell
As when, by night and negligence, the fire
Is spied in populous cities.

Roderigo. What, ho, Brabantio! Signior Brabantio,
75 ho!

Iago. Awake! What, ho, Brabantio! Thieves! Thieves!
Look to your house, your daughter, and your bags!
Thieves! Thieves!

      Brabantio above° [at a window].

Brabantio. What is the reason of this terrible summons?
80 What is the matter there?

Roderigo. Signior, is all your family within?

Iago. Are your doors locked?

Brabantio.   Why, wherefore ask you
this?

Iago. Zounds, sir, y'are robbed! For shame. Put on
your gown!
Your heart is burst, you have lost half your soul.
85 Even now, now, very now, an old black ram
Is tupping your white ewe. Arise, arise!
Awake the snorting citizens with the bell,
Or else the devil will make a grandsire of you.
Arise, I say!

Brabantio.   What, have you lost your wits?

Roderigo. Most reverend signior, do you know my
90 voice?

Brabantio. Not I. What are you?

---

⁷² *timorous* frightening ⁷⁸ s.d. *above* (i.e., on the small upper stage
above and to the rear of the main platform stage, which resembled the
projecting upper story of an Elizabethan house)

Roderigo. My name is Roderigo.

Brabantio.   The worser welcome!
I have charged thee not to haunt about my doors.
In honest plainness thou hast heard me say
My daughter is not for thee; and now, in madness,   95
Being full of supper and distemp'ring draughts,°
Upon malicious knavery dost thou come
To start° my quiet.

Roderigo. Sir, sir, sir——

Brabantio.   But thou must needs be sure
My spirits and my place° have in their power   100
To make this bitter to thee.

Roderigo.   Patience, good sir.

Brabantio. What tell'st thou me of robbing? This is
   Venice;
My house is not a grange.°

Roderigo.   Most grave Brabantio,
In simple and pure soul I come to you.

Iago. Zounds, sir, you are one of those that will not 105
serve God if the devil bid you. Because we come
to do you service and you think we are ruffians,
you'll have your daughter covered with a Barbary°
horse, you'll have your nephews° neigh to you,
you'll have coursers for cousins,° and gennets for 110
germans.°

Brabantio. What profane wretch art thou?

Iago. I am one, sir, that comes to tell you your daughter
and the Moor are making the beast with two backs.

Brabantio. Thou art a villain.

Iago.   You are—a senator.   115

Brabantio. This thou shalt answer. I know thee,
   Roderigo.

---

96 *distemp'ring draughts* unsettling drinks **98** *start* disrupt **100** *place*
rank, i.e., of senator **103** *grange* isolated house **108** *Barbary* Arabian,
i.e., Moorish **109** *nephews* i.e., grandsons **110** *cousins* relations
110–11 *gennets for germans* Spanish horses for blood relatives

Roderigo. Sir, I will answer anything. But I beseech
you,
If't be your pleasure and most wise consent,
As partly I find it is, that your fair daughter,
120 At this odd-even° and dull watch o' th' night,
Transported, with no worse nor better guard
But with a knave of common hire, a gondolier,
To the gross clasps of a lascivious Moor—
If this be known to you, and your allowance,
125 We then have done you bold and saucy wrongs;
But if you know not this, my manners tell me
We have your wrong rebuke. Do not believe
That from the sense of all civility°
I thus would play and trifle with your reverence.
130 Your daughter, if you have not given her leave,
I say again, hath made a gross revolt,
Tying her duty, beauty, wit, and fortunes
In an extravagant° and wheeling stranger
Of here and everywhere. Straight satisfy yourself.
135 If she be in her chamber, or your house,
Let loose on me the justice of the state
For thus deluding you.

Brabantio.   Strike on the tinder, ho!
Give me a taper! Call up all my people!
This accident° is not unlike my dream.
140 Belief of it oppresses me already.
Light, I say! Light!   *Exit* [*above*].

Iago.   Farewell, for I must leave you.
It seems not meet, nor wholesome to my place,
To be produced—as, if I stay, I shall—
Against the Moor. For I do know the State,
145 However this may gall him with some check,°
Cannot with safety cast° him; for he's embarked
With such loud reason to the Cyprus wars,

---

120 *odd-even* between night and morning   128 *sense of all civility* feeling of what is proper   133 *extravagant* vagrant, wandering (Othello is
not Venetian and thus may be considered a wandering soldier of fortune)   139 *accident* happening   145 *check* restraint   146 *cast* dismiss

Which even now stands in act,° that for their souls
Another of his fathom° they have none
To lead their business; in which regard,   *150*
Though I do hate him as I do hell-pains,
Yet, for necessity of present life,
I must show out a flag and sign of love,
Which is indeed but sign. That you shall surely find him,
Lead to the Sagittary° the raisèd search;   *155*
And there will I be with him. So farewell.   *Exit.*

*Enter Brabantio [in his nightgown], with Servants
and torches.*

Brabantio. It is too true an evil. Gone she is;
And what's to come of my despisèd time
Is naught but bitterness. Now, Roderigo,
Where didst thou see her?—O unhappy girl!—   *160*
With the Moor, say'st thou?—Who would be a father?—
How didst thou know 'twas she?—O, she deceives me
Past thought!—What said she to you? Get moe° tapers!
Raise all my kindred!—Are they married, think you?

Roderigo. Truly I think they are.   *165*

Brabantio. O heaven! How got she out? O treason of the blood!
Fathers, from hence trust not your daughters' minds
By what you see them act.° Is there not charms
By which the property° of youth and maidhood
May be abused? Have you not read, Roderigo,   *170*
Of some such thing?

Roderigo.   Yes, sir, I have indeed.

Brabantio. Call up my brother.—O, would you had had her!—

---

148 *stands in act* takes place   149 *fathom* ability   155 *Sagittary* (probably the name of an inn)   163 *moe* more   168 *act* do   169 *property* true nature

Some one way, some another.—Do you know
Where we may apprehend her and the Moor?

175 *Roderigo.* I think I can discover him, if you please
To get good guard and go along with me.

Brabantio. Pray you lead on. At every house I'll call;
I may command at most.—Get weapons, ho!
And raise some special officers of might.—
180   On, good Roderigo; I will deserve your pains.°

                                        Exeunt.

Scene II. [*A street.*]

Enter Othello, Iago, Attendants with torches.

Iago. Though in the trade of war I have slain men,
Yet do I hold it very stuff° o' th' conscience
To do no contrived murder. I lack iniquity
Sometime to do me service. Nine or ten times
I had thought t' have yerked° him here, under the
5   ribs.

Othello. 'Tis better as it is.

Iago.   Nay, but he prated,
And spoke such scurvy and provoking terms
Against your honor, that with the little godliness
    I have
I did full hard forbear him. But I pray you, sir,
10   Are you fast married? Be assured of this,
That the magnifico° is much beloved,
And hath in his effect a voice potential
As double as the Duke's.° He will divorce you,
Or put upon you what restraint or grievance

180 *deserve your pains* be worthy of (and reward) your efforts
I.ii.² *stuff* essence   ⁵ *yerked* stabbed   ¹¹ *magnifico* nobleman   ¹²⁻¹³ *hath
. . . Duke's* i.e., can be as effective as the Duke

The law, with all his might to enforce it on,   15
Will give him cable.°

Othello.   Let him do his spite.
My services which I have done the Signiory°
Shall out-tongue his complaints. 'Tis yet to know° —
Which when I know that boasting is an honor
I shall promulgate—I fetch my life and being   20
From men of royal siege;° and my demerits°
May speak unbonneted to as proud a fortune
As this that I have reached.° For know, Iago,
But that I love the gentle Desdemona,
I would not my unhousèd° free condition   25
Put into circumscription and confine
For the seas' worth. But look, what lights come
    yond?

        Enter Cassio, with [Officers and] torches.

Iago. Those are the raisèd father and his friends.
    You were best go in.

Othello.   Not I. I must be found.
My parts, my title, and my perfect soul°   30
Shall manifest me rightly. Is it they?

Iago. By Janus, I think no.

Othello. The servants of the Duke? And my lieutenant?
    The goodness of the night upon you, friends.
    What is the news?

Cassio.   The Duke does greet you, general;   35
    And he requires your haste-posthaste appearance
    Even on the instant.

Othello.   What is the matter, think you?

Cassio. Something from Cyprus, as I may divine.
    It is a business of some heat. The galleys

---

16 *cable* range, scope   17 *Signiory* the rulers of Venice   18 *yet to know* unknown as yet   21 *siege* rank   21 *demerits* deserts   22-23 *May . . . reached,* i.e., are the equal of the family I have married into   25 *unhousèd* unconfined   30 *perfect soul* clear, unflawed conscience

40   Have sent a dozen sequent° messengers
        This very night at one another's heels,
        And many of the consuls, raised and met,
        Are at the Duke's already. You have been hotly
            called for.
        When, being not at your lodging to be found,
45   The Senate hath sent about three several° quests
        To search you out.

Othello.   'Tis well I am found by you.
        I will but spend a word here in the house,
        And go with you.   [*Exit.*]

Cassio.   Ancient, what makes he here?
Iago. Faith, he tonight hath boarded a land carack.°
50   If it prove lawful prize, he's made forever.

Cassio. I do not understand.

Iago.   He's married.

Cassio.   To who?
            [*Enter Othello.*]

Iago. Marry,° to—Come, captain, will you go?

Othello.   Have with you.

Cassio. Here comes another troop to seek for you.

    Enter Brabantio, Roderigo, with Officers and torches.

Iago. It is Brabantio. General, be advised.
        He comes to bad intent.

55 *Othello.*   Holla! Stand there!

Roderigo. Signior, it is the Moor.

Brabantio.   Down with him, thief!
                [*They draw swords.*]

Iago. You, Roderigo? Come, sir, I am for you.

Othello. Keep up your bright swords, for the dew will
        rust them.

---

⁴⁰ *sequent* successive ⁴⁵ *several* separate ⁴⁹ *carack* treasure ship
⁵² *Marry* By Mary (an interjection)

Good signior, you shall more command with years
Than with your weapons.   60

Brabantio. O thou foul thief, where hast thou stowed
      my daughter?
Damned as thou art, thou hast enchanted her!
For I'll refer me to all things of sense,°
If she in chains of magic were not bound,
Whether a maid so tender, fair, and happy,   65
So opposite to marriage that she shunned
The wealthy, curlèd darlings of our nation,
Would ever have, t' incur a general mock,°
Run from her guardage to the sooty bosom
Of such a thing as thou—to fear, not to delight.   70
Judge me the world if 'tis not gross in sense°
That thou hast practiced ° on her with foul charms,
Abused her delicate youth with drugs or minerals
That weaken motion.° I'll have't disputed on;
'Tis probable, and palpable to thinking.   75
I therefore apprehend and do attach° thee
For an abuser of the world, a practicer
Of arts inhibited and out of warrant.°
Lay hold upon him. If he do resist,
Subdue him at his peril.

Othello.   Hold your hands,   80
Both you of my inclining and the rest.
Were it my cue to fight, I should have known it
Without a prompter. Whither will you that I go
To answer this your charge?

Brabantio.   To prison, till fit time
Of law and course of direct session   85
Call thee to answer.

Othello.   What if I do obey?
How may the Duke be therewith satisfied,
Whose messengers are here about my side

---

[63] *refer . . . sense* i.e., base (my argument) on all ordinary understanding of nature [68] *general mock* public shame [71] *gross in sense*
obvious [72] *practiced* used tricks [74] *motion* thought, i.e., reason
[76] *attach* arrest [78] *inhibited . . . warrant* prohibited and illegal (black
magic)

Upon some present° business of the state
To bring me to him?

90 *Officer.*   'Tis true, most worthy signior.
The Duke's in council, and your noble self
I am sure is sent for.

Brabantio.   How? The Duke in council?
In this time of the night? Bring him away.
Mine's not an idle cause. The Duke himself,
95   Or any of my brothers° of the state,
Cannot but feel this wrong as 'twere their own;
For if such actions may have passage free,
Bondslaves and pagans shall our statesmen be.
                                        Exeunt.

Scene III. [*A council chamber.*]

Enter Duke, Senators, and Officers [set at a table,
with lights and Attendants].

Duke. There's no composition° in this news
That gives them credit.°

First Senator.   Indeed, they are disproportioned.
My letters say a hundred and seven galleys.

Duke. And mine a hundred forty.

Second Senator.   And mine two hundred.
5   But though they jump° not on a just accompt° —
As in these cases where the aim° reports
'Tis oft with difference—yet do they all confirm
A Turkish fleet, and bearing up to Cyprus.

Duke. Nay, it is possible enough to judgment.°
10   I do not so secure me in the error,

89 *present* immediate   95 *brothers* i.e., the other senators   I.iii.¹ *compo-*
sition agreement   ² *gives them credit* makes them believable   5 *jump*
agree   5 *just accompt* exact counting   6 *aim* approximation   9 *to judg-*
ment when carefully considered

But the main article I do approve
In fearful sense.°

Sailor. (*Within*) What, ho! What, ho! What, ho!

Enter Sailor.

Officer. A messenger from the galleys.

Duke.   Now? What's the business?

Sailor. The Turkish preparation makes for Rhodes.
So was I bid report here to the State   *15*
By Signior Angelo.

Duke. How say you by this change?

First Senator.   This cannot be
By no assay of reason. 'Tis a pageant°
To keep us in false gaze.° When we consider
Th' importancy of Cyprus to the Turk,   *20*
And let ourselves again but understand
That, as it more concerns the Turk than Rhodes,
So may he with more facile question° bear it,
For that it stands not in such warlike brace,°
But altogether lacks th' abilities   *25*
That Rhodes is dressed in. If we make thought of
  this,
We must not think the Turk is so unskillful
To leave that latest which concerns him first,
Neglecting an attempt of ease and gain
To wake and wage a danger profitless.   *30*

Duke. Nay, in all confidence he's not for Rhodes.

Officer. Here is more news.

Enter a Messenger.

Messenger. The Ottomites, reverend and gracious,
Steering with due course toward the isle of Rhodes,
Have there injointed them with an after° fleet.   *35*

10-12 *I do . . sense* i.e., just because the numbers disagree in the reports, I do not doubt that the principal information (that the Turkish fleet is out) is fearfully true   18 *pageant* show, pretense   19 *in false gaze* looking the wrong way   23 *facile question* easy struggle   24 *warlike brace* "military posture"   35 *after* following

First Senator. Ay, so I thought. How many, as you
    guess?

Messenger. Of thirty sail; and now they do restem
    Their backward course, bearing with frank ap-
        pearance
    Their purposes toward Cyprus. Signior Montano,
40   Your trusty and most valiant servitor,
    With his free duty° recommends° you thus,
    And prays you to believe him.

Duke. 'Tis certain then for Cyprus.
    Marcus Luccicos, is not he in town?

45 *First Senator.* He's now in Florence.

Duke. Write from us to him; post-posthaste dispatch.

First Senator. Here comes Brabantio and the valiant
    Moor.

    Enter Brabantio, Othello, Cassio, Iago, Roderigo,
          and Officers.

Duke. Valiant Othello, we must straight° employ you
    Against the general° enemy Ottoman.
    [*To Brabantio*] I did not see you. Welcome, gentle
50   signior.
    We lacked your counsel and your help tonight.

Brabantio. So did I yours. Good your grace, pardon
    me.
    Neither my place, nor aught I heard of business,
    Hath raised me from my bed; nor doth the general
        care
55   Take hold on me; for my particular grief
    Is of so floodgate and o'erbearing nature
    That it engluts and swallows other sorrows,
    And it is still itself.

Duke.   Why, what's the matter?

Brabantio. My daughter! O, my daughter!

---

⁴¹ *free duty* unlimited respect   ⁴¹ *recommends* informs   ⁴⁸ *straight* at
once   ⁴⁹ *general* universal

Senators.   Dead?

Brabantio.   Ay, to me.
    She is abused, stol'n from me, and corrupted   60
    By spells and medicines bought of mountebanks;
    For nature so prepost'rously to err,
    Being not deficient, blind, or lame of sense,
    Sans° witchcraft could not.

Duke. Whoe'er he be that in this foul proceeding   65
    Hath thus beguiled your daughter of herself,
    And you of her, the bloody book of law
    You shall yourself read in the bitter letter
    After your own sense; yea, though our proper° son
    Stood in your action.°

Brabantio.   Humbly I thank your Grace.   70
    Here is the man—this Moor, whom now, it seems,
    Your special mandate for the state affairs
    Hath hither brought.

All.   We are very sorry for't.

Duke. [*To Othello*] What in your own part can you
    say to this?

Brabantio. Nothing, but this is so.   75

Othello. Most potent, grave, and reverend signiors,
    My very noble and approved° good masters,
    That I have ta'en away this old man's daughter,
    It is most true; true I have married her.
    The very head and front° of my offending   80
    Hath this extent, no more. Rude am I in my speech,
    And little blessed with the soft phrase of peace,
    For since these arms of mine had seven years' pith°
    Till now some nine moons wasted,° they have used
    Their dearest° action in the tented field;   85
    And little of this great world can I speak

More than pertains to feats of broils and battle;
And therefore little shall I grace my cause
In speaking for myself. Yet, by your gracious
     patience,
90   I will a round° unvarnished tale deliver
Of my whole course of love—what drugs, what
     charms,
What conjuration, and what mighty magic,
For such proceeding I am charged withal,
I won his daughter—

Brabantio.   A maiden never bold,
95   Of spirit so still and quiet that her motion
Blushed at herself;° and she, in spite of nature,
Of years, of country, credit, everything,
To fall in love with what she feared to look on!
It is a judgment maimed and most imperfect
100 That will confess perfection so could err
Against all rules of nature, and must be driven
To find out practices of cunning hell
Why this should be. I therefore vouch again
That with some mixtures pow'rful o'er the blood,
105 Or with some dram, conjured to this effect,
He wrought upon her.

Duke.   To vouch this is no proof,
Without more wider and more overt test
Than these thin habits° and poor likelihoods
Of modern° seeming do prefer against him.

110 *First Senator.* But, Othello, speak.
Did you by indirect and forcèd courses
Subdue and poison this young maid's affections?
Or came it by request, and such fair question°
As soul to soul affordeth?

Othello.   I do beseech you,
115 Send for the lady to the Sagittary

---

⁹⁰ *round* blunt   ⁹⁵⁻⁹⁶ *her motion/Blushed at herself* i.e., she was so modest that she blushed at every thought (and movement)   ¹⁰⁸ *habits* clothing   ¹⁰⁹ *modern* trivial   ¹¹³ *question* discussion

And let her speak of me before her father.
If you do find me foul in her report,
The trust, the office, I do hold of you
Not only take away, but let your sentence
Even fall upon my life.

Duke.   Fetch Desdemona hither.   *120*

Othello. Ancient, conduct them; you best know the
    place.
        [*Exit Iago, with two or three Attendants.*]

And till she come, as truly as to heaven
I do confess the vices of my blood,
So justly to your grave ears I'll present
How I did thrive in this fair lady's love,   *125*
And she in mine.

Duke.   Say it, Othello.

Othello. Her father loved me; oft invited me;
    Still° questioned me the story of my life
    From year to year, the battle, sieges, fortune
    That I have passed.   *130*
    I ran it through, even from my boyish days
    To th' very moment that he bade me tell it.
    Wherein I spoke of most disastrous chances,
    Of moving accidents by flood and field,
    Of hairbreadth scapes i' th' imminent° deadly
       breach,   *135*
    Of being taken by the insolent foe
    And sold to slavery, of my redemption thence
    And portance° in my travel's history,
    Wherein of anters° vast and deserts idle,°
    Rough quarries, rocks, and hills whose heads touch
       heaven,   *140*
    It was my hint to speak. Such was my process.
    And of the Cannibals that each other eat,
    The Anthropophagi,° and men whose heads

---

128 *Still* regularly   135 *imminent* threatening   138 *portance* manner of
acting   139 *anters* caves   139 *idle* empty, sterile   143 *Anthropophagi*
man-eaters

Grew beneath their shoulders. These things to hear
145 Would Desdemona seriously incline;
But still the house affairs would draw her thence;
Which ever as she could with haste dispatch,
She'd come again, and with a greedy ear
Devour up my discourse. Which I observing,
150 Took once a pliant hour, and found good means
To draw from her a prayer of earnest heart
That I would all my pilgrimage dilate,°
Whereof by parcels she had something heard,
But not intentively.° I did consent,
155 And often did beguile her of her tears
When I did speak of some distressful stroke
That my youth suffered. My story being done,
She gave me for my pains a world of kisses.
She swore in faith 'twas strange, 'twas passing°
      strange;
160 'Twas pitiful, 'twas wondrous pitiful.
She wished she had not heard it; yet she wished
That heaven had made her such a man. She thanked
      me,
And bade me, if I had a friend that loved her,
I should but teach him how to tell my story,
165 And that would woo her. Upon this hint I spake.
She loved me for the dangers I had passed,
And I loved her that she did pity them.
This only is the witchcraft I have used.
Here comes the lady. Let her witness it.

Enter Desdemona, Iago, Attendants.

170 *Duke.* I think this tale would win my daughter too.
Good Brabantio, take up this mangled matter at the
      best.°
Men do their broken weapons rather use
Than their bare hands.

---

152 *dilate* relate in full   154 *intentively* at length and in sequence
159 *passing* surpassing   171 *Take . . . best* i.e., make the best of this
disaster

Brabantio.   I pray you hear her speak.
  If she confess that she was half the wooer,
  Destruction on my head if my bad blame   *175*
  Light on the man. Come hither, gentle mistress.
  Do you perceive in all this noble company
  Where most you owe obedience?

Desdemona.   My noble father,
  I do perceive here a divided duty.
  To you I am bound for life and education;   *180*
  My life and education both do learn me
  How to respect you. You are the lord of duty,
  I am hitherto your daughter. But here's my husband,
  And so much duty as my mother showed
  To you, preferring you before her father,   *185*
  So much I challenge° that I may profess
  Due to the Moor my lord.

Brabantio.   God be with you. I have done.
  Please it your Grace, on to the state affairs.
  I had rather to adopt a child that get° it.
  Come hither, Moor.   *190*
  I here do give thee that with all my heart
  Which, but thou hast already, with all my heart
  I would keep from thee. For your sake,° jewel,
  I am glad at soul I have no other child,
  For thy escape would teach me tyranny,   *195*
  To hang clogs on them. I have done, my lord.

Duke. Let me speak like yourself and lay a sentence°
  Which, as a grise° or step, may help these lovers.
  When remedies are past, the griefs are ended
  By seeing the worst, which late on hopes depended.°   *200*
  To mourn a mischief that is past and gone
  Is the next° way to draw new mischief on.
  What cannot be preserved when fortune takes,

---

186 *challenge* claim as right   189 *get* beget   193 *For your sake* because
of you   197 *lay a sentence* provide a maxim   198 *grise* step   200 *late
on hopes depended* was supported by hope (of a better outcome) until
lately   202 *next* closest, surest

Patience her injury a mock'ry makes.
The robbed that smiles, steals something from the
205   thief;
He robs himself that spends a bootless° grief.

Brabantio. So let the Turk of Cyprus us beguile:
We lose it not so long as we can smile.
He bears the sentence well that nothing bears
210   But the free comfort which from thence he hears;
But he bears both the sentence and the sorrow
That to pay grief must of poor patience borrow.
These sentences, to sugar, or to gall,
Being strong on both sides, are equivocal.
215   But words are words. I never yet did hear
That the bruisèd heart was piercèd° through the ear.
I humbly beseech you, proceed to th' affairs of state.

Duke. The Turk with a most mighty preparation makes
for Cyprus. Othello, the fortitude° of the place is
220   best known to you; and though we have there a
substitute° of most allowed sufficiency,° yet opinion, a more sovereign mistress of effects, throws a
more safer voice on you.° You must therefore be
content to slubber° the gloss of your new fortunes
225   with this more stubborn and boisterous° expedition.

Othello. The tyrant Custom, most grave senators,
Hath made the flinty and steel couch of war
My thrice-driven° bed of down. I do agnize°
A natural and prompt alacrity
230   I find in hardness and do undertake
This present wars against the Ottomites.

---

²⁰⁶ *bootless* valueless   ²¹⁶ *piercèd* (some editors emend to *pieced,* i.e.,
"healed." But *pierced* makes good sense: Brabantio is saying in effect
that his heart cannot be further hurt [pierced] by the indignity of the
useless, conventional advice the Duke offers him. *Pierced* can also
mean, however, "lanced" in the medical sense, and would then mean
"treated")   ²¹⁹ *fortitude* fortification   ²²¹ *substitute* viceroy   ²²¹ *most
allowed sufficiency* generally acknowledged capability   ²²¹⁻²³ *opinion
. . . you* i.e., the general opinion, which finally controls affairs, is that
you would be the best man in this situation   ²²⁴ *slubber* besmear
²²⁵ *stubborn and boisterous* rough and violent   ²²⁸ *thrice-driven* i.e.,
softest   ²²⁸ *agnize* know in myself

Most humbly, therefore, bending to your state,
I crave fit disposition for my wife,
Due reference of place, and exhibition,°
With such accommodation and besort   235
As levels with° her breeding.

Duke.   Why, at her father's.

Brabantio. I will not have it so.

Othello.   Nor I.

Desdemona.   Nor would I there reside,
To put my father in impatient thoughts
By being in his eye. Most gracious Duke,
To my unfolding° lend your prosperous° ear,   240
And let me find a charter° in your voice,
T' assist my simpleness.

Duke.   What would you, Desdemona?

Desdemona. That I love the Moor to live with him,
My downright violence, and storm of fortunes,
May trumpet to the world. My heart's subdued   245
Even to the very quality of my lord.°
I saw Othello's visage in his mind,
And to his honors and his valiant parts
Did I my soul and fortunes consecrate.
So that, dear lords, if I be left behind,   250
A moth of peace, and he go to the war,
The rites° for why I love him are bereft me,
And I a heavy interim shall support
By his dear absence. Let me go with him.

Othello. Let her have your voice.°   255
Vouch with me, heaven, I therefore beg it not
To please the palate of my appetite,
Nor to comply with heat° —the young affects°

---

²³⁴ *exhibition* grant of funds   ²³⁶ *levels with* is suitable to   ²⁴⁰ *unfolding* explanation   ²⁴⁰ *prosperous* favoring   ²⁴¹ *charter* permission   ²⁴⁵⁻⁴⁶ *My . . . lord* i.e., I have become one in nature and being with the man I married (therefore, I too would go to the wars like a soldier)   ²⁵² *rites* (may refer either to the marriage rites or to the rites, formalities, of war)   ²⁵⁵ *voice* consent   ²⁵⁸ *heat* lust   ²⁵⁸ *affects* passions

In me defunct—and proper satisfaction;°
260   But to be free and bounteous to her mind;
And heaven defend° your good souls that you think
I will your serious and great business scant
When she is with me. No, when light-winged toys
Of feathered Cupid seel° with wanton° dullness
265   My speculative and officed instrument,°
That my disports corrupt and taint my business,
Let housewives make a skillet of my helm,
And all indign° and base adversities
Make head° against my estimation!°—

270 *Duke.* Be it as you shall privately determine,
Either for her stay or going. Th' affair cries haste,
And speed must answer it.

First Senator.   You must away tonight.

Othello. With all my heart.

Duke. At nine i' th' morning here we'll meet again
275   Othello, leave some officer behind,
And he shall our commission bring to you,
And such things else of quality and respect
As doth import you.

Othello.   So please your grace, my ancient;
A man he is of honesty and trust.
280   To his conveyance I assign my wife,
With what else needful your good grace shall think
To be sent after me.

Duke.   Let it be so.
Good night to every one. [*To Brabantio*] And, noble
signior,
If virtue no delighted° beauty lack,
285   Your son-in-law is far more fair than black.

First Senator. Adieu, brave Moor. Use Desdemona
well.

---

259 *proper satisfaction* i.e., consummation of the marriage 261 *defend* forbid 264 *seel* sew up 264 *wanton* lascivious 265 *speculative . . . instrument* i.e., sight (and, by extension, the mind) 268 *indign* un-worthy 269 *Make head* form an army, i.e., attack 269 *estimation* reputation 284 *delighted* delightful

Brabantio. Look to her, Moor, if thou hast eyes to see:
 She has deceived her father, and may thee.
     [*Exeunt Duke, Senators, Officers, &c.*]

Othello. My life upon her faith! Honest Iago,
 My Desdemona must I leave to thee.   *290*
 I prithee let thy wife attend on her,
 And bring them after in the best advantage.°
 Come, Desdemona. I have but an hour
 Of love, of wordly matter, and direction
 To spend with thee. We must obey the time. *295*
     Exit [*Moor with Desdemona*].

Roderigo. Iago?

Iago. What say'st thou, noble heart?

Roderigo. What will I do, think'st thou?

Iago. Why, go to bed and sleep.

Roderigo. I will incontinently° drown myself. *300*

Iago. If thou dost, I shall never love thee after. Why,
 thou silly gentleman?

Roderigo. It is silliness to live when to live is torment;
 and then have we a prescription to die when death is
 our physician.   *305*

Iago. O villainous! I have looked upon the world for
 four times seven years, and since I could distinguish
 betwixt a benefit and an injury, I never found man
 that knew how to love himself. Ere I would say I
 would drown myself for the love of a guinea hen, *310*
 I would change my humanity with a baboon.

Roderigo. What should I do? I confess it is my shame
 to be so fond, but it is not in my virtue° to amend it.

Iago. Virtue? A fig! 'Tis in ourselves that we are thus,
 or thus. Our bodies are our gardens, to the which *315*
 our wills are gardeners; so that if we will plant
 nettles or sow lettuce, set hyssop and weed up thyme,

---

²⁹² *advantage* opportunity ³⁰⁰ *incontinently* at once ³¹³ *virtue* strength
(Roderigo is saying that his nature controls him)

supply it with one gender of herbs or distract° it
with many—either to have it sterile with idleness or
320　manured with industry—why, the power and corri-
gible° authority of this lies in our wills. If the balance of our lives had not one scale of reason to poise
another of sensuality, the blood and baseness of
our natures would conduct us to most prepost'rous
325　conclusions.° But we have reason to cool our raging
motions, our carnal stings or unbitted° lusts,
whereof I take this that you call love to be a sect
or scion.°

Roderigo. It cannot be.

330　*Iago.* It is merely a lust of the blood and a permission of
the will. Come, be a man! Drown thyself? Drown
cats and blind puppies! I have professed me thy
friend, and I confess me knit to thy deserving with
cables of perdurable toughness. I could never better
335　stead° thee than now. Put money in thy purse.
Follow thou the wars; defeat thy favor° with an
usurped° beard. I say, put money in thy purse.
It cannot be long that Desdemona should continue
her love to the Moor. Put money in thy purse. Nor
340　he his to her. It was a violent commencement in
her and thou shalt see an answerable° sequestra-
tion—put but money in thy purse. These Moors
are changeable in their wills—fill thy purse with
money. The food that to him now is as luscious as
345　locusts° shall be to him shortly as bitter as coloquintida.° She must change for youth; when she is
sated with his body, she will find the errors of her
choice. Therefore, put money in thy purse. If thou
wilt needs damn thyself, do it a more delicate way
350　than drowning. Make all the money thou canst. If

---

³¹⁸ *distract* vary ³²⁰⁻²¹ *corrigible* corrective ³²⁵ *conclusions* ends
³²⁶ *unbitted* i.e., uncontrolled ³²⁷⁻²⁸ *sect or scion* offshoot ³³⁵ *stead*
serve ³³⁶ *defeat thy favor* disguise your face ³³⁷ *usurped* assumed
³⁴¹ *answerable* similar ³⁴⁵ *locusts* (a sweet fruit) ³⁴⁵⁻⁴⁶ *coloquintida*
(a purgative derived from a bitter apple)

sanctimony° and a frail vow betwixt an erring°
barbarian and supersubtle Venetian be not too hard
for my wits, and all the tribe of hell, thou shalt enjoy
her. Therefore, make money. A pox of drowning
thyself, it is clean out of the way. Seek thou rather   355
to be hanged in compassing° thy joy than to be
drowned and go without her.

Roderigo. Wilt thou be fast to my hopes, if I depend
on the issue?

Iago. Thou art sure of me. Go, make money. I have   360
told thee often, and I retell thee again and again, I
hate the Moor. My cause is hearted;° thine hath no
less reason. Let us be conjunctive° in our revenge
against him. If thou canst cuckold him, thou dost
thyself a pleasure, me a sport. There are many   365
events in the womb of time, which will be delivered.
Traverse, go, provide thy money! We will have more
of this tomorrow. Adieu.

Roderigo. Where shall we meet i' th' morning?

Iago. At my lodging.   370

Roderigo. I'll be with thee betimes.

Iago. Go to, farewell. Do you hear, Roderigo?

Roderigo. I'll sell all my land.   *Exit.*

Iago. Thus do I ever make my fool my purse;
For I mine own gained knowledge° should profane   375
If I would time expend with such snipe
But for my sport and profit. I hate the Moor,
And it is thought abroad that 'twixt my sheets
H'as done my office. I know not if't be true,
But I, for mere suspicion in that kind,   380
Will do, as if for surety.° He holds me well;
The better shall my purpose work on him.

---

³⁵¹ *sanctimony* sacred bond (of marriage)   ³⁵¹ *erring* wandering
³⁵⁶ *compassing* encompassing, achieving   ³⁶² *hearted* deep-seated in the
heart   ³⁶³ *conjunctive* joined   ³⁷⁵ *gained knowledge* i.e., practical,
worldly wisdom   ³⁸¹ *surety* certainty

Cassio's a proper° man. Let me see now:
To get his place, and to plume up my will°
385 In double knavery. How? How? Let's see.
After some time, to abuse Othello's ears
That he is too familiar with his wife.
He hath a person and a smooth dispose°
To be suspected—framed° to make women false.
390 The Moor is of a free and open nature
That thinks men honest that but seem to be so;
And will as tenderly be led by th' nose
As asses are.
I have't! It is engendered! Hell and night
395 Must bring this monstrous birth to the world's light.
                                                    [*Exit.*]

[383] *proper* handsome   [384] *plume up my will* (many explanations have been offered for this crucial line, which in Q1 reads "make up my will." The general sense is something like "to make more proud and gratify my ego")   [388] *dispose* manner   [389] *framed* designed

ACT II

Scene I. [*Cyprus.*]

Enter Montano and two Gentlemen, [one above].°

Montano. What from the cape can you discern at sea?

First Gentleman. Nothing at all, it is a high-wrought
    flood.
  I cannot 'twixt the heaven and the main
  Descry a sail.

Montano. Methinks the wind hath spoke aloud at land;   *5*
  A fuller blast ne'er shook our battlements.
  If it hath ruffianed so upon the sea,
  What ribs of oak, when mountains melt on them,
  Can hold the mortise? What shall we hear of this?

Second Gentleman. A segregation° of the Turkish
    fleet.   *10*
  For do but stand upon the foaming shore,
  The chidden billow seems to pelt the clouds;
  The wind-shaked surge, with high and monstrous
    main,°
  Seems to cast water on the burning Bear
  And quench the guards of th' ever-fixèd pole.°   *15*

II.i. s.d. (the Folio arrangement of this scene requires that the First
Gentleman stand above—on the upper stage—and act as a lookout re-
porting sights which cannot be seen by Montano standing below on the
main stage)   ¹⁰ *segregation* separation   ¹³ *main* (both "ocean" and
"strength")   ¹⁴⁻¹⁵ *Seems . . . pole* (the constellation Ursa Minor contains two stars which are the *guards,* or companions, of the *pole,* or
North Star)

I never did like molestation view
On the enchafèd flood.

Montano.   If that the Turkish fleet
Be not ensheltered and embayed, they are drowned;
It is impossible to bear it out.

Enter a [third] Gentleman.

20 *Third Gentleman.* News, lads! Our wars are done.
The desperate tempest hath so banged the Turks
That their designment halts. A noble ship of Venice
Hath seen a grievous wrack and sufferance°
On most part of their fleet.

Montano. How? Is this true?

25 *Third Gentleman.*   The ship is here put in,
A Veronesa; Michael Cassio,
Lieutenant to the warlike Moor Othello,
Is come on shore; the Moor himself at sea,
And is in full commission here for Cyprus.

30 *Montano.* I am glad on't. 'Tis a worthy governor.

Third Gentleman. But this same Cassio, though he
    speak of comfort
Touching the Turkish loss, yet he looks sadly
And prays the Moor be safe, for they were parted
With foul and violent tempest.

Montano.   Pray heavens he be;
35 For I have served him, and the man commands
Like a full soldier. Let's to the seaside, ho!
As well to see the vessel that's come in
As to throw out our eyes for brave Othello,
Even till we make the main and th' aerial blue
An indistinct regard.°

40 *Third Gentleman.*   Come, let's do so;
For every minute is expectancy
Of more arrivancie.°

---

²³ *sufferance* damage ³⁹⁻⁴⁰ *the main . . . regard* i.e., the sea and sky
become indistinguishable ⁴² *arrivancie* arrivals

Enter Cassio.

Cassio. Thanks, you the valiant of the warlike isle,
    That so approve° the Moor. O, let the heavens
    Give him defense against the elements,   *45*
    For I have lost him on a dangerous sea.

Montano. Is he well shipped?

Cassio. His bark is stoutly timbered, and his pilot
    Of very expert and approved allowance;°
    Therefore my hopes, not surfeited to death,°   *50*
    Stand in bold cure.°   (*Within*) A sail, a sail, a sail!

Cassio. What noise?

First Gentleman. The town is empty; on the brow o'
    th' sea
    Stand ranks of people, and they cry, "A sail!"

Cassio. My hopes do shape him for the governor.   *55*
                            [*A shot.*]

Second Gentleman. They do discharge their shot of
    courtesy:
    Our friends at least.

Cassio.   I pray you, sir, go forth
    And give us truth who 'tis that is arrived.

Second Gentleman. I shall.   *Exit.*

Montano. But, good lieutenant, is your general wived?   *60*

Cassio. Most fortunately. He hath achieved a maid
    That paragons° description and wild fame;°
    One that excels the quirks of blazoning pens,°
    And in th' essential vesture of creation°
    Does tire the ingener.°

---

⁴⁴ *approve* ("honor" or, perhaps, "are as warlike and valiant as your governor")   ⁴⁹ *approved allowance* known and tested   ⁵⁰ *not surfeited to death* i.e., not so great as to be in danger   ⁵¹ *Stand in bold cure* i.e., are likely to be restored   ⁶² *paragons* exceeds   ⁶² *wild fame* extravagant report   ⁶³ *quirks of blazoning pens* ingenuities of praising pens   ⁶⁴ *essential vesture of creation* i.e., essential human nature as given by the Creator   ⁶⁵ *tire the ingener* (a difficult line which probably means something like "outdo the human ability to imagine and picture")

Enter [Second] Gentleman.

65   How now? Who has put in?

Second Gentleman. 'Tis one Iago, ancient to the
general.

Cassio. H'as had most favorable and happy speed:
Tempests themselves, high seas, and howling winds,
The guttered° rocks and congregated° sands,
70   Traitors ensteeped° to enclog the guiltless keel,
As having sense° of beauty, do omit
Their mortal° natures, letting go safely by
The divine Desdemona.

Montano.   What is she?

Cassio. She that I spake of, our great captain's captain,
75   Left in the conduct of the bold Iago,
Whose footing° here anticipates our thoughts
A se'nnight's° speed. Great Jove, Othello guard,
And swell his sail with thine own pow'rful breath,
That he may bless this bay with his tall° ship,
80   Make love's quick pants in Desdemona's arms,
Give renewed fire to our extincted spirits.

Enter Desdemona, Iago, Roderigo, and Emilia.

O, behold! The riches of the ship is come on shore!
You men of Cyprus, let her have your knees.
                                   [*Kneeling.*]
Hail to thee, lady! and the grace of heaven,
85   Before, behind thee, and on every hand,
Enwheel thee round.

Desdemona.   I thank you, valiant Cassio.
What tidings can you tell of my lord?

Cassio. He is not yet arrived, nor know I aught
But that he's well and will be shortly here.

90   *Desdemona.* O but I fear. How lost you company?

---

⁶⁹ *guttered* jagged   ⁶⁹ *congregated* gathered   ⁷⁰ *ensteeped* submerged
⁷¹ *sense* awareness   ⁷² *mortal* deadly   ⁷⁶ *footing* landing   ⁷⁷ *se'nnight's*
week's   ⁷⁹ *tall* brave

Cassio. The great contention of sea and skies
    Parted our fellowship. (*Within*) A sail, a sail!
    [*A shot.*]
                         But hark. A sail!

Second Gentleman. They give this greeting to the
    citadel;
    This likewise is a friend.

Cassio.   See for the news.   95
                    [*Exit Gentleman.*]
    Good ancient, you are welcome. [*To Emilia*] Wel-
    come, mistress.
    Let it not gall your patience, good Iago,
    That I extend° my manners. 'Tis my breeding°
    That gives me this bold show of courtesy. [*Kisses
    Emilia.*]

Iago. Sir, would she give you so much of her lips   *100*
    As of her tongue she oft bestows on me,
    You would have enough.

Desdemona.   Alas, she has no speech.

Iago. In faith, too much.
    I find it still when I have leave to sleep.°
    Marry, before your ladyship,° I grant,   *105*
    She puts her tongue a little in her heart
    And chides with thinking.

Emilia.   You have little cause to say so.

Iago. Come on, come on! You are pictures° out of
    door,
    Bells in your parlors, wildcats in your kitchens,
    Saints in your injuries,° devils being offended,   *110*

---

⁹⁸ *extend* stretch ⁹⁸ *breeding* careful training in manners (Cassio is
considerably more the polished gentleman than Iago, and aware of it)
¹⁰⁴ *still . . . sleep* i.e., even when she allows me to sleep she continues
to scold ¹⁰⁵ *before your ladyship* in your presence ¹⁰⁸ *pictures* models
(of virtue) ¹¹⁰ *in your injuries* when you injure others

Players in your housewifery,° and housewives in
your beds.

Desdemona. O, fie upon thee, slanderer!

Iago. Nay, it is true, or else I am a Turk:
You rise to play, and go to bed to work.

Emilia. You shall not write my praise.

115 *Iago.*   No, let me not.

Desdemona. What wouldst write of me, if thou shouldst
praise me?

Iago. O gentle lady, do not put me to't,
For I am nothing if not critical.

Desdemona. Come on, assay. There's one gone to the
harbor?

Iago. Ay, madam.

120 *Desdemona.* [*Aside*] I am not merry; but I do beguile
The thing I am by seeming otherwise.—
Come, how wouldst thou praise me?

Iago. I am about it; but indeed my invention
Comes from my pate as birdlime° does from
frieze° —

125 It plucks out brains and all. But my Muse labors,
And thus she is delivered:
If she be fair° and wise: fairness and wit,
The one's for use, the other useth it.

Desdemona. Well praised. How if she be black° and
witty?

130 *Iago.* If she be black, and thereto have a wit,
She'll find a white that shall her blackness fit.

Desdemona. Worse and worse!

---

111 *housewifery* (this word can mean "careful, economical household
management," and Iago would then be accusing women of only pretending to be good housekeepers, while in bed they are either [1] economical of their favors, or more likely [2] serious and dedicated workers)
124 *birdlime* a sticky substance put on branches to catch birds
124 *frieze* rough cloth   127 *fair* light-complexioned   129 *black* brunette

Emilia. How if fair and foolish?

Iago. She never yet was foolish that was fair,
For even her folly helped her to an heir.   *135*

Desdemona. These are old fond° paradoxes to make
fools laugh i' th' alehouse. What miserable praise
hast thou for her that's foul and foolish?

Iago. There's none so foul, and foolish thereunto,
But does foul pranks which fair and wise ones do.   *140*

Desdemona. O heavy ignorance. Thou praisest the
worst best. But what praise couldst thou bestow on
a deserving woman indeed—one that in the authority of her merit did justly put on the vouch of very
malice itself?°   *145*

Iago. She that was ever fair, and never proud;
Had tongue at will, and yet was never loud;
Never lacked gold, and yet went never gay;
Fled from her wish, and yet said "Now I may";
She that being angered, her revenge being nigh,   *150*
Bade her wrong stay, and her displeasure fly;
She that in wisdom never was so frail
To change the cod's head for the salmon's tail;°
She that could think, and nev'r disclose her mind;
See suitors following, and not look behind: *155*
She was a wight° (if ever such wights were)—

Desdemona. To do what?

Iago. To suckle fools and chronicle small beer.°

Desdemona. O most lame and impotent conclusion.
Do not learn of him, Emilia, though he be thy hus-   *160*
band. How say you, Cassio? Is he not a most profane
and liberal° counselor?

---

136 *fond* foolish   143–45 *one . . . itself* i.e., a woman so honest and
deserving that even malice would be forced to approve of her   153 *To
. . . tail* i.e., to exchange something valuable for something useless
156 *wight* person   158 *chronicle small beer* i.e., keep household accounts
(the most trivial of occupations in Iago's opinion)   162 *liberal* licentious

Cassio. He speaks home,° madam. You may relish
him more in° the soldier than in the scholar. [*Takes
Desdemona's hand.*]

165 *Iago.* [*Aside*] He takes her by the palm. Ay, well said,
whisper! With as little a web as this will I ensnare
as great a fly as Cassio. Ay, smile upon her, do! I
will gyve° thee in thine own courtship.—You say
true; 'tis so, indeed!—If such tricks as these strip
170 you out of your lieutenantry, it had been better you
had not kissed your three fingers so oft—which now
again you are most apt to play the sir° in. Very
good! Well kissed! An excellent curtsy!° 'Tis so,
indeed. Yet again your fingers to your lips? Would
175 they were clyster pipes° for your sake! [*Trumpets
within.*] The Moor! I know his trumpet.°

Cassio. 'Tis truly so.

Desdemona. Let's meet him and receive him.

Cassio. Lo, where he comes.

Enter Othello and Attendants.

Othello. O my fair warrior!

180 *Desdemona.*   My dear Othello.

Othello. It gives me wonder great as my content
To see you here before me. O my soul's joy!
If after every tempest come such calms,
May the winds blow till they have wakened death.
185 And let the laboring bark climb hills of seas
Olympus-high, and duck again as low
As hell's from heaven. If it were now to die,
'Twere now to be most happy; for I fear
My soul hath her content so absolute
190 That not another comfort like to this
Succeeds in unknown fate.

---

163 *speaks home* thrusts deeply with his speech   163–64 *relish him more
in* enjoy him more as   168 *gyve* bind   172 *the sir* the fashionable gentleman   173 *curtsy* courtesy, i.e., bow   175 *clyster pipes* enema tubes
176 *his trumpet* (great men had their own distinctive calls)

Desdemona.   The heavens forbid
  But that our loves and comforts should increase
  Even as our days do grow.

Othello.   Amen to that, sweet powers!
  I cannot speak enough of this content;
  It stops me here [*touches his heart*]; it is too much
      of joy.   *195*
  And this, and this, the greatest discords be
                                        [*They kiss.*]
  That e'er our hearts shall make!

Iago.   [*Aside*] O, you are well tuned now!
  But I'll set down the pegs° that make this music,
  As honest as I am.

Othello.   Come, let us to the castle.
  News, friends! Our wars are done; the Turks are
      drowned.   *200*
  How does my old acquaintance of this isle?
  Honey, you shall be well desired in Cyprus;
  I have found great love amongst them. O my sweet,
  I prattle out of fashion, and I dote
  In mine own comforts. I prithee, good Iago,   *205*
  Go to the bay and disembark my coffers.
  Bring thou the master to the citadel;
  He is a good one, and his worthiness
  Does challenge° much respect. Come, Desdemona,
  Once more well met at Cyprus.   *210*
  Exit Othello and Desdemona [*and all but Iago and*
                                        Roderigo].

Iago. [*To an Attendant*] Do thou meet me presently
  at the harbor. [*To Roderigo*] Come hither. If thou
  be'st valiant (as they say base men being in love
  have then a nobility in their natures more than is
  native to them), list me. The lieutenant tonight *215*
  watches on the court of guard.° First, I must tell thee
  this: Desdemona is directly in love with him.

Roderigo. With him? Why, 'tis not possible.

---

¹⁹⁸ *set down the pegs* loosen the strings (to produce discord)   ²⁰⁹ *challenge* require, exact   ²¹⁶ *court of guard* guardhouse

Iago. Lay thy finger thus [*puts his finger to his lips*],
220 and let thy soul be instructed. Mark me with what
violence she first loved the Moor but for bragging
and telling her fantastical lies. To love him still for
prating? Let not thy discreet heart think it. Her
eye must be fed. And what delight shall she have to
225 look on the devil? When the blood is made dull with
the act of sport, there should be a game° to inflame
it and to give satiety a fresh appetite, loveliness in
favor,° sympathy in years,° manners, and beauties;
all which the Moor is defective in. Now for want of
230 these required conveniences,° her delicate tender-
ness will find itself abused, begin to heave the
gorge,° disrelish and abhor the Moor. Very nature
will instruct her in it and compel her to some second
choice. Now, sir, this granted—as it is a most preg-
235 nant° and unforced position—who stands so eminent in the degree of this fortune as Cassio does?
A knave very voluble; no further conscionable°
than in putting on the mere form of civil and hu-
mane° seeming for the better compass of his salt°
240 and most hidden loose° affection. Why, none! Why,
none! A slipper° and subtle knave, a finder of
occasion, that has an eye can stamp and counterfeit
advantages, though true advantage never present
itself. A devilish knave. Besides, the knave is hand-
245 some, young, and hath all those requisites in him
that folly and green minds look after. A pestilent
complete knave, and the woman hath found him
already.

Roderigo. I cannot believe that in her; she's full of
250 most blessed condition.

Iago. Blessed fig's-end! The wine she drinks is made of
grapes. If she had been blessed, she would never

---

²²⁶ *game* sport (with the added sense of "gamey," "rank") ²²⁸ *favor*
countenance, appearance ²²⁸ *sympathy in years* sameness of age
²³⁰ *conveniences* advantages ²³¹⁻³² *heave the gorge* vomit ²³⁴⁻³⁵ *preg-
nant* likely ²³⁷ *no further conscionable* having no more conscience
²³⁸⁻³⁹ *humane* polite ²³⁹ *salt* lecherous ²⁴⁰ *loose* immoral ²⁴¹ *slip-
per* slippery

have loved the Moor. Blessed pudding! Didst thou
not see her paddle with the palm of his hand? Didst
not mark that?   255

Roderigo. Yes, that I did; but that was but courtesy.

Iago. Lechery, by this hand! [Extends his index finger.]
An index° and obsure prologue to the history of
lust and foul thoughts. They met so near with their
lips that their breaths embraced together. Villainous 260
thoughts, Roderigo. When these mutualities so
marshal the way, hard at hand comes the master and
main exercise, th' incorporate° conclusion: Pish!
But, sir, be you ruled by me. I have brought you
from Venice. Watch you tonight; for the command,   265
I'll lay't upon you. Cassio knows you not. I'll not be
far from you. Do you find some occasion to anger
Cassio, either by speaking too loud, or tainting°
his discipline, or from what other course you please
which the time shall more favorably minister.   270

Roderigo. Well.

Iago. Sir, he's rash and very sudden in choler,° and
haply may strike at you. Provoke him that he may;
for even out of that will I cause these of Cyprus to
mutiny, whose qualification shall come into no true 275
taste° again but by the displanting of Cassio. So
shall you have a shorter journey to your desires by
the means I shall then have to prefer them; and the
impediment most profitably removed without the
which there were no expectation of our prosperity.   280

Roderigo. I will do this if you can bring it to any
opportunity.

Iago. I warrant thee. Meet me by and by at the citadel.
I must fetch his necessaries ashore. Farewell.

Roderigo. Adieu.   Exit.   285

Iago. That Cassio loves her, I do well believe 't;

---

258 *index* pointer   263 *incorporate* carnal   268 *tainting* discrediting
272 *choler* anger   275–76 *qualification . . . taste* i.e., appeasement will not
be brought about (wine was "qualified" by adding water)

That she loves him, 'tis apt and of great credit.
The Moor, howbeit that I endure him not,
Is of a constant, loving, noble nature,
290 And I dare think he'll prove to Desdemona
A most dear° husband. Now I do love her too;
Not out of absolute° lust, though peradventure°
I stand accountant for as great a sin,
But partly led to diet° my revenge,
295 For that I do suspect the lusty Moor
Hath leaped into my seat; the thought whereof
Doth, like a poisonous mineral, gnaw my inwards;
And nothing can or shall content my soul
Till I am evened with him, wife for wife.
300 Or failing so, yet that I put the Moor
At least into a jealousy so strong
That judgment cannot cure. Which thing to do,
If this poor trash of Venice, whom I trace°
For his quick hunting, stand the putting on,
305 I'll have our Michael Cassio on the hip,
Abuse him to the Moor in the right garb°
(For I fear Cassio with my nightcap too),
Make the Moor thank me, love me, and reward me
For making him egregiously an ass
310 And practicing upon° his peace and quiet,
Even to madness. 'Tis here, but yet confused:
Knavery's plain face is never seen till used.   *Exit.*

---

291 *dear* expensive   292 *out of absolute* absolutely out of   292 *peradventure* perchance   294 *diet* feed   303 *trace* (most editors emend to "trash," meaning to hang weights on a dog to slow his hunting; but "trace" clearly means something like "put on the trace" or "set on the track")   306 *right garb* i.e., "proper fashion"   310 *practicing upon* scheming to destroy

Scene II. [*A street.*]

Enter Othello's Herald, with a proclamation.

Herald. It is Othello's pleasure, our noble and valiant
   general, that upon certain tidings now arrived im-
   porting the mere perdition° of the Turkish fleet,
   every man put himself into triumph. Some to dance,
   some to make bonfires, each man to what sport and   5
   revels his addition° leads him. For, besides these
   beneficial news, it is the celebration of his nuptial.
   So much was his pleasure should be proclaimed.
   All offices° are open, and there is full liberty of
   feasting from this present hour of five till the bell   10
   have told eleven. Bless the isle of Cyprus and our
   noble general Othello!   *Exit.*

Scene III. [*The citadel of Cyprus.*]

Enter Othello, Desdemona, Cassio, and Attendants.

Othello. Good Michael, look you to the guard tonight.
   Let's teach ourselves that honorable stop,
   Not to outsport discretion.

Cassio.   Iago hath direction what to do;
   But notwithstanding, with my personal eye   5
   Will I look to't.

Othello.   Iago is most honest.
   Michael, good night. Tomorrow with your earliest
   Let me have speech with you. [*To Desdemona*]
      Come, my dear love,

II.ii.³ *mere perdition* absolute destruction ⁶ *addition* rank ⁹ *offices*
kitchens and storerooms of food

The purchase made, the fruits are to ensue,
10 That profit's yet to come 'tween me and you.
Good night.

        Exit [*Othello with Desdemona and Attendants*].

                Enter Iago.

Cassio. Welcome, Iago. We must to the watch.

Iago. Not this hour, lieutenant; 'tis not yet ten o' th'
clock. Our general cast° us thus early for the love
15 of his Desdemona; who let us not therefore blame.
He hath not yet made wanton the night with her, and
she is sport for Jove.

Cassio. She's a most exquisite lady.

Iago. And, I'll warrant her, full of game.

20 *Cassio.* Indeed, she's a most fresh and delicate creature.

Iago. What an eye she has! Methinks it sounds a parley
to provocation.

Cassio. An inviting eye; and yet methinks right modest.

Iago. And when she speaks, is it not an alarum° to
25 love?

Cassio. She is indeed perfection.

Iago. Well, happiness to their sheets! Come, lieutenant,
I have a stoup° of wine, and here without are a
brace of Cyprus gallants that would fain have a
30 measure to the health of black Othello.

Cassio. Not tonight, good Iago. I have very poor and
unhappy brains for drinking; I could well wish
courtesy would invent some other custom of entertainment.

35 *Iago.* O, they are our friends. But one cup! I'll drink
for you.

Cassio. I have drunk but one cup tonight, and that was
craftily qualified° too; and behold what innovation

II.iii.¹⁴ *cast* dismissed   ²⁴ *alarum* the call to action, "general quarters"
²⁸ *stoup* two-quart tankard   ³⁸ *qualified* diluted

it makes here. I am unfortunate in the infirmity and
dare not task my weakness with any more.   40

Iago. What, man! 'Tis a night of revels, the gallants
   desire it.

Cassio. Where are they?

Iago. Here, at the door. I pray you call them in.

Cassio. I'll do't, but it dislikes me.   *Exit.*   45

Iago. If I can fasten but one cup upon him
   With that which he hath drunk tonight already,
   He'll be as full of quarrel and offense
   As my young mistress' dog. Now, my sick fool
      Roderigo,
   Whom love hath turned almost the wrong side out,   50
   To Desdemona hath tonight caroused
   Potations pottle-deep;° and he's to watch.
   Three else° of Cyprus, noble swelling spirits,
   That hold their honors in a wary distance,°
   The very elements of this warlike isle,   55
   Have I tonight flustered with flowing cups,
   And they watch too. Now, 'mongst this flock of
      drunkards
   Am I to put our Cassio in some action
   That may offend the isle. But here they come.

   Enter Cassio, Montano, and Gentlemen.

   If consequence do but approve my dream,   60
   My boat sails freely, both with wind and stream.

Cassio. 'Fore God, they have given me a rouse° already.

Montano. Good faith, a little one; not past a pint, as
   I am a soldier.

Iago. Some wine, ho!   65
   [*Sings*] And let me the canakin clink, clink;
            And let me the canakin clink.

---

⁵²*pottle-deep* to the bottom of the cup   ⁵³ *else* others   ⁵⁴ *hold . . .
distance* are scrupulous in maintaining their honor   ⁶² *rouse* drink

A soldier's a man;
O man's life's but a span,
70   Why then, let a soldier drink.
Some wine, boys!

Cassio. 'Fore God, an excellent song!

Iago. I learned it in England, where indeed they are
most potent in potting. Your Dane, your German,
75   and your swag-bellied° Hollander—Drink, ho!—
are nothing to your English.

Cassio. Is your Englishman so exquisite° in his drinking?

Iago. Why, he drinks you with facility your Dane dead
80   drunk; he sweats not to overthrow your Almain; he
gives your Hollander a vomit ere the next pottle can
be filled.

Cassio. To the health of our general!

Montano. I am for it, lieutenant, and I'll do you justice.

85   *Iago.* O sweet England!
[*Sings*] King Stephen was and a worthy peer;
His breeches cost him but a crown;
He held them sixpence all too dear,
With that he called the tailor lown.°
90   He was a wight of high renown,
And thou art but of low degree:
'Tis pride that pulls the country down;
And take thine auld cloak about thee.
Some wine, ho!

95   *Cassio.* 'Fore God, this is a more exquisite song than
the other.

Iago. Will you hear't again?

Cassio. No, for I hold him to be unworthy of his place
that does those things. Well, God's above all; and
100   there be souls must be saved, and there be souls
must not be saved.

---

⁷⁵ *swag-bellied* hanging   ⁷⁷ *exquisite* superb   ⁸⁹ *lown* lout

Iago. It's true, good lieutenant.

Cassio. For mine own part—no offense to the general,
nor any man of quality—I hope to be saved.

Iago. And so do I too, lieutenant.   *105*

Cassio. Ay, but, by your leave, not before me. The lieutenant is to be saved before the ancient. Let's have
no more of this; let's to our affairs.—God forgive us
our sins!—Gentlemen, let's look to our business.
Do not think, gentlemen, I am drunk. This is my *110*
ancient; this is my right hand, and this is my left.
I am not drunk now. I can stand well enough, and
I speak well enough.

Gentlemen. Excellent well!

Cassio. Why, very well then. You must not think then *115*
that I am drunk.   *Exit.*

Montano. To th' platform, masters. Come, let's set
the watch.

Iago. You see this fellow that is gone before.
He's a soldier fit to stand by Caesar
And give direction; and do but see his vice.
'Tis to his virtue a just equinox,°   *120*
The one as long as th' other. 'Tis pity of him.
I fear the trust Othello puts him in,
On some odd time of his infirmity,
Will shake this island.

Montano.   But is he often thus?   *125*

Iago. 'Tis evermore his prologue to his sleep:
He'll watch the horologe a double set°
If drink rock not his cradle.

Montano.   It were well
The general were put in mind of it.
Perhaps he sees it not, or his good nature
Prizes the virtue that appears in Cassio   *130*
And looks not on his evils. Is not this true?

---

¹²¹ *just equinox* exact balance (of dark and light)   ¹²⁷ *watch . . . set*
stay awake twice around the clock

Enter Roderigo.

Iago. [*Aside*] How now, Roderigo?
I pray you after the lieutenant, go! [*Exit Roderigo.*]

135 *Montano.* And 'tis great pity that the noble Moor
Should hazard such a place as his own second
With one of an ingraft° infirmity.
It were an honest action to say so
To the Moor.

Iago.   Not I, for this fair island!
140 I do love Cassio well and would do much
To cure him of this evil.   (Help! Help! *Within.*)
                    But hark? What noise?

Enter Cassio, pursuing Roderigo.

Cassio. Zounds, you rogue! You rascal!

Montano. What's the matter, lieutenant?

Cassio. A knave teach me my duty? I'll beat the knave
145 into a twiggen° bottle.

Roderigo. Beat me?

Cassio. Dost thou prate, rogue?   [*Strikes him.*]

Montano. Nay, good lieutenant! I pray you, sir, hold
your hand.
                              [*Stays him.*]

150 *Cassio.* Let me go, sir, or I'll knock you o'er the
mazzard.°

Montano. Come, come, you're drunk!

Cassio. Drunk?   [*They fight.*]

Iago. [*Aside to Roderigo*] Away, I say! Go out and
155 cry a mutiny!
                              [*Exit Roderigo.*]
Nay, good lieutenant. God's will, gentlemen!
Help, ho! Lieutenant. Sir. Montano.
Help, masters! Here's a goodly watch indeed!
                              [*A bell rung.*]

137 *ingraft* ingrained   145 *twiggen* wicker-covered   151 *mazzard* head

Who's that which rings the bell? Diablo, ho!
The town will rise. God's will, lieutenant,   160
You'll be ashamed forever.

Enter Othello and Attendants.

Othello.   What is the matter here?

Montano. Zounds, I bleed still. I am hurt to the death.
He dies.   [*He and Cassio fight again.*]

Othello. Hold for your lives!

Iago. Hold, ho! Lieutenant. Sir. Montano. Gentlemen!   165
Have you forgot all place of sense and duty?
Hold! The general speaks to you. Hold, for shame!

Othello. Why, how now, ho? From whence ariseth this?
Are we turned Turks, and to ourselves do that
Which heaven hath forbid the Ottomites?°   170
For Christian shame put by this barbarous brawl!
He that stirs next to carve for his own rage
Holds his soul light;° he dies upon his motion.
Silence that dreadful bell! It frights the isle
From her propriety.° What is the matter, masters?   175
Honest Iago, that looks dead with grieving,
Speak. Who began this? On thy love, I charge thee.

Iago. I do not know. Friends all, but now, even now,
In quarter° and in terms like bride and groom
Devesting them for bed; and then, but now—   180
As if some planet had unwitted men—
Swords out, and tilting one at other's breasts
In opposition bloody. I cannot speak
Any beginning to this peevish odds,°
And would in action glorious I had lost   185
Those legs that brought me to a part of it!

Othello. How comes it, Michael, you are thus forgot?

Cassio. I pray you pardon me; I cannot speak.

Othello. Worthy Montano, you were wont to be civil;
The gravity and stillness of your youth   190

---

170 *heaven . . . Ottomites* i.e., by sending the storm which dispersed
the Turks   173 *Holds his soul light* values his soul lightly   175 *propriety*
proper order   179 *In quarter* on duty   184 *odds* quarrel

The world hath noted, and your name is great
In mouths of wisest censure.° What's the matter
That you unlace° your reputation thus
And spend your rich opinion° for the name
195 Of a night-brawler? Give me answer to it.

Montano. Worthy Othello, I am hurt to danger.
Your officer, Iago, can inform you,
While I spare speech, which something now offends°
          me,
Of all that I do know; nor know I aught
200 By me that's said or done amiss this night,
Unless self-charity be sometimes a vice,
And to defend ourselves it be a sin
When violence assails us.

Othello.   Now, by heaven,
My blood begins my safer guides to rule,
205 And passion, having my best judgment collied,°
Assays to lead the way. If I once stir
Or do but lift this arm, the best of you
Shall sink in my rebuke. Give me to know
How this foul rout began, who set it on;
210 And he that is approved in this offense,
Though he had twinned with me, both at a birth,
Shall lose me. What? In a town of war
Yet wild, the people's hearts brimful of fear,
To manage° private and domestic quarrel?
215 In night, and on the court and guard of safety?
'Tis monstrous. Iago, who began't?

Montano. If partially affined, or leagued in office,°
Thou dost deliver more or less than truth,
Thou art no soldier.

Iago.   Touch me not so near.
220 I had rather have this tongue cut from my mouth
Than it should do offense to Michael Cassio.

---

¹⁹²*censure* judgment   ¹⁹³*unlace* undo (the term refers specifically to
the dressing of a wild boar killed in the hunt)   ¹⁹⁴*opinion* reputation
¹⁹⁸*offends* harms, hurts   ²⁰⁵*collied* darkened   ²¹⁴*manage* conduct
²¹⁷*If . . . office* if you are partial because you are related ("affined")
or the brother officer (of Cassio)

Yet I persuade myself to speak the truth
Shall nothing wrong him. This it is, general.
Montano and myself being in speech,
There comes a fellow crying out for help,   225
And Cassio following him with determined sword
To execute upon him. Sir, this gentleman
Steps in to Cassio and entreats his pause.
Myself the crying fellow did pursue,
Lest by his clamor—as it so fell out—   230
The town might fall in fright. He, swift of foot,
Outran my purpose; and I returned then rather
For that I heard the clink and fall of swords,
And Cassio high in oath; which till tonight
I ne'er might say before. When I came back—   235
For this was brief—I found them close together
At blow and thrust, even as again they were
When you yourself did part them.
More of this matter cannot I report;
But men are men; the best sometimes forget.   240
Though Cassio did some little wrong to him,
As men in rage strike those that wish them best,
Yet surely Cassio I believe received
From him that fled some strange indignity,
Which patience could not pass.°

Othello.   I know, Iago,   245
Thy honesty and love doth mince° this matter,
Making it light to Cassio. Cassio, I love thee;
But never more be officer of mine.

Enter Desdemona, attended.

Look if my gentle love be not raised up.
I'll make thee an example.

Desdemona.   What is the matter, dear.   250

Othello. All's well, sweeting; come away to bed.
   [*To Montano*] Sir, for your hurts, myself will be
      your surgeon.
   Lead him off.   [*Montano led off.*]

---

²⁴⁵ *pass* allow to pass   ²⁴⁶ *mince* cut up (i.e., tell only part of)

Iago, look with care about the town
255   And silence those whom this vile brawl distracted.
Come, Desdemona: 'tis the soldiers' life
To have their balmy slumbers waked with strife.

                    Exit [with all but Iago and Cassio].

Iago. What, are you hurt, lieutenant?

Cassio. Ay, past all surgery.

260   *Iago.* Marry, God forbid!

Cassio. Reputation, reputation, reputation! O, I have
lost my reputation! I have lost the immortal part of
myself, and what remains is bestial. My reputation,
Iago, my reputation.

265   *Iago.* As I am an honest man, I had thought you had
received some bodily wound. There is more sense°
in that than in reputation. Reputation is an idle and
most false imposition,° oft got without merit and
lost without deserving. You have lost no reputation
270   at all unless you repute yourself such a loser. What,
man, there are more ways to recover the general
again. You are but now cast in his mood°—a
punishment more in policy° than in malice—even
so as one would beat his offenseless dog to affright
275   an imperious lion. Sue to him again, and he's yours.

Cassio. I will rather sue to be despised than to deceive
so good a commander with so slight, so drunken,
and so indiscreet an officer. Drunk! And speak
parrot!° And squabble! Swagger! Swear! and dis-
280   course fustian° with one's own shadow! O thou
invisible spirit of wine, if thou hast no name to be
known by, let us call thee devil!

Iago. What was he that you followed with your sword?
What had he done to you?

285   *Cassio.* I know not.

Iago. Is't possible?

---

²⁶⁶ *sense* physical feeling   ²⁶⁸ *imposition* external thing   ²⁷² *cast in his
mood* dismissed because of his anger   ²⁷³ *in policy* politically necessary
²⁷⁸⁻⁷⁹ *speak parrot* gabble without sense   ²⁷⁹⁻⁸⁰ *discourse fustian* speak
nonsense ("fustian" was a coarse cotton cloth used for stuffing)

Cassio. I remember a mass of things, but nothing distinctly: a quarrel, but nothing wherefore. O God,
   that men should put an enemy in their mouths to
   steal away their brains! that we should with joy,   290
   pleasance, revel, and applause transform ourselves
   into beasts!

Iago. Why, but you are now well enough. How came
   you thus recovered?

Cassio. It hath pleased the devil drunkenness to give   295
   place to the devil wrath. One unperfectness shows
   me another, to make me frankly despise myself.

Iago. Come, you are too severe a moraler. As the time,
   the place, and the condition of this country stands,
   I could heartily wish this had not befall'n; but since   300
   it is as it is, mend it for your own good.

Cassio. I will ask him for my place again: he shall tell
   me I am a drunkard. Had I as many mouths as
   Hydra, such an answer would stop them all. To be
   now a sensible man, by and by a fool, and presently   305
   a beast! O strange! Every inordinate cup is unblest,
   and the ingredient is a devil.

Iago. Come, come, good wine is a good familiar
   creature if it be well used. Exclaim no more against
   it. And, good lieutenent, I think you think I love   310
   you.

Cassio. I have well approved it, sir. I drunk?

Iago. You or any man living may be drunk at a time,
   man. I tell you what you shall do. Our general's
   wife is now the general. I may say so in this respect,   315
   for that he hath devoted and given up himself to the
   contemplation, mark, and devotement of her parts°
   and graces. Confess yourself freely to her; importune
   her help to put you in your place again. She is of
   so free, so kind, so apt, so blessed a disposition she   320
   holds it a vice in her goodness not to do more than

---

³¹⁷ *devotement of her parts* devotion to her qualities

she is requested. This broken joint between you
and her husband entreat her to splinter;° and my
fortunes against any lay° worth naming, this crack
325   of your love shall grow stronger than it was before.

Cassio. You advise me well.

Iago. I protest, in the sincerity of love and honest
kindness.

Cassio. I think it freely; and betimes in the morning I
330   will beseech the virtuous Desdemona to undertake
for me. I am desperate of my fortunes if they check°
me.

Iago. You are in the right. Good night, lieutenant; I
must to the watch.

335   *Cassio.* Good night, honest Iago.   *Exit Cassio.*

Iago. And what's he then that says I play the villain,
    When this advice is free° I give, and honest,
    Probal to° thinking, and indeed the course
    To win the Moor again? For 'tis most easy
340   Th' inclining° Desdemona to subdue
    In any honest suit; she's framed as fruitful°
    As the free elements.° And then for her
    To win the Moor—were't to renounce his baptism,
    All seals and symbols of redeemèd sin—
345   His soul is so enfettered to her love
    That she may make, unmake, do what she list,
    Even as her appetite° shall play the god
    With his weak function.° How am I then a villain
    To counsel Cassio to this parallel course,
350   Directly to his good? Divinity of hell!
    When devils will the blackest sins put on,°
    They do suggest at first with heavenly shows,°
    As I do now. For whiles this honest fool
    Plies Desdemona to repair his fortune,
355   And she for him pleads strongly to the Moor,

---

³²³ *splinter* splint   ³²⁴ *lay* wager   ³³¹ *check* repulse   ³³⁷ *free* generous
and open   ³³⁸ *Probal to* provable by   ³⁴⁰ *inclining* inclined (to be help-
ful)   ³⁴¹ *framed as fruitful* made as generous   ³⁴² *elements* i.e., basic
nature   ³⁴⁷ *appetite* liking   ³⁴⁸ *function* thought   ³⁵¹ *put on* advance,
further   ³⁵² *shows* appearances

I'll pour this pestilence into his ear:
That she repeals him° for her body's lust;
And by how much she strives to do him good,
She shall undo her credit with the Moor.
So will I turn her virtue into pitch,　　　　　　　　360
And out of her own goodness make the net
That shall enmesh them all. How now, Roderigo?

Enter Roderigo.

Roderigo. I do follow here in the chase, not like a
hound that hunts, but one that fills up the cry.° My
money is almost spent; I have been tonight exceed-　365
ingly well cudgeled; and I think the issue will be,
I shall have so much experience for my pains; and
so, with no money at all, and a little more wit,
return again to Venice.

Iago. How poor are they that have not patience!　　370
What wound did ever heal but by degrees?
Thou know'st we work by wit, and not by witch-
　　craft;
And wit depends on dilatory time.
Does't not go well? Cassio hath beaten thee,
And thou by that small hurt hath cashiered Cassio.　375
Though other things grow fair against the sun,
Yet fruits that blossom first will first be ripe.
Content thyself awhile. By the mass, 'tis morning!
Pleasure and action make the hours seem short.
Retire thee; go where thou art billeted.　　　　　380
Away, I say! Thou shalt know more hereafter.
Nay, get thee gone! 　　　　　*Exit Roderigo.*
　　　　　Two things are to be done:
My wife must move° for Cassio to her mistress;
I'll set her on;
Myself awhile° to draw the Moor apart　　　　　385
And bring him jump° when he may Cassio find
Soliciting his wife. Ay, that's the way!
Dull not device by coldness and delay.　　　*Exit.*

---

357 *repeals him* asks for (Cassio's reinstatement)　364 *fills up the cry*
makes up one of the hunting pack, adding to the noise but not actually tracking　383 *move* petition　385 *awhile* at the same time
386 *jump* at the precise moment and place

ACT III

Scene I. [*A street.*]

Enter Cassio [and] Musicians.

Cassio. Masters, play here. I will content your pains.°
Something that's brief; and bid "Good morrow,
general." [*They play.*]

[*Enter Clown.*°]

Clown. Why, masters, have your instruments been in
Naples° that they speak i' th' nose thus?

5 *Musician.* How, sir, how?

Clown. Are these, I pray you, wind instruments?

Musician. Ay, marry, are they, sir.

Clown. O, thereby hangs a tale.

Musician. Whereby hangs a tale, sir?

10 *Clown.* Marry, sir, by many a wind instrument that I
know. But, masters, here's money for you; and the
general so likes your music that he desires you,
for love's sake, to make no more noise with it.

Musician. Well, sir, we will not.

15 *Clown.* If you have any music that may not be heard,
to't again. But, as they say, to hear music the
general does not greatly care.

III.i.¹ *content your pains* reward your efforts ² s.d. *Clown* fool
⁴ *Naples* (this may refer either to the Neapolitan nasal tone, or to syph-
ilis—rife in Naples—which breaks down the nose)

90

Musician. We have none such, sir.

Clown. Then put up your pipes in your bag, for I'll
    away. Go, vanish into air, away!   20

                                    Exit Musicians.

Cassio. Dost thou hear me, mine honest friend?

Clown. No. I hear not your honest friend. I hear you.

Cassio. Prithee keep up thy quillets.° There's a poor
    piece of gold for thee. If the gentlewoman that
    attends the general's wife be stirring, tell her there's   25
    one Cassio entreats her a little favor of speech.
    Wilt thou do this?

Clown. She is stirring, sir. If she will stir hither, I shall
    seem to notify unto her.°   *Exit Clown.*

                    Enter Iago.

Cassio. In happy time, Iago.

Iago.   You have not been abed then?   30

Cassio. Why no, the day had broke before we parted.
    I have made bold, Iago, to send in to your wife;
    My suit to her is that she will to virtuous Desdemona
    Procure me some access.

Iago.   I'll send her to you presently,
    And I'll devise a mean to draw the Moor   35
    Out of the way, that your converse and business
    May be more free.

Cassio. I humbly thank you for 't.   *Exit [Iago].*
                            I never knew
    A Florentine° more kind and honest.

                    Enter Emilia.

Emilia. Good morrow, good lieutenant. I am sorry   40
    For your displeasure;° but all will sure be well.
    The general and his wife are talking of it,

---

23 *quillets* puns 29 *seem . . . her* (the Clown is mocking Cassio's
overly elegant manner of speaking) 39 *Florentine* i.e., Iago is as kind
as if he were from Cassio's home town, Florence 41 *displeasure* dis-
comforting

And she speaks for you stoutly. The Moor replies
That he you hurt is of great fame in Cyprus
45 And great affinity,° and that in wholesome wisdom
He might not but refuse you. But he protests he loves
    you,
And needs no other suitor but his likings
To bring you in again.

Cassio.   Yet I beseech you,
If you think fit, or that it may be done,
50 Give me advantage of some brief discourse
With Desdemona alone.

Emilia.   Pray you come in.
I will bestow you where you shall have time
To speak your bosom° freely.

Cassio.   I am much bound to you.
                            [*Exeunt.*]

Scene II. [*The citadel.*]

Enter Othello, Iago, and Gentlemen.

Othello. These letters give, Iago, to the pilot
And by him do my duties to the Senate.
That done, I will be walking on the works;
Repair° there to me.

Iago.   Well, my good lord, I'll do't.

5 *Othello.* This fortification, gentlemen, shall we see't?

Gentlemen. We'll wait upon your lordship.   *Exeunt.*

---

⁴⁵ *affinity* family   ⁵³ *bosom* inmost thoughts   III.ii.⁴ *Repair* go

Scene III. [*The citadel.*]

Enter Desdemona, Cassio, and Emilia.

Desdemona. Be thou assured, good Cassio, I will do
  All my abilities in thy behalf.

Emilia. Good madam, do. I warrant it grieves my husband
  As if the cause were his.

Desdemona. O, that's an honest fellow. Do not doubt,
  Cassio,   5
  But I will have my lord and you again
  As friendly as you were.

Cassio.   Bounteous madam,
  Whatever shall become of Michael Cassio,
  He's never anything but your true servant.

Desdemona. I know't; I thank you. You do love my   10
  lord.
  You have known him long, and be you well assured
  He shall in strangeness stand no farther off
  Than in a politic distance.°

Cassio.   Ay, but, lady,
  That policy may either last so long,
  Or feed upon such nice° and waterish diet,   15
  Or breed itself so out of circumstances,°
  That, I being absent, and my place supplied,°
  My general will forget my love and service.

Desdemona. Do not doubt° that; before Emilia here
  I give thee warrant of thy place. Assure thee,   20
  If I do vow a friendship, I'll perform it

III.iii.¹²⁻¹³ *He . . . distance* i.e., he shall act no more distant to you
than is necessary for political reasons   ¹⁵ *nice* trivial   ¹⁶ *Or . . . circumstances* i.e., or grow so on the basis of accidental happenings and
political needs   ¹⁷ *supplied* filled   ¹⁹ *doubt* imagine

To the last article. My lord shall never rest;
I'll watch him tame° and talk him out of patience;
His bed shall seem a school, his board a shrift;°
25 I'll intermingle everything he does
With Cassio's suit. Therefore be merry, Cassio,
For thy solicitor shall rather die
Than give thy cause away.

     Enter Othello and Iago [at a distance].

Emilia. Madam, here comes my lord.

30 *Cassio.* Madam, I'll take my leave.

Desdemona. Why, stay, and hear me speak.

Cassio. Madam, not now. I am very ill at ease,
    Unfit for mine own purposes.

Desdemona. Well, do your discretion.   *Exit Cassio.*

Iago. Ha! I like not that.

35 *Othello.*   What dost thou say?

Iago. Nothing, my lord; or if—I know not what.

Othello. Was not that Cassio parted from my wife?

Iago. Cassio, my lord? No, sure, I cannot think it
    That he would steal away so guilty-like,
    Seeing your coming.

40 *Othello.*   I do believe 'twas he.

Desdemona. [*Coming to them*] How now, my lord?
    I have been talking with a suitor here,
    A man that languishes in your displeasure.

Othello. Who is't you mean?

Desdemona. Why, your lieutenant, Cassio. Good my
45   lord,
    If I have any grace or power to move you,
    His present° reconciliation take.
    For if he be not one that truly loves you,

---

23 *watch him tame* (animals were tamed by being kept awake)
24 *board a shrift* table (seem) a confessional   47 *present* immediate

  That errs in ignorance, and not in cunning,
  I have no judgment in an honest face.   *50*
  I prithee call him back.

Othello.   Went he hence now?

Desdemona. I' sooth so humbled
  That he hath left part of his grief with me
  To suffer with him. Good love, call him back.

Othello. Not now, sweet Desdemon; some other time. *55*

Desdemona. But shall't be shortly?

Othello.   The sooner, sweet, for you.

Desdemona. Shall't be tonight at supper?

Othello.   No, not tonight.

Desdemona. Tomorrow dinner then?

Othello.   I shall not dine at home;
  I meet the captains at the citadel.

Desdemona. Why then, tomorrow night, on Tuesday
   morn,   *60*
  On Tuesday noon, or night, on Wednesday morn.
  I prithee name the time, but let it not
  Exceed three days. In faith, he's penitent;
  And yet his trespass, in our common reason
  (Save that, they say, the wars must make example *65*
  Out of her best), is not almost a fault
  T' incur a private check.° When shall he come?
  Tell me, Othello. I wonder in my soul
  What you would ask me that I should deny
  Or stand so mamm'ring° on. What? Michael Cassio, *70*
  That came awooing with you, and so many a time,
  When I have spoke of you dispraisingly,
  Hath ta'en your part—to have so much to do
  To bring him in? By'r Lady, I could do much—

Othello. Prithee no more. Let him come when he will! *75*
  I will deny thee nothing.

---

⁶⁶⁻⁶⁷ *is . . . check* is almost not serious enough for a private rebuke
(let alone a public disgrace) ⁷⁰ *mamm'ring* hesitating

Desdemona.   Why, this is not a boon;
   'Tis as I should entreat you wear your gloves,
   Or feed on nourishing dishes, or keep you warm,
   Or sue to you to do a peculiar profit°
80 To your own person. Nay, when I have a suit
   Wherein I mean to touch your love indeed,
   It shall be full of poise° and difficult weight,
   And fearful to be granted.

Othello.   I will deny thee nothing!
   Whereon I do beseech thee grant me this,
85 To leave me but a little to myself.

Desdemona. Shall I deny you? No. Farewell, my lord.

Othello. Farewell, my Desdemona: I'll come to thee
   straight.°

Desdemona. Emilia, come. Be as your fancies teach
   you;
   Whate'er you be, I am obedient. *Exit* [*with Emilia*].

90 *Othello.* Excellent wretch! Perdition catch my soul
   But I do love thee! And when I love thee not,
   Chaos is come again.

Iago. My noble lord——

Othello.   What dost thou say, Iago?

Iago. Did Michael Cassio, when you wooed my lady,
95 Know of your love?

Othello. He did, from first to last. Why dost thou ask?

Iago. But for a satisfaction of my thought,
   No further harm.

Othello.   Why of thy thought, Iago?

Iago. I did not think he had been acquainted with her.

100 *Othello.* O, yes, and went between us° very oft.

Iago. Indeed?

Othello. Indeed? Ay, indeed! Discern'st thou aught in
   that?

---

⁷⁹ *peculiar profit*   particularly personal good   ⁸² *poise*   weight
⁸⁷ *straight* at once   ¹⁰⁰ *between us* i.e., as messenger

Is he not honest?

Iago.   Honest, my lord?

Othello.   Honest? Ay, honest.

Iago. My lord, for aught I know.

Othello. What dost thou think?

Iago.   Think, my lord?

Othello.   Think, my lord? *105*
By heaven, thou echoest me,
As if there were some monster in thy thought
Too hideous to be shown. Thou dost mean some-
     thing.
I heard thee say even now, thou lik'st not that,
When Cassio left my wife. What didst not like? *110*
And when I told thee he was of my counsel°
Of my whole course of wooing, thou cried'st "In-
     deed?"
And didst contract and purse thy brow together,
As if thou then hadst shut up in thy brain
Some horrible conceit.° If thou dost love me, *115*
Show me thy thought.

Iago. My lord, you know I love you.

Othello.   I think thou dost;
And, for I know thou'rt full of love and honesty
And weigh'st thy words before thou giv'st them
     breath,
Therefore these stops° of thine fright me the more; *120*
For such things in a false disloyal knave
Are tricks of custom;° but in a man that's just
They're close dilations,° working from the heart
That passion cannot rule.

Iago.   For Michael Cassio,
I dare be sworn, I think that he is honest. *125*

Othello. I think so too.

---

[111] *of my counsel* in my confidence   [115] *conceit* thought   [120] *stops* interruptions   [122] *of custom* customary   [123] *close dilations* expressions of hidden thoughts

Iago.   Men should be what they seem;
  Or those that be not, would they might seem none!

Othello. Certain, men should be what they seem.

Iago. Why then, I think Cassio's an honest man.

130 *Othello.* Nay, yet there's more in this?
  I prithee speak to me as to thy thinkings,
  As thou dost ruminate, and give thy worst of
    thoughts
  The worst of words.

Iago.   Good my lord, pardon me:
  Though I am bound to every act of duty,
135 I am not bound to that all slaves are free to.
  Utter my thoughts? Why, say they are vile and false,
  As where's that palace whereinto foul things
  Sometimes intrude not? Who has that breast so pure
  But some uncleanly apprehensions
140 Keep leets and law days,° and in sessions sit
  With meditations lawful?

Othello. Thou dost conspire against thy friend, Iago,
  If thou but think'st him wronged, and mak'st his ear
  A stranger to thy thoughts.

Iago.   I do beseech you—
145 Though I perchance am vicious in my guess
  (As I confess it is my nature's plague
  To spy into abuses, and of my jealousy
  Shape faults that are not), that your wisdom
  From one that so imperfectly conceits
150 Would take no notice, nor build yourself a trouble
  Out of his scattering and unsure observance.
  It were not for your quiet nor your good,
  Nor for my manhood, honesty, and wisdom,
  To let you know my thoughts.

Othello.   What dost thou mean?

155 *Iago.* Good name in man and woman, dear my lord,
  Is the immediate jewel of their souls.

_____

140 *leets and law days* meetings of local courts

Who steals my purse steals trash; 'tis something,
   nothing;
'Twas mine, 'tis his, and has been slave to thousands;
But he that filches from me my good name
Robs me of that which not enriches him   160
And makes me poor indeed.

Othello. By heaven, I'll know thy thoughts!

Iago. You cannot, if my heart were in your hand;
   Nor shall not whilst 'tis in my custody.

Othello. Ha!

Iago.   O, beware, my lord, of jealousy!   165
   It is the green-eyed monster, which doth mock
   The meat it feeds on. That cuckold lives in bliss
   Who, certain of his fate, loves not his wronger;
   But O, what damnèd minutes tells° he o'er
   Who dotes, yet doubts—suspects, yet fondly° loves!   170

Othello. O misery.

Iago. Poor and content is rich, and rich enough;
   But riches fineless° is as poor as winter
   To him that ever fears he shall be poor.
   Good God the souls of all my tribe defend   175
   From jealousy!

Othello.   Why? Why is this?
   Think'st thou I'd make a life of jealousy,
   To follow still° the changes of the moon
   With fresh suspicions? No! To be once in doubt
   Is to be resolved. Exchange me for a goat   180
   When I shall turn the business of my soul
   To such exsufflicate and blown° surmises,
   Matching thy inference. 'Tis not to make me jealous
   To say my wife is fair, feeds well, loves company,
   Is free of speech, sings, plays, and dances;   185
   Where virtue is, these are more virtuous.
   Nor from mine own weak merits will I draw
   The smallest fear or doubt of her revolt,

---

[169] *tells* counts [170] *fondly* foolishly [173] *fineless* infinite [178] *To follow still* to change always (as the phases of the moon) [182] *exsufflicate and blown* inflated and flyblown

For she had eyes, and chose me. No, Iago;
190 I'll see before I doubt; when I doubt, prove;
And on the proof there is no more but this:
Away at once with love or jealousy!

Iago. I am glad of this; for now I shall have reason
To show the love and duty that I bear you
195 With franker spirit. Therefore, as I am bound,
Receive it from me. I speak not yet of proof.
Look to your wife; observe her well with Cassio;
Wear your eyes thus: not jealous nor secure.
I would not have your free and noble nature
200 Out of self-bounty° be abused. Look to't.
I know our country disposition well:
In Venice they do let heaven see the pranks
They dare not show their husbands; their best con-
        science
Is not to leave't undone, but kept unknown.°

205 *Othello.* Dost thou say so?

Iago. She did deceive her father, marrying you;
And when she seemed to shake and fear your looks,
She loved them most.

Othello.   And so she did.

Iago.   Why, go to then!
She that so young could give out such a seeming
210 To seel° her father's eyes up close as oak°—
He thought 'twas witchcraft. But I am much to
        blame.
I humbly do beseech you of your pardon
For too much loving you.

Othello.   I am bound to thee forever.

Iago. I see this hath a little dashed your spirits.

Othello. Not a jot, not a jot.

215 *Iago.*   Trust me, I fear it has.

²⁰⁰ *self-bounty* innate kindness (which attributes his own motives to
others)   ²⁰³⁻⁴ *their . . . unknown* i.e., their morality does not forbid
adultery, but it does forbid being found out   ²¹⁰ *seel* hoodwink   ²¹⁰ *oak*
(a close-grained wood)

I hope you will consider what is spoke
Comes from my love. But I do see y' are moved.
I am to pray you not to strain° my speech
To grosser issues, nor to larger reach°
Than to suspicion.   220

Othello. I will not.

Iago.   Should you do so, my lord,
My speech should fall into such vile success
Which my thoughts aimed not. Cassio's my worthy
    friend—
My lord, I see y' are moved.

Othello.   No, not much moved.
I do not think but Desdemona's honest.   225

Iago. Long live she so. And long live you to think so.

Othello. And yet, how nature erring from itself——

Iago. Ay, there's the point, as (to be bold with you)
Not to affect many proposèd matches
Of her own clime, complexion, and degree,°   230
Whereto we see in all things nature tends° —
Foh! one may smell in such a will most rank,
Foul disproportions, thoughts unnatural.
But, pardon me, I do not in position°
Distinctly° speak of her; though I may fear   235
Her will, recoiling to her better judgment,
May fall to match° you with her country forms,°
And happily° repent.

Othello.   Farewell, farewell!
If more thou dost perceive, let me know more.
Set on thy wife to observe. Leave me, Iago.   240

Iago. My lord, I take my leave.   [*Going.*]

---

²¹⁸ *strain* enlarge the meaning of ²¹⁹ *reach* meaning ²³⁰ *degree* social
station ²³¹ *in . . . tends* i.e., all things in nature seek out their own
kind ²³⁴ *position* general argument ²³⁵ *Distinctly* specifically ²³⁷ *fall
to match* happen to compare ²³⁷ *country forms* i.e., the familiar
appearances of her countrymen ²³⁸ *happily* by chance

Othello. Why did I marry? This honest creature doubtless
  Sees and knows more, much more, than he unfolds.

Iago. [*Returns.*] My lord, I would I might entreat your
  honor
245   To scan this thing no farther. Leave it to time.
  Although 'tis fit that Cassio have his place,
  For sure he fills it up with great ability,
  Yet, if you please to hold him off awhile,
  You shall by that perceive him and his means.
250   Note if your lady strain his entertainment°
  With any strong or vehement importunity;
  Much will be seen in that. In the meantime
  Let me be thought too busy in my fears
  (As worthy cause I have to fear I am)
255   And hold her free, I do beseech your honor.

Othello. Fear not my government.°

Iago.   I once more take my leave.
                            Exit.

Othello. This fellow's of exceeding honesty,
  And knows all qualities,° with a learnèd spirit
  Of human dealings. If I do prove her haggard,°
260   Though that her jesses° were my dear heartstrings,
  I'd whistle her off and let her down the wind°
  To prey at fortune. Haply for° I am black
  And have not those soft parts° of conversation
  That chamberers° have, or for I am declined
265   Into the vale of years—yet that's not much—
  She's gone. I am abused, and my relief
  Must be to loathe her. O curse of marriage,
  That we can call these delicate creatures ours,
  And not their appetites! I had rather be a toad

---

250 *strain his entertainment* urge strongly that he be reinstated
256 *government* self-control 258 *qualities* natures, types of people
259 *haggard* a partly trained hawk which has gone wild again 260 *jesses*
straps which held the hawk's legs to the trainer's wrist 261 *I'd . . .
wind* I would release her (like an untamable hawk) and let her fly free
262 *Haply for* it may be because 263 *soft parts* gentle qualities and
manners 264 *chamberers* courtiers—or perhaps, accomplished seducers

And live upon the vapor of a dungeon   270
Than keep a corner in the thing I love
For others' uses. Yet 'tis the plague to great ones;
Prerogatived are they less than the base.
'Tis destiny unshunnable, like death.
Even then this forkèd° plague is fated to us   275
When we do quicken.° Look where she comes.

Enter Desdemona and Emilia.

If she be false, heaven mocked itself!
I'll not believe't.

Desdemona.   How now, my dear Othello?
Your dinner, and the generous islanders
By you invited, do attend° your presence.   280

Othello. I am to blame.

Desdemona.   Why do you speak so faintly?
Are you not well?

Othello. I have a pain upon my forehead, here.°

Desdemona. Why, that's with watching; 'twill away
 again.
Let me but bind it hard, within this hour   285
It will be well.

Othello.   Your napkin° is too little;
 [*He pushes the handkerchief away, and it falls.*]
Let it° alone. Come, I'll go in with you.

Desdemona. I am very sorry that you are not well.
       Exit [with Othello].

Emilia. I am glad I have found this napkin;
This was her first remembrance from the Moor. 290
My wayward husband hath a hundred times
Wooed me to steal it; but she so loves the token

---

²⁷⁵ *forkèd* horned (the sign of the cuckold was horns) ²⁷⁶ *do quicken*
are born ²⁸⁰ *attend* wait ²⁸³ *here* (he points to his imaginary horns)
²⁸⁶ *napkin* elaborately worked handkerchief ²⁸⁷ *it* (it makes a considerable difference in the interpretation of later events whether this
"it" refers to Othello's forehead or to the handkerchief; nothing in the
text makes the reference clear)

(For he conjured her she should ever keep it)
That she reserves it evermore about her
295   To kiss and talk to. I'll have the work ta'en out°
And give't Iago. What he will do with it,
Heaven knows, not I; I nothing° but to please his
     fantasy.°

Enter Iago.

Iago. How now? What do you here alone?

Emilia. Do not you chide; I have a thing for you.

Iago. You have a thing for me? It is a common
300   thing——

Emilia. Ha?

Iago. To have a foolish wife.

Emilia. O, is that all? What will you give me now
    For that same handkerchief?

Iago.   What handkerchief?

305 *Emilia.* What handkerchief!
    Why, that the Moor first gave to Desdemona,
    That which so often you did bid me steal.

Iago. Hast stol'n it from her?

Emilia. No, but she let it drop by negligence,
310   And to th' advantage,° I, being here, took't up.
    Look, here 't is.

Iago.   A good wench. Give it me.

Emilia. What will you do with't, that you have been
     so earnest
    To have me filch it?

Iago.   Why, what is that to you?
                         [Takes it.]

Emilia. If it be not for some purpose of import,°
315   Give't me again. Poor lady, she'll run mad
    When she shall lack° it.

---

²⁹⁵ *work ta'en out* needlework copied   ²⁹⁷ *I nothing* I wish nothing
²⁹⁷ *fantasy* fancy, whim   ³¹⁰ *to th' advantage* being lucky   ³¹⁴ *import*
importance   ³¹⁶ *lack* miss

Iago.   Be not acknown on't.°
  I have use for it. Go, leave me.   *Exit Emilia.*
  I will in Cassio's lodging lose this napkin
  And let him find it. Trifles light as air
  Are to the jealous confirmations strong   320
  As proofs of Holy Writ. This may do something.
  The Moor already changes with my poison:
  Dangerous conceits are in their natures poisons,
  Which at the first are scarce found to distaste,°
  But, with a little,° act upon the blood,   325
  Burn like the mines of sulfur. I did say so.

             Enter Othello.

  Look where he comes! Not poppy nor mandragora,°
  Nor all the drowsy syrups of the world,
  Shall ever medicine thee to that sweet sleep
  Which thou owedst° yesterday.

Othello.   Ha! ha! False to me?   330

Iago. Why, how now, general? No more of that.

Othello. Avaunt! be gone! Thou hast set me on the
    rack.
  I swear 'tis better to be much abused
  Than but to know't a little.

Iago.   How now, my lord?

Othello. What sense had I of her stol'n hours of lust?   335
  I saw't not, thought it not, it harmed not me;
  I slept the next night well, fed well, was free and
    merry;
  I found not Cassio's kisses on her lips.
  He that is robbed, not wanting° what is stol'n,
  Let him not know't, and he's not robbed at all.   340

Iago. I am sorry to hear this.

---

316 *Be not acknown on't* forget you ever saw it   324 *are scarce found to distaste* scarcely can be tasted   325 *with a little* in a short time   327 *poppy nor mandragora* (soporifics)   330 *owedst* possessed   339 *wanting* missing

Othello. I had been happy if the general camp,
Pioners° and all, had tasted her sweet body,
So I had nothing known. O now, forever
345 Farewell the tranquil mind! Farewell content!
Farewell the plumèd troops, and the big wars
That makes ambition virtue! O, farewell!
Farewell the neighing steed and the shrill trump,
The spirit-stirring drum, th' ear-piercing fife,
350 The royal banner, and all quality,
Pride, pomp, and circumstance° of glorious war!
And O you mortal engines° whose rude throats
Th' immortal Jove's dread clamors° counterfeit,
Farewell! Othello's occupation's gone!

355 *Iago.* Is't possible, my lord?

Othello. Villain, be sure thou prove my love a whore!
Be sure of it; give me the ocular proof;
Or, by the worth of mine eternal soul,
Thou hadst been better have been born a dog
Than answer my waked wrath!

360 *Iago.*   Is't come to this?

Othello. Make me to see't; or at the least so prove it
That the probation° bear no hinge nor loop
To hang a doubt on—or woe upon thy life!

Iago. My noble lord——

365 *Othello.* If thou dost slander her and torture me,
Never pray more; abandon all remorse;
On horror's head horrors accumulate;
Do deeds to make heaven weep, all earth amazed;
For nothing canst thou to damnation add
Greater than that.

370 *Iago.*   O grace! O heaven forgive me!
Are you a man? Have you a soul or sense?
God b' wi' you! Take mine office. O wretched fool,
That lov'st to make thine honesty a vice!
O monstrous world! Take note, take note, O world,

---

343 *Pioners* (the basest manual laborers in the army, who dug trenches and mines) 351 *circumstance* pageantry 352 *mortal engines* lethal weapons, i.e., cannon 353 *clamors* i.e., thunder 362 *probation* proof

To be direct and honest is not safe.   *375*
I thank you for this profit, and from hence
I'll love no friend, sith° love breeds such offense.

Othello. Nay, stay. Thou shouldst be honest.

Iago. I should be wise; for honesty's a fool
And loses that it works for.

Othello.   By the world,   *380*
I think my wife be honest, and think she is not;
I think that thou art just, and think thou art not.
I'll have some proof. My name, that was as fresh
As Dian's° visage, is now begrimed and black
As mine own face. If there be cords, or knives,   *385*
Poison, or fire, or suffocating streams,
I'll not endure it. Would I were satisfied!

Iago. I see you are eaten up with passion.
I do repent me that I put it to you.
You would be satisfied?

Othello.   Would? Nay, and I will.   *390*

Iago. And may; but how? How satisfied, my lord?
Would you, the supervisor,° grossly gape on?
Behold her topped?

Othello.   Death and damnation! O!

Iago. It were a tedious° difficulty, I think,
To bring them to that prospect.° Damn them then,   *395*
If ever mortal eyes do see them bolster°
More than their own! What then? How then?
What shall I say? Where's satisfaction?
It is impossible you should see this,
Were they as prime° as goats, as hot as monkeys,   *400*
As salt° as wolves in pride,° and fools as gross
As ignorance made drunk. But yet, I say,

---

³⁷⁷ *sith* since ³⁸⁴ *Dian's* Diana's (goddess of the moon and of chastity) ³⁹² *supervisor* onlooker ³⁹⁴ *tedious* hard to arrange ³⁹⁵ *prospect* sight (where they can be seen) ³⁹⁶ *bolster* go to bed ⁴⁰⁰⁻⁰¹ *prime, salt* lustful ⁴⁰¹ *pride* heat

If imputation and strong circumstances
Which lead directly to the door of truth
405 Will give you satisfaction, you might have't.

Othello. Give me a living reason she's disloyal.

Iago. I do not like the office.°
But sith I am entered in this cause so far,
Pricked° to't by foolish honesty and love,
410 I will go on. I lay with Cassio lately,
And being troubled with a raging tooth,
I could not sleep.
There are a kind of men so loose of soul
That in their sleeps will mutter their affairs.
415 One of this kind is Cassio.
In sleep I heard him say, "Sweet Desdemona,
Let us be wary, let us hide our loves!"
And then, sir, would he gripe° and wring my hand,
Cry "O sweet creature!" Then kiss me hard,
420 As if he plucked up kisses by the roots
That grew upon my lips; laid his leg o'er my thigh,
And sigh, and kiss, and then cry, "Cursèd fate
That gave thee to the Moor!"

Othello. O monstrous! monstrous!

Iago.   Nay, this was but his dream.

425 *Othello.* But this denoted a foregone conclusion,°
'Tis a shrewd doubt,° though it be but a dream.

Iago. And this may help to thicken other proofs
That do demonstrate° thinly.

Othello.   I'll tear her all to pieces!

Iago. Nay, yet be wise. Yet we see nothing done;
430 She may be honest yet. Tell me but this:
Have you not sometimes seen a handkerchief
Spotted with strawberries in your wife's hand?

Othello. I gave her such a one; 'twas my first gift.

---

⁴⁰⁷ *office* duty   ⁴⁰⁹ *Pricked* spurred   ⁴¹⁸ *gripe* seize   ⁴²⁵ *foregone conclusion* consummated fact   ⁴²⁶ *shrewd doubt* penetrating guess   ⁴²⁸ *demonstrate* show, appear

Iago. I know not that; but such a handkerchief—
  I am sure it was your wife's—did I today   *435*
  See Cassio wipe his beard with.

Othello.   If it be that——

Iago. If it be that, or any that was hers,
  It speaks against her with the other proofs.

Othello. O, that the slave had forty thousand lives!
  One is too poor, too weak for my revenge.   *440*
  Now do I see 'tis true. Look here, Iago:
  All my fond love thus do I blow to heaven.
  'Tis gone.
  Arise, black vengeance, from the hollow hell!
  Yield up, O Love, thy crown and hearted° throne   *445*
  To tyrannous hate! Swell, bosom, with thy fraught,°
  For 'tis of aspics'° tongues.

Iago.   Yet be content.°

Othello. O, blood, blood, blood!

Iago. Patience, I say. Your mind may change.

Othello. Never, Iago. Like to the Pontic Sea,°   *450*
  Whose icy current and compulsive course
  Nev'r keeps retiring ebb, but keeps due on
  To the Propontic and the Hellespont,
  Even so my bloody thoughts, with violent pace,
  Shall nev'r look back, nev'r ebb to humble love,   *455*
  Till that a capable and wide° revenge
  Swallow them up. [*He kneels.*] Now, by yond marble heaven,
  In the due reverence of a sacred vow
  I here engage my words.

Iago.   Do not rise yet.
                     [*Iago kneels.*]
  Witness, you ever-burning lights above,   *460*

---

[445] *hearted* seated in the heart   [446] *fraught* burden   [447] *aspics'* asps'
[447] *content* patient, quiet   [450] *Pontic Sea* the Black Sea (famous for the strong and constant current with which it flows through the Bosporus into the Mediterranean, where the water level is lower)   [456] *capable and wide* sufficient and far-reaching

You elements that clip° us round about,
Witness that here Iago doth give up
The execution° of his wit, hands, heart
To wronged Othello's service! Let him command,
465 And to obey shall be in me remorse,°
What bloody business ever.°   [*They rise.*]

Othello.   I greet thy love,
Not with vain thanks but with acceptance boun-
teous,°
And will upon the instant put thee to't.°
Within these three days let me hear thee say
470 That Cassio's not alive.

Iago. My friend is dead. 'Tis done at your request.
But let her live.

Othello.   Damn her, lewd minx! O, damn her!
Damn her!
Come, go with me apart. I will withdraw
To furnish me with some swift means of death
475 For the fair devil. Now art thou my lieutenant.

Iago. I am your own forever.   *Exeunt.*

Scene IV. [*A street.*]

Enter Desdemona, Emilia, and Clown.

Desdemona. Do you know, sirrah, where Lieutenant
Cassio lies?°

Clown. I dare not say he lies anywhere.

Desdemona. Why, man?

5   *Clown.* He's a soldier, and for me to say a soldier lies,
'tis stabbing.

---

⁴⁶¹ *clip* enfold ⁴⁶³ *execution* workings, action ⁴⁶⁵ *remorse* pity
⁴⁶⁶ *ever* soever ⁴⁶⁷ *bounteous* absolute ⁴⁶⁸ *to't* i.e., to the work you
have said you are prepared to do   III.iv.² *lies* lodges

Desdemona. Go to. Where lodges he?

Clown. To tell you where he lodges is to tell you where
　I lie.

Desdemona. Can anything be made of this?　　　　　　10

Clown. I know not where he lodges, and for me to
　devise a lodging, and say he lies here or he lies there,
　were to lie in mine own throat.°

Desdemona. Can you enquire him out, and be edified°
　by report?　　　　　　　　　　　　　　　　　15

Clown. I will catechize the world for him; that is, make
　questions, and by them answer.

Desdemona. Seek him, bid him come hither. Tell him
　I have moved° my lord on his behalf and hope all
　will be well.　　　　　　　　　　　　　　　20

Clown. To do this is within the compass° of man's wit,
　and therefore I will attempt the doing it. *Exit Clown.*

Desdemona. Where should° I lose the handkerchief,
　Emilia?

Emilia. I know not, madam.

Desdemona. Believe me, I had rather have lost my
　purse　　　　　　　　　　　　　　　　　　25
　Full of crusadoes.° And but my noble Moor
　Is true of mind, and made of no such baseness
　As jealous creatures are, it were enough
　To put him to ill thinking.

Emilia.　　　　　　　　　Is he not jealous?

Desdemona. Who? He? I think the sun where he was
　born　　　　　　　　　　　　　　　　　　30
　Drew all such humors° from him.

Emilia.　　　　　　　　　Look where he comes.

---

¹³ *lie in mine own throat* (to lie in the throat is to lie absolutely and
completely)　¹⁴ *edified* enlightened (Desdemona mocks the Clown's
overly elaborate diction)　¹⁹ *moved* pleaded with　²¹ *compass* reach
²³ *should* might　²⁶ *crusadoes* Portuguese gold coins　³¹ *humors* char-
acteristics

Enter Othello.

Desdemona. I will not leave him now till Cassio
 Be called to him. How is't with you, my lord?

Othello. Well, my good lady. [*Aside*] O, hardness to
 dissemble!° —
How do you, Desdemona?

35 *Desdemona.*   Well, my good lord.

Othello. Give me your hand. This hand is moist,°
 my lady.

Desdemona. It hath felt no age nor known no sorrow.

Othello. This argues° fruitfulness and liberal° heart.
 Hot, hot, and moist. This hand of yours requires
40 A sequester° from liberty; fasting and prayer;
 Much castigation; exercise devout;
 For here's a young and sweating devil here
 That commonly rebels. 'Tis a good hand,
 A frank one.

Desdemona. You may, indeed, say so;
45 For 'twas that hand that gave away my heart.

Othello. A liberal hand! The hearts of old gave hands,
 But our new heraldry° is hands, not hearts.

Desdemona. I cannot speak of this. Come now, your
 promise!

Othello. What promise, chuck?

Desdemona. I have sent to bid Cassio come speak with
50 you.

Othello. I have a salt and sorry rheum° offends me.
 Lend me thy handkerchief.

---

[34] *hardness to dissemble* (Othello may refer here either to the difficulty he has in maintaining his appearance of composure, or to
what he believes to be Desdemona's hardened hypocrisy) [36] *moist*
(a moist, hot hand was taken as a sign of a lustful nature) [38] *argues*
suggests [38] *liberal* free, open (but also with a suggestion of "licentious";
from here on in this scene Othello's words bear a double meaning,
seeming to be normal but accusing Desdemona of being unfaithful)
[40] *sequester* separation [47] *heraldry* heraldic symbolism [51] *a salt and
sorry rheum* a heavy, running head cold

Desdemona.   Here, my lord.

Othello. That which I gave you.

Desdemona.   I have it not about me.

Othello. Not?

Desdemona. No, indeed, my lord.

Othello.   That's a fault.
That handkerchief   55
Did an Egyptian to my mother give.
She was a charmer,° and could almost read
The thoughts of people. She told her, while she
   kept it
'Twould make her amiable° and subdue my father
Entirely to her love; but if she lost it   60
Or made a gift of it, my father's eye
Should hold her loathèd, and his spirits should hunt
After new fancies. She, dying, gave it me,
And bid me, when my fate would have me wived,
To give it her. I did so; and take heed on't;   65
Make it a darling like your precious eye.
To lose't or give't away were such perdition
As nothing else could match.

Desdemona.   Is't possible?

Othello. 'Tis true. There's magic in the web° of it.
A sibyl that had numbered in the world   70
The sun to course two hundred compasses,
In her prophetic fury° sewed the work;
The worms were hallowed that did breed the silk,
And it was dyed in mummy° which the skillful
Conserved of maidens' hearts.

Desdemona.   Indeed? Is't true?   75

Othello. Most veritable. Therefore look to't well.

Desdemona. Then would to God that I had never
   seen't!

---

[57] *charmer* magician [59] *amiable* desirable [69] *web* weaving [72] *prophetic fury* seized by the spirit and able to prophesy [74] *mummy* liquid drained from embalmed bodies

Othello. Ha! Wherefore?

Desdemona. Why do you speak so startingly and rash?

80 *Othello.* Is't lost? Is't gone? Speak, is it out o' th' way?

Desdemona. Heaven bless us!

Othello. Say you?

Desdemona. It is not lost. But what an if it were?

Othello. How?

85 *Desdemona.* I say it is not lost.

Othello. Fetch't, let me see't!

Desdemona. Why, so I can; but I will not now.
   This is a trick to put me from my suit:
   Pray you let Cassio be received again.

90 *Othello.* Fetch me the handkerchief! My mind misgives.

Desdemona. Come, come!
   You'll never meet a more sufficient° man——

Othello. The handkerchief!

Desdemona.   A man that all his time
   Hath founded his good fortunes on your love,
95   Shared dangers with you——

Othello. The handkerchief!

Desdemona. I'faith, you are to blame.

Othello. Away!   *Exit Othello.*

Emilia. Is not this man jealous?

100 *Desdemona.* I nev'r saw this before.
   Sure there's some wonder in this handkerchief;
   I am most unhappy in the loss of it.

Emilia. 'Tis not a year or two shows us a man.
   They are all but stomachs, and we all but food;
105   They eat us hungerly, and when they are full,
   They belch us.

92 *sufficient* complete, with all proper qualities

Enter Iago and Cassio.

           Look you, Cassio and my husband.

Iago. There is no other way; 'tis she must do't.
And lo the happiness! Go and importune her.

Desdemona. How now, good Cassio? What's the news
   with you?

Cassio. Madam, my former suit. I do beseech you   *110*
That by your virtuous means I may again
Exist, and be a member of his love
Whom I with all the office° of my heart
Entirely honor. I would not be delayed.
If my offense be of such mortal kind   *115*
That nor my service past, nor present sorrows,
Nor purposed merit in futurity,
Can ransom me into his love again,
But to know so must be my benefit.°
So shall I clothe me in a forced content,   *120*
And shut myself up in some other course
To fortune's alms.

Desdemona.   Alas, thrice-gentle Cassio,
My advocation° is not now in tune.
My lord is not my lord; nor should I know him
Were he in favor° as in humor altered.   *125*
So help me every spirit sanctified
As I have spoken for you all my best
And stood within the blank° of his displeasure
For my free speech. You must awhile be patient.
What I can do I will; and more I will   *130*
Than for myself I dare. Let that suffice you.

Iago. Is my lord angry?

Emilia.   He went hence but now,
And certainly in strange unquietness.

Iago. Can he be angry? I have seen the cannon
When it hath blown his ranks into the air   *135*
And, like the devil, from his very arm

[113] *office* duty [119] *benefit* good [123] *advocation* advocacy [125] *favor* countenance [128] *blank* bull's-eye of a target

Puffed his own brother. And is he angry?
Something of moment° then. I will go meet him.
There's matter in't indeed if he be angry.

Desdemona. I prithee do so.   *Exit [Iago].*
140   Something sure of state,°
Either from Venice or some unhatched practice°
Made demonstrable here in Cyprus to him,
Hath puddled° his clear spirit; and in such cases
Men's natures wrangle with inferior things,
145   Though great ones are their object. 'Tis even so.
For let our finger ache, and it endues°
Our other, healthful members even to a sense
Of pain. Nay, we must think men are not gods,
Nor of them look for such observancy
150   As fits the bridal. Beshrew me much, Emilia,
I was, unhandsome warrior as I am,
Arraigning his unkindness with my soul;
But now I find I had suborned the witness,
And he's indicted falsely.

Emilia.   Pray heaven it be
155   State matters, as you think, and no conception
Nor no jealous toy° concerning you.

Desdemona. Alas the day! I never gave him cause.

Emilia. But jealous souls will not be answered so;
They are not ever jealous for the cause,
160   But jealous for they're jealous. It is a monster
Begot upon itself, born on itself.

Desdemona. Heaven keep the monster from Othello's
mind!

Emilia. Lady, amen.

Desdemona. I will go seek him. Cassio, walk here
about.
165   If I do find him fit,° I'll move your suit
And seek to effect it to my uttermost.

---

¹³⁸ *moment* importance   ¹⁴⁰ *of state* state affairs   ¹⁴¹ *unhatched practice* undisclosed plot   ¹⁴³ *puddled* muddied   ¹⁴⁶ *endues* leads   ¹⁵⁶ *toy*
trifle   ¹⁶⁵ *fit* receptive

Cassio. I humbly thank your ladyship.
                    Exit [Desdemona with Emilia].

                Enter Bianca.

Bianca. Save you, friend Cassio!

Cassio.   What make you from
    home?
    How is't with you, my most fair Bianca?
    I' faith, sweet love, I was coming to your house.   170

Bianca. And I was going to your lodging, Cassio.
    What, keep a week away? Seven days and nights?
    Eightscore eight hours? And lovers' absent hours
    More tedious than the dial eightscore times?
    O weary reck'ning.°

Cassio.   Pardon me, Bianca.   175
    I have this while with leaden thoughts been pressed,
    But I shall in a more continuate° time
    Strike off this score° of absence. Sweet Bianca,
                [Gives her Desdemona's handkerchief.]
    Take me this work out.

Bianca.   O Cassio, whence came this?
    This is some token from a newer friend.   180
    To the felt absence now I feel a cause.
    Is't come to this? Well, well.

Cassio.   Go to, woman!
    Throw your vile guesses in the devil's teeth,
    From whence you have them. You are jealous now
    That this is from some mistress, some remembrance.   185
    No, by my faith, Bianca.

Bianca.   Why, whose is it?

Cassio. I know not neither; I found it in my chamber.
    I like the work well; ere it be demanded,°
    As like enough it will, I would have it copied.
    Take it and do't, and leave me for this time.   190

---

175 *reck'ning* addition   177 *continuate* uninterrupted   178 *Strike off this score* i.e., pay this bill (the *score* being the account of drinks kept in a tavern)   188 *demanded* asked for (by the person who lost it)

Bianca. Leave you? Wherefore?

Cassio. I do attend here on the general
  And think it no addition, nor my wish,
  To have him see me womaned.

Bianca.   Why, I pray you?

Cassio. Not that I love you not.

195 *Bianca.*   But that you do not love me!
  I pray you bring° me on the way a little,
  And say if I shall see you soon at night.

Cassio. 'Tis but a little way that I can bring you,
  For I attend here; but I'll see you soon.

200 *Bianca.* 'Tis very good. I must be circumstanced.°

                                    Exeunt omnes.

---

196 *bring* accompany   200 *circumstanced* accept things as they are

ACT IV

Scene I. [*A street.*]

Enter Othello and Iago.

Iago. Will you think so?

Othello.   Think so, Iago?

Iago.   What,
To kiss in private?

Othello.   An unauthorized° kiss?

Iago. Or to be naked with her friend in bed
An hour or more, not meaning any harm?

Othello. Naked in bed, Iago, and not mean harm?   5
It is hypocrisy against the devil.
They that mean virtuously, and yet do so,
The devil their virtue tempts, and they tempt heaven.

Iago. If they do nothing, 'tis a venial slip.
But if I give my wife a handkerchief——   10

Othello. What then?

Iago. Why, then 'tis hers, my lord; and being hers,
She may, I think, bestow't on any man.

Othello. She is protectress of her honor too.
May she give that?   15

Iago. Her honor is an essence that's not seen;
They have it very oft that have it not.
But for the handkerchief——

V.i.² *unauthorized* illicit

119

Othello. By heaven, I would most gladly have forgot it!
20   Thou said'st—O, it comes o'er my memory
      As doth the raven° o'er the infected house,
      Boding to all—he had my handkerchief.

Iago. Ay, what of that?

Othello.   That's not so good now.

Iago. What if I had said I had seen him do you wrong?
25   Or heard him say—as knaves be such abroad°
      Who having, by their own importunate suit,
      Or voluntary dotage° of some mistress,
      Convincèd or supplied° them, cannot choose
      But they must blab——

Othello.   Hath he said anything?

30 *Iago.* He hath, my lord; but be you well assured,
      No more than he'll unswear.

Othello.   What hath he said?

Iago. Why, that he did—I know not what he did.

Othello. What? what?

Iago. Lie——

Othello. With her?

35 *Iago.*   With her, on her; what you will.

Othello. Lie with her? Lie on her?—We say lie on her
      when they belie her.—Lie with her! Zounds, that's
      fulsome.° —Handkerchief—confessions—handker-
      chief!—To confess, and be hanged for his labor—
40   first to be hanged, and then to confess! I tremble at
      it. Nature would not invest herself in such shadow-
      ing passion without some instruction.° It is not
      words that shakes me thus.—Pish! Noses, ears, and

---

²¹ *raven* (a harbinger of death)   ²⁵ *abroad* i.e., in the world   ²⁷ *vol-
untary dotage* weakness of the will   ²⁸*Convincèd or supplied* persuaded
or gratified (the mistress)   ³⁸ *fulsome* foul, repulsive   ⁴¹⁻⁴² *Nature
. . . instruction* i.e., my mind would not become so darkened (with
anger) unless there were something in this (accusation); (it should be
remembered that Othello believes in the workings of magic and supernatural forces)

lips? Is't possible?—Confess?—Handkerchief?—O
devil!   *Falls in a trance.*   45

Iago. Work on.
  My med'cine works! Thus credulous fools are
    caught,
  And many worthy and chaste dames even thus,
  All guiltless, meet reproach.° What, ho! My lord!
  My lord, I say! Othello!

                        Enter Cassio.

                            How now, Cassio?   50

Cassio. What's the matter?

Iago. My lord is fall'n into an epilepsy.
  This is his second fit; he had one yesterday.

Cassio. Rub him about the temples.

Iago. The lethargy° must have his quiet course.   55
  If not, he foams at mouth, and by and by
  Breaks out to savage madness. Look, he stirs.
  Do you withdraw yourself a little while.
  He will recover straight. When he is gone,
  I would on great occasion° speak with you.   60
                          [*Exit Cassio.*]
  How is it, general? Have you not hurt your head?

Othello. Dost thou mock° me?

Iago.   I mock you not, by heaven.
  Would you would bear your fortune like a man.

Othello. A hornèd man's a monster and a beast.

Iago. There's many a beast then in a populous city,   65
  And many a civil° monster.

Othello. Did he confess it?

Iago.   Good, sir, be a man.
  Think every bearded fellow that's but yoked
  May draw° with you. There's millions now alive

---

⁴⁹ *reproach* shame ⁵⁵ *lethargy* coma ⁶⁰ *great occasion* very important matter ⁶² *mock* (Othello takes Iago's comment as a reference to
his horns—which it is) ⁶⁶ *civil* city-dwelling ⁶⁹ *draw* i.e., like the
hornèd ox

70   That nightly lie in those unproper° beds
       Which they dare swear peculiar.° Your case is
         better.
       O, 'tis the spite of hell, the fiend's arch-mock,
       To lip a wanton in a secure couch,
       And to suppose her chaste. No, let me know;
75   And knowing what I am, I know what she shall be.

    Othello. O, thou art wise! 'Tis certain.

    Iago.   Stand you awhile apart;
       Confine yourself but in a patient list.°
       Whilst you were here, o'erwhelmèd with your
         grief—
       A passion most unsuiting such a man—
80   Cassio came hither. I shifted him away°
       And laid good 'scuses upon your ecstasy;°
       Bade him anon return, and here speak with me;
       The which he promised. Do but encave° yourself
       And mark the fleers,° the gibes, and notable°
         scorns
85   That dwell in every region of his face.
       For I will make him tell the tale anew:
       Where, how, how oft, how long ago, and when
       He hath, and is again to cope your wife.
       I say, but mark his gesture. Marry patience,
90   Or I shall say you're all in all in spleen,°
       And nothing of a man.

    Othello.   Dost thou hear, Iago?
       I will be found most cunning in my patience;
       But—dost thou hear?—most bloody.

    Iago.   That's not amiss;
       But yet keep time in all. Will you withdraw?

    [*Othello moves to one side, where his remarks are not
                      audible to Cassio and Iago.*]

70 *unproper* i.e., not exclusively the husband's   71 *peculiar* their own alone   77 *a patient list* the bounds of patience   80 *shifted him away* got rid of him by a strategem   81 *ecstasy* trance (the literal meaning, "outside oneself," bears on the meaning of the change Othello is undergoing)   83 *encave* hide   84 *fleers* mocking looks or speeches   84 *notable* obvious   90 *spleen* passion, particularly anger

Now will I question Cassio of Bianca,　　　　　　　95
A huswife° that by selling her desires
Buys herself bread and cloth. It is a creature
That dotes on Cassio, as 'tis the strumpet's plague
To beguile many and be beguiled by one.
He, when he hears of her, cannot restrain　　　　　100
From the excess of laughter. Here he comes.

Enter Cassio.

As he shall smile, Othello shall go mad;
And his unbookish° jealousy must conster°
Poor Cassio's smiles, gestures, and light behaviors
Quite in the wrong. How do you, lieutenant?　　　105

Cassio. The worser that you give me the addition°
Whose want even kills me.

Iago. Ply Desdemona well, and you are sure on't.
Now, if this suit lay in Bianca's power,
How quickly should you speed!

Cassio.　　　　　　　　　　　Alas, poor caitiff!°　　110

Othello. Look how he laughs already!

Iago. I never knew woman love man so.

Cassio. Alas, poor rogue! I think, i' faith, she loves me.

Othello. Now he denies it faintly, and laughs it out.

Iago. Do you hear, Cassio?

Othello.　　　　　　　　　Now he importunes him　115
To tell it o'er. Go to! Well said, well said!

Iago. She gives it out that you shall marry her.
Do you intend it?

Cassio. Ha, ha, ha!

Othello. Do ye triumph, Roman? Do you triumph?　120

Cassio. I marry? What, a customer?° Prithee bear

---

⁹⁶ *huswife* housewife (but with the special meaning here of "prostitute")
¹⁰³ *unbookish* ignorant　¹⁰³ *conster* construe　¹⁰⁶ *addition* title
¹¹⁰ *caitiff* wretch　¹²¹ *customer* one who sells, a merchant (here, a prostitute)

some charity to my wit; do not think it so unwhole-
some. Ha, ha, ha!

Othello. So, so, so, so. They laugh that win.

125 *Iago.* Why, the cry goes that you marry her.

Cassio. Prithee, say true.

Iago. I am a very villain else.

Othello. Have you scored° me? Well.

Cassio. This is the monkey's own giving out. She is
130   persuaded I will marry her out of her own love and
flattery, not out of my promise.

Othello. Iago beckons me; now he begins the story.
     [*Othello moves close enough to hear.*]

Cassio. She was here even now; she haunts me in every
place. I was the other day talking on the sea bank
135   with certain Venetians, and thither comes the
bauble,° and falls me thus about my neck——

Othello. Crying "O dear Cassio!" as it were. His ges-
ture imports it.

Cassio. So hangs, and lolls, and weeps upon me; so
140   shakes and pulls me! Ha, ha, ha!

Othello. Now he tells how she plucked him to my
chamber. O, I see that nose of yours, but not that
dog I shall throw it to.

Cassio. Well, I must leave her company.

145 *Iago.* Before me!° Look where she comes.

                    Enter Bianca.

Cassio. 'Tis such another fitchew!° Marry a perfumed
one? What do you mean by this haunting of me?

Bianca. Let the devil and his dam haunt you! What did
you mean by that same handkerchief you gave me
150   even now? I was a fine fool to take it. I must take

---

¹²⁸ *scored* marked, defaced   ¹³⁶ *bauble* plaything   ¹⁴⁵ *Before me!* (an
exclamation of surprise)   ¹⁴⁶ *fitchew* polecat, i.e., strong-smelling
creature

out the work? A likely piece of work that you should
find it in your chamber and know not who left it
there! This is some minx's token, and I must take
out the work? There! [*She throws down the handkerchief.*] Give it your hobbyhorse.° Wheresoever   *155*
you had it, I'll take out no work on't.

Cassio. How now, my sweet Bianca? How now? how
now?

Othello. By heaven, that should be my handkerchief!

Bianca. If you'll come to supper tonight, you may; if   *160*
you will not, come when you are next prepared
for.°   *Exit.*

Iago. After her, after her!

Cassio. Faith, I must; she'll rail in the streets else.

Iago. Will you sup there?   *165*

Cassio. Yes, I intend so.

Iago. Well, I may chance to see you, for I would very
fain speak with you.

Cassio. Prithee come. Will you?

Iago. Go to, say no more.   [*Exit Cassio.*]   *170*

Othello. [*Comes forward.*] How shall I murder him,
Iago?

Iago. Did you perceive how he laughed at his vice?

Othello. O Iago!

Iago. And did you see the handkerchief?   *175*

Othello. Was that mine?

Iago. Yours, by this hand! And to see how he prizes
the foolish woman your wife! She gave it him, and
he hath giv'n it his whore.

Othello. I would have him nine years a-killing!—A   *180*
fine woman, a fair woman, a sweet woman?

---

155 *hobbyhorse* prostitute   161-62 *next prepared for* next expected—i.e.,
never

Iago. Nay, you must forget that.

Othello. Ay, let her rot, and perish, and be damned
tonight; for she shall not live. No, my heart is turned
185   to stone; I strike it, and it hurts my hand. O, the
world hath not a sweeter creature! She might lie by
an emperor's side and command him tasks.

Iago. Nay, that's not your way.°

Othello. Hang her! I do but say what she is. So deli-
190   cate with her needle. An admirable musician. O, she
will sing the savageness out of a bear! Of so high
and plenteous wit and invention° ——

Iago. She's the worse for all this.

Othello. O, a thousand, a thousand times. And then,
195   of so gentle a condition?°

Iago. Ay, too gentle.

Othello. Nay, that's certain. But yet the pity of it,
Iago. O Iago, the pity of it, Iago.

Iago. If you are so fond over her iniquity, give her
200   patent to offend; for if it touch° not you, it comes
near nobody.

Othello. I will chop her into messes!° Cuckold me!

Iago. O, 'tis foul in her.

Othello. With mine officer!

205 *Iago.* That's fouler.

Othello. Get me some poison, Iago, this night. I'll not
expostulate with her, lest her body and beauty unprovide my mind° again. This night, Iago!

Iago. Do it not with poison. Strangle her in her bed,
210   even the bed she hath contaminated.

Othello. Good, good! The justice of it pleases. Very
good!

---

188 *way* proper course   192 *invention* imagination   195 *gentle a condition*
(1) well born (2) of a gentle nature   200 *touch* affects   202 *messes* bits
207–08 *unprovide my mind* undo my resolution

Iago. And for Cassio, let me be his undertaker.° You
    shall hear more by midnight.

Othello. Excellent good!   [*A trumpet.*]
                What trumpet is that same?   *215*

Iago. I warrant something from Venice.

    Enter Lodovico, Desdemona, and Attendants.

                      'Tis Lodovico.
    This comes from the Duke. See, your wife's with
    him.

Lodovico. God save you, worthy general.

Othello.   With° all my heart, sir.

Lodovico. The Duke and the senators of Venice greet
    you.   [*Gives him a letter.*]

Othello. I kiss the instrument of their pleasures.   *220*
             [*Opens the letter and reads.*]

Desdemona. And what's the news, good cousin Lodo-
    vico?

Iago. I am very glad to see you, signior.
    Welcome to Cyprus.

Lodovico. I thank you. How does Lieutenant Cassio?

Iago.   Lives, sir.

Desdemona. Cousin, there's fall'n between him and
    my lord   *225*
    An unkind° breach; but you shall make all well.

Othello. Are you sure of that?

Desdemona. My lord?

Othello. [*Reads*] "This fail you not to do, as you
    will——"

Lodovico. He did not call; he's busy in the paper.   *230*
    Is there division 'twixt my lord and Cassio?

---

[213] *undertaker* (not "burier" but "one who undertakes to do something") [218] *With* i.e., I greet you with [226] *unkind* unnatural

Desdemona. A most unhappy one. I would do much
    T' atone° them, for the love I bear to Cassio.

Othello. Fire and brimstone!

Desdemona.   My lord?

Othello.   Are you wise?

Desdemona. What, is he angry?

235 *Lodovico.*   May be th' letter moved him;
    For, as I think, they do command him home,
    Deputing Cassio in his government.°

Desdemona. Trust me, I am glad on't.

Othello.   Indeed?

Desdemona.   My lord?

Othello. I am glad to see you mad.

Desdemona.   Why, sweet Othello——

240 *Othello.* Devil!   [*Strikes her.*]

Desdemona. I have not deserved this.

Lodovico. My lord, this would not be believed in
    Venice,
    Though I should swear I saw't. 'Tis very much.
    Make her amends; she weeps.

Othello.   O devil, devil!
245 If that the earth could teem° with woman's tears,
    Each drop she falls° would prove a crocodile.°
    Out of my sight!

Desdemona.   I will not stay to offend you.   [*Going.*]

Lodovico. Truly, an obedient lady.
    I do beseech your lordship call her back.

Othello. Mistress!

Desdemona.   My lord?

250 *Othello.*   What would you with her, sir?

---

233 *atone* reconcile   237 *government* office   245 *teem* conceive   246 *falls* drops   246 *crocodile* (the crocodile was supposed to shed false tears to lure its victims)

Lodovico. Who? I, my lord?

Othello. Ay! You did wish that I would make her turn.
　　Sir, she can turn, and turn, and yet go on
　　And turn again; and she can weep, sir, weep;
　　And she's obedient; as you say, obedient.   255
　　Very obedient. Proceed you in your tears.
　　Concerning this, sir—O well-painted passion!
　　I am commanded home.—Get you away;
　　I'll send for you anon.—Sir, I obey the mandate
　　And will return to Venice.—Hence, avaunt!   260
　　　　　　　　　　　　　　[*Exit Desdemona.*]
　　Cassio shall have my place. And, sir, tonight
　　I do entreat that we may sup together.
　　You are welcome, sir, to Cyprus.—Goats and mon-
　　　keys!   *Exit.*

Lodovico. Is this the noble Moor whom our full Senate
　　Call all in all sufficient? Is this the nature   265
　　Whom passion could not shake? whose solid virtue
　　The shot of accident nor dart of chance
　　Could neither graze nor pierce?

Iago.   He is much changed.

Lodovico. Are his wits safe? Is he not light of brain?

Iago. He's that he is; I may not breathe my censure.   270
　　What he might be (if, what he might, he is not)
　　I would to heaven he were!

Lodovico.   What, strike his wife?

Iago. Faith, that was not so well; yet would I knew
　　That stroke would prove the worst.

Lodovico.   Is it his use?°
　　Or did the letters work upon his blood°   275
　　And new-create his fault?

Iago.   Alas, alas!
　　It is not honesty in me to speak
　　What I have seen and known. You shall observe
　　　him,

274 *use* habit   275 *blood* passion

And his own courses° will denote him so
280   That I may save my speech. Do but go after
And mark how he continues.

Lodovico. I am sorry that I am deceived in him.

                               Exeunt.

Scene II. [*The citadel.*]

Enter Othello and Emilia.

Othello. You have seen nothing then?

Emilia. Nor ever heard, nor ever did suspect.

Othello. Yes, you have seen Cassio and she together.

Emilia. But then I saw no harm, and then I heard
5   Each syllable that breath made up° between them.

Othello. What, did they never whisper?

Emilia.   Never, my lord.

Othello. Nor send you out o' th' way?

Emilia. Never.

Othello. To fetch her fan, her gloves, her mask, nor
nothing?

10   *Emilia.* Never, my lord.

Othello. That's strange.

Emilia. I durst, my lord, to wager she is honest,
Lay down my soul at stake.° If you think other,
Remove your thought. It doth abuse your bosom.
15   If any wretch have put this in your head,
Let heaven requite it with the serpent's curse,°
For if she be not honest,° chaste, and true,

---

²⁷⁹ *courses* actions   IV.ii.⁵ *that breath made up* spoken   ¹³ *at stake* as
the wager   ¹⁶ *serpent's curse* (God's curse on the serpent after the fall
in Eden)   ¹⁷ *honest* chaste

There's no man happy. The purest of their wives
Is foul as slander.

Othello.   Bid her come hither. Go.

                              Exit Emilia.

She says enough; yet she's a simple bawd°   20
That cannot say as much. This is a subtle whore,
A closet lock and key of villainous secrets,
And yet she'll kneel and pray; I have seen her do't.

          Enter Desdemona and Emilia.

Desdemona. My lord, what is your will?

Othello.   Pray you, chuck, come hither.

Desdemona. What is your pleasure?

Othello.   Let me see your eyes.   25
Look in my face.

Desdemona.   What horrible fancy's this?

Othello. [*To Emilia*] Some of your function,° mis-
          tress:
Leave procreants alone and shut the door;
Cough or cry hem if anybody come.
Your mystery,° your mystery! Nay, dispatch!   30

                              Exit Emilia.

Desdemona. Upon my knee, what doth your speech
          import?
I understand a fury in your words.°

Othello. Why, what art thou?

Desdemona.   Your wife, my lord; your true
And loyal wife.

Othello.   Come, swear it, damn thyself;
Lest, being like one of heaven, the devils themselves   35
Should fear to seize thee. Therefore be double-
          damned:
Swear thou art honest.

Desdemona.   Heaven doth truly know it.

²⁰ *bawd* procuress   ²⁷ *Some of your function* do your proper work (as
the operator of a brothel)   ³⁰ *mystery* trade   ³² *words* (Q1 adds to
this line, "But not the words")

Othello. Heaven truly knows that thou art false as hell.

Desdemona. To whom, my lord? With whom? How am
　　I false?

40　*Othello.* Ah, Desdemon! Away! Away! Away!

Desdemona. Alas the heavy day! Why do you weep?
　　Am I the motive° of these tears, my lord?
　　If haply° you my father do suspect
　　An instrument of this your calling back,
45　Lay not your blame on me. If you have lost him,
　　I have lost him too.

Othello.　　　　　　　Had it pleased heaven
　　To try me with affliction, had they rained
　　All kinds of sores and shames on my bare head,
　　Steeped° me in poverty to the very lips,
50　Given to captivity me and my utmost hopes,
　　I should have found in some place of my soul
　　A drop of patience. But, alas, to make me
　　The fixèd figure for the time of scorn°
　　To point his slow and moving finger at.
55　Yet could I bear that too, well, very well.
　　But there where I have garnered up my heart,
　　Where either I must live or bear no life,
　　The fountain from the which my current runs
　　Or else dries up—to be discarded thence,
60　Or keep it as a cistern for foul toads
　　To knot and gender° in—turn thy complexion there,
　　Patience, thou young and rose-lipped cherubin!
　　I here look grim as hell!°

Desdemona. I hope my noble lord esteems me honest.

65　*Othello.* O, ay, as summer flies are in the shambles,°
　　That quicken even with blowing.° O thou weed,

---

[42] *motive* cause　[43] *haply* by chance　[49] *Steeped* submerged　[53] *The
. . . scorn* the very image of scorn in our time　[61] *knot and gender*
twist in bunches and procreate　[61-63] *turn . . . hell* (the rough sense
would seem to be, "even Patience would grow pale, turn complexion, at
Desdemona's perfidy, but that Othello looks grimly on")　[65] *shambles*
abattoirs　[66] *quicken even with blowing* become impregnated as soon
as they lay their eggs

Who art so lovely fair, and smell'st so sweet,
That the sense aches at thee, would thou hadst never
    been born!

Desdemona. Alas, what ignorant° sin have I com-
    mitted?

Othello. Was this fair paper, this most goodly book,   70
    Made to write "whore" upon? What committed?
    Committed? O thou public commoner,°
    I should make very forges of my cheeks
    That would to cinders burn up modesty,
    Did I but speak thy deeds. What committed?   75
    Heaven stops the nose at it, and the moon winks;°
    The bawdy wind that kisses all it meets
    Is hushed within the hollow mine of earth
    And will not hear 't. What committed?

Desdemona. By heaven, you do me wrong!   80

Othello. Are not you a strumpet?

Desdemona.   No, as I am a Christian!
    If to preserve this vessel for my lord
    From any other foul unlawful touch
    Be not to be a strumpet, I am none.

Othello. What, not a whore?

Desdemona.   No, as I shall be saved!   85

Othello. Is 't possible?

Desdemona. O, heaven forgive us!

Othello.   I cry you mercy° then.
    I took you for that cunning whore of Venice
    That married with Othello. [*Calling*] You, mistress,

                    Enter Emilia.

That have the office opposite to Saint Peter   90
And keep the gate of hell! You, you, ay, you!
We have done our course; there's money for your
    pains.   [*Throws her some coins.*]

---

⁶⁹ *ignorant* unknowing ⁷² *commoner* prostitute ⁷⁶ *winks* closes its
eyes (the moon was the symbol of chastity) ⁸⁷ *cry you mercy* ask
your pardon

I pray you turn the key and keep our counsel.

Exit.

Emilia. Alas, what does this gentleman conceive?
How do you, madam? How do you, my good lady?

Desdemona. Faith, half asleep.

Emilia. Good madam, what's the matter with my lord?

Desdemona. With who?

Emilia. Why, with my lord, madam.

Desdemona. Who is thy lord?

Emilia.   He that is yours, sweet lady.

Desdemona. I have none. Do not talk to me, Emilia.
I cannot weep, nor answers have I none
But what should go by water.° Prithee tonight
Lay on my bed my wedding sheets, remember;
And call thy husband hither.

Emilia.   Here's a change indeed!

Exit.

Desdemona. 'Tis meet I should be used so, very meet.
How have I been behaved, that he might stick
The small'st opinion on my least misuse?°

Enter Iago and Emilia.

Iago. What is your pleasure, madam? How is't with
you?

Desdemona. I cannot tell. Those that do teach young
babes
Do it with gentle means and easy tasks.
He might have chid me so; for, in good faith,
I am a child to chiding.

Iago.   What is the matter, lady?

Emilia. Alas, Iago, my lord hath so bewhored her,

---

103 *water* tears   107–08 *stick . . . misuse* base any doubt on my smallest
fault

Thrown such despite° and heavy terms upon her 115
That true hearts cannot bear it.

Desdemona. Am I that name, Iago?

Iago. What name, fair lady?

Desdemona. Such as she said my lord did say I was.

Emilia. He called her whore. A beggar in his drink
Could not have laid such terms upon his callet.° 120

Iago. Why did he so?

Desdemona. I do not know; I am sure I am none such.

Iago. Do not weep, do not weep. Alas the day.

Emilia. Hath she forsook so many noble matches,
Her father and her country, and her friends, 125
To be called whore? Would it not make one weep?

Desdemona. It is my wretched fortune.

Iago. Beshrew° him for 't!
How comes this trick upon him?

Desdemona. Nay, heaven doth know.

Emilia. I will be hanged if some eternal villain,
Some busy and insinuating rogue,
Some cogging,° cozening slave, to get some office, 130
Have not devised this slander. I will be hanged else.

Iago. Fie, there is no such man! It is impossible.

Desdemona. If any such there be, heaven pardon him.

Emilia. A halter pardon him! And hell gnaw his bones! 135
Why should he call her whore? Who keeps her com-
pany?
What place? What time? What form? What likeli-
hood?
The Moor's abused by some most villainous knave,
Some base notorious knave, some scurvy fellow.
O heavens, that such companions° thou'dst unfold,° 140
And put in every honest hand a whip
To lash the rascals naked through the world
Even from the east to th' west!

¹⁵ *despite* abuse ¹²⁰ *callet* slut ¹²⁷ *Beshrew* curse ¹³¹ *cogging* cheat-
ng ¹⁴⁰ *companions* fellows, rogues ¹⁴⁰ *unfold* disclose

Iago.   Speak within door.°

Emilia. O, fie upon them! Some such squire° he was
145   That turned your wit the seamy side without
       And made you to suspect me with the Moor.

Iago. You are a fool. Go to.

Desdemona.   Alas, Iago,
       What shall I do to win my lord again?
       Good friend, go to him, for, by this light of heaven,
150   I know not how I lost him. Here I kneel:
       If e'er my will did trespass 'gainst his love
       Either in discourse of thought° or actual deed,
       Or that mine eyes, mine ears, or any sense
       Delighted them in any other form;
155   Or that I do not yet, and ever did,
       And ever will (though he do shake me off
       To beggarly divorcement) love him dearly,
       Comfort forswear me. Unkindness may do much,
       And his unkindness may defeat° my life,
160   But never taint my love. I cannot say "whore."
       It does abhor me now I speak the word;
       To do the act that might the addition earn
       Not the world's mass of vanity could make me.

Iago. I pray you be content. 'Tis but his humor.°
165   The business of the state does him offense.

Desdemona. If 'twere no other.

Iago.   It is but so, I warrant.
                                   [*Trumpets within.*]
       Hark how these instruments summon to supper.
       The messengers of Venice stay the meat.°
       Go in, and weep not. All things shall be well.
                          [*Exeunt Desdemona and Emilia.*]

                          Enter Roderigo.

170   How now, Roderigo?

---

143 *within door* more quietly and moderately   144 *squire* (a term of
contempt)   152 *discourse of thought* thinking   159 *defeat* destroy
164 *humor* mood   168 *stay the meat* await the meal

Roderigo. I do not find that thou deal'st justly with me.

Iago. What in the contrary?

Roderigo. Every day thou daff'st° me with some de- vice,° Iago, and rather, as it seems to me now, keep'st from me all conveniency° than suppliest me 175 with the least advantage of hope. I will indeed no longer endure it; nor am I yet persuaded to put up° in peace what already I have foolishly suffered.

Iago. Will you hear me, Roderigo?

Roderigo. I have heard too much, and your words 180 and performances are no kin together.

Iago. You charge me most unjustly.

Roderigo. With naught but truth. I have wasted my- self out of my means. The jewels you have had from me to deliver Desdemona would half have corrupted 185 a votarist.° You have told me she hath received them, and returned me expectations and comforts of sudden respect° and acquaintance; but I find none.

Iago. Well, go to; very well.   190

Roderigo. Very well? Go to? I cannot go to, man; nor 'tis not very well. Nay, I think it is scurvy, and begin to find myself fopped° in it.

Iago. Very well.

Roderigo. I tell you 'tis not very well. I will make my- 195 self known to Desdemona. If she will return me my jewels, I will give over my suit and repent my unlawful solicitation. If not, assure yourself I will seek satisfaction of you.

Iago. You have said now?   200

Roderigo. Ay, and said nothing but what I protest° intendment of doing.

---

173 *daff'st* put off   173-74 *device* scheme   175 *conveniency* what is need- ul   177 *put up* accept   186 *votarist* nun   188 *sudden respect* immediate consideration   193 *fopped* duped   201 *protest* aver

Iago. Why, now I see there's mettle° in thee, and even
from this instant do build on thee a better opinion
205　than ever before. Give me thy hand, Roderigo. Thou
hast taken against me a most just exception;° but
yet I protest I have dealt most directly° in thy
affair.

Roderigo. It hath not appeared.

210 *Iago.* I grant indeed it hath not appeared, and your
suspicion is not without wit and judgment. But,
Roderigo, if thou hast that in thee indeed which I
have greater reason to believe now than ever—I
mean purpose, courage, and valor—this night show
215　it. If thou the next night following enjoy not Desdemona, take me from this world with treachery and
devise engines for° my life.

Roderigo. Well, what is it? Is it within reason and
compass?°

220 *Iago.* Sir, there is especial commission come from
Venice to depute Cassio in Othello's place.

Roderigo. Is that true? Why, then Othello and Desdemona return again to Venice.

Iago. O, no; he goes into Mauritania and taketh away
225　with him the fair Desdemona, unless his abode be
lingered here by some accident; wherein none can
be so determinate° as the removing of Cassio.

Roderigo. How do you mean, removing him?

Iago. Why, by making him uncapable of Othello's
230　place—knocking out his brains.

Roderigo. And that you would have me to do?

Iago. Ay, if you dare do yourself a profit and a right.
He sups tonight with a harlotry,° and thither will I
go to him. He knows not yet of his honorable for-
235　tune. If you will watch his going thence, which I

---

²⁰³ *mettle* spirit　²⁰⁶ *exception* objection　²⁰⁷ *directly* straightforwardly
²¹⁷ *engines for* schemes against　²¹⁹ *compass* possibility　²²⁷ *determi-
nate* effective　²³³ *harlotry* female

will fashion to fall out° between twelve and one,
you may take him at your pleasure. I will be near
to second° your attempt, and he shall fall between
us. Come, stand not amazed at it, but go along with
me. I will show you such a necessity in his death   240
that you shall think yourself bound to put it on him.
It is now high supper time, and the night grows
to waste. About it.

Roderigo. I will hear further reason for this.

Iago. And you shall be satisfied.   *Exeunt.* 245

Scene III. [*The citadel.*]

*Enter Othello, Lodovico, Desdemona, Emilia, and
Attendants.*

Lodovico. I do beseech you, sir, trouble yourself no
further.

Othello. O, pardon me; 'twill do me good to walk.

Lodovico. Madam, good night. I humbly thank your
ladyship.

Desdemona. Your honor is most welcome.

Othello. Will you walk, sir? O, Desdemona.   5

Desdemona. My lord?

Othello. Get you to bed on th' instant; I will be returned forthwith. Dismiss your attendant there.
Look't be done.

Desdemona. I will, my lord.   10
          Exit [Othello, with Lodovico and Attendants].

Emilia. How goes it now? He looks gentler than he did.

²³⁶ *fall out* occur   ²³⁸ *second* support

Desdemona. He says he will return incontinent,°
   And hath commanded me to go to bed,
   And bade me to dismiss you.

Emilia.   Dismiss me?

15 *Desdemona.* It was his bidding; therefore, good Emilia,
   Give me my nightly wearing, and adieu.
   We must not now displease him.

Emilia. I would you had never seen him!

Desdemona. So would not I. My love doth so approve
   him
   That even his stubbornness, his checks,° his
20   frowns—
   Prithee unpin me—have grace and favor.

Emilia. I have laid these sheets you bade me on the
   bed.

Desdemona. All's one.° Good Father, how foolish
   are our minds!
   If I do die before, prithee shroud me
   In one of these same sheets.

25 *Emilia.*   Come, come! You talk.

Desdemona. My mother had a maid called Barbary.
   She was in love; and he she loved proved mad
   And did forsake her. She had a song of "Willow";
   An old thing 'twas, but it expressed her fortune,
30   And she died singing it. That song tonight
   Will not go from my mind; I have much to do
   But to go hang my head all at one side
   And sing it like poor Barbary. Prithee dispatch.

Emilia. Shall I go fetch your nightgown?

35 *Desdemona.* No, unpin me here.
   This Lodovico is a proper man.

Emilia. A very handsome man.

Desdemona. He speaks well.

IV.iii.[12] *incontinent* at once   [20] *checks* rebukes   [23] *All's one* no matter

Emilia. I know a lady in Venice would have walked
   barefoot to Palestine for a touch of his nether lip.   40

Desdemona. [*Sings*]
   "The poor soul sat singing by a sycamore tree,
      Sing all a green willow;
   Her hand on her bosom, her head on her knee,
      Sing willow, willow, willow.
   The fresh streams ran by her and murmured
         her moans;   45
      Sing willow, willow, willow;
   Her salt tears fell from her, and soft'ned the
         stones—
      Sing willow, willow, willow—"
Lay by these.   [*Gives Emilia her clothes.*]
   "Willow, Willow"——   50
Prithee hie° thee; he'll come anon.°
   "Sing all a green willow must be my garland.
   Let nobody blame him; his scorn I approve"——
Nay, that's not next. Hark! Who is't that knocks?

Emilia. It is the wind.   55

Desdemona. [*Sings*]
   "I called my love false love; but what said he
         then?
      Sing willow, willow, willow:
   If I court moe° women, you'll couch with moe
         men."
So, get thee gone; good night. Mine eyes do itch.
Doth that bode weeping?

Emilia.   'Tis neither here nor there.   60

Desdemona. I have heard it said so. O, these men,
   these men.
Dost thou in conscience think, tell me, Emilia,
That there be women do abuse their husbands
In such gross kind?

Emilia.   There be some such, no question.

---

⁵¹ *hie* hurry   ⁵¹ *anon* at once   ⁵⁸ *moe* more

Desdemona. Wouldst thou do such a deed for all the
65   world?

Emilia. Why, would not you?

Desdemona.   No, by this heavenly light!

Emilia. Nor I neither by this heavenly light.
I might do't as well i' th' dark.

Desdemona. Wouldst thou do such a deed for all the
world?

70 *Emilia.* The world's a huge thing; it is a great price for
a small vice.

Desdemona. In troth, I think thou wouldst not.

Emilia. In troth, I think I should; and undo't when I
had done. Marry, I would not do such a thing for
75   a joint-ring,° nor for measures of lawn,° nor for
gowns, petticoats, nor caps, nor any petty exhibition,° but for all the whole world? Why, who
would not make her husband a cuckold to make him
a monarch? I should venture purgatory for't.

80 *Desdemona.* Beshrew me if I would do such a wrong
for the whole world.

Emilia. Why, the wrong is but a wrong i' th' world;
and having the world for your labor, 'tis a wrong
in your own world, and you might quickly make
85   it right.

Desdemona. I do not think there is any such woman.

Emilia. Yes, a dozen; and as many to th' vantage as
would store° the world they played for.
But I do think it is their husbands' faults
90   If wives do fall. Say that they slack their duties
And pour our treasures into foreign° laps;
Or else break out in peevish jealousies,
Throwing restraint upon us; or say they strike us,

---

75 *joint-ring* (a ring with two interlocking halves)   75 *lawn* fine linen
76-77 *exhibition* payment   87-88 *to . . . store* in addition as would fill
91 *foreign* alien, i.e., other than the wife

Or scant our former having in despite°—
Why, we have galls; and though we have some
    grace,   95
Yet have we some revenge. Let husbands know
Their wives have sense like them. They see, and
    smell,
And have their palates both for sweet and sour,
As husbands have. What is it that they do
When they change° us for others? Is it sport?   100
I think it is. And doth affection° breed it?
I think it doth. Is't frailty that thus errs?
It is so too. And have not we affections?
Desires for sport? and frailty? as men have?
Then let them use us well; else let them know,   105
The ills we do, their ills instruct us so.°

Desdemona. Good night, good night. Heaven me such
    uses° send,
Not to pick bad from bad, but by bad mend. *Exeunt.*

---

⁹⁴ *scant . . . despite* reduce, in spite, our household allowance (?)
¹⁰⁰ *change* exchange   ¹⁰¹ *affection* strong feeling, desire   ¹⁰⁶ *instruct
us so* teach us to do likewise   ¹⁰⁷ *uses* practices

ACT V

Scene I. [*A street.*]

Enter Iago and Roderigo.

Iago. Here, stand behind this bulk;° straight will he
    come.
    Wear thy good rapier bare, and put it home.
    Quick, quick! Fear nothing; I'll be at thy elbow.
    It makes us, or it mars us, think on that,
5   And fix most firm thy resolution.

Roderigo. Be near at hand; I may miscarry in't.

Iago. Here, at thy hand. Be bold, and take thy stand.
                         [*Moves to one side.*]

Roderigo. I have no great devotion to the deed,
    And yet he hath given me satisfying reasons.
10   'Tis but a man gone. Forth my sword! He dies!

Iago. I have rubbed this young quat° almost to the
    sense,°
    And he grows angry. Now, whether he kill Cassio,
    Or Cassio him, or each do kill the other,
    Every way makes my gain. Live Roderigo,
15   He calls me to a restitution large
    Of gold and jewels that I bobbed° from him
    As gifts to Desdemona.
    It must not be. If Cassio do remain,

V.i.[1] *bulk* projecting stall of a shop   [11] *quat* pimple   [11] *to the sense*
raw   [16] *bobbed* swindled

He hath a daily beauty in his life
That makes me ugly; and besides, the Moor   20
May unfold me to him; there stand I in much peril.
No, he must die. But so, I hear him coming.

Enter Cassio.

Roderigo. I know his gait. 'Tis he. Villain, thou diest!
                              [*Thrusts at Cassio.*]

Cassio. That thrust had been mine enemy indeed
   But that my coat° is better than thou know'st.   25
   I will make proof of thine.   [*Fights with Roderigo.*]

Roderigo.   O, I am slain!°

Cassio. I am maimed forever. Help, ho! Murder!
   Murder!

Enter Othello [to one side].

Othello. The voice of Cassio. Iago keeps his word.

Roderigo. O, villain that I am!

Othello.   It is even so.

Cassio. O help, ho! Light! A surgeon!   30

Othello. 'Tis he. O brave Iago, honest and just,
   That hast such noble sense of thy friend's wrong!
   Thou teachest me. Minion,° your dear lies dead,
   And your unblest° fate hies.° Strumpet, I come.
   Forth of my heart those charms, thine eyes, are
      blotted.   35
   Thy bed, lust-stained, shall with lust's blood be
      spotted.
                              Exit Othello.

²⁵ *coat* i.e., a mail shirt or bulletproof vest   ²⁶ *slain* (most editors add
here a stage direction which has Iago wounding Cassio in the leg from
behind, but remaining unseen. However, nothing in the text requires
this, and Cassio's wound can be given him in the fight with Roderigo,
for presumably when Cassio attacks Roderigo the latter would not
simply accept the thrust but would parry. Since Iago enters again at
line 46, he must exit at some point after line 22)   ³³ *Minion* hussy, i.e.,
Desdemona   ³⁴ *unblest* unsanctified   ³⁴ *hies* approaches swiftly

Enter Lodovico and Gratiano.

Cassio. What, ho? No watch? No passage?° Murder! Murder!

Gratiano. 'Tis some mischance. The voice is very direful.

Cassio. O, help!

40 *Lodovico.* Hark!

Roderigo. O wretched villain!

Lodovico. Two or three groan. 'Tis heavy night.
These may be counterfeits. Let's think't unsafe
To come into the cry without more help.

45 *Roderigo.* Nobody come? Then shall I bleed to death.

Lodovico. Hark!

Enter Iago [with a light].

Gratiano. Here's one comes in his shirt, with light and weapons.

Iago. Who's there? Whose noise is this that cries on murder?

Lodovico. We do not know.

Iago.   Do not you hear a cry?

Cassio. Here, here! For heaven's sake, help me!

50 *Iago.*   What's the matter?

Gratiano. This is Othello's ancient, as I take it.

Lodovico. The same indeed, a very valiant fellow.

Iago. What are you here that cry so grievously?

Cassio. Iago? O, I am spoiled, undone by villains.
55   Give me some help.

Iago. O me, lieutenant! What villains have done this?

Cassio. I think that one of them is hereabout
And cannot make away.

---

³⁷ *passage* passers-by

Iago.   O treacherous villains!
  [*To Lodovico and Gratiano*] What are you there?
    Come in, and give some help.

Roderigo. O, help me there!   60

Cassio. That's one of them.

Iago.   O murd'rous slave! O vil-
    lain!   [*Stabs Roderigo.*]

Roderigo. O damned Iago! O inhuman dog!

Iago. Kill men i' th' dark?—Where be these bloody
    thieves?—
  How silent is this town!—Ho! Murder! Murder!—
  What may you be? Are you of good or evil?   65

Lodovico. As you shall prove us, praise us.

Iago. Signior Lodovico?

Lodovico. He, sir.

Iago. I cry you mercy. Here's Cassio hurt by villains.

Gratiano. Cassio?   70

Iago. How is't, brother?

Cassio. My leg is cut in two.

Iago.   Marry, heaven forbid!
  Light, gentlemen. I'll bind it with my shirt.

               Enter Bianca.

Bianca. What is the matter, ho? Who is't that cried?

Iago. Who is't that cried?   75

Bianca. O my dear Cassio! My sweet Cassio!
  O Cassio, Cassio, Cassio!

Iago. O notable strumpet!—Cassio, may you suspect
  Who they should be that have thus mangled you?

Cassio. No.   80

Gratiano. I am sorry to find you thus. I have been to
    seek you.

Iago. Lend me a garter. So. O for a chair
  To bear him easily hence.

Bianca. Alas, he faints! O Cassio, Cassio, Cassio!

85 *Iago.* Gentlemen all, I do suspect this trash
  To be a party in this injury.—
  Patience awhile, good Cassio.—Come, come.
  Lend me a light. Know we this face or no?
  Alas, my friend and my dear countryman
90 Roderigo? No.—Yes, sure.—Yes, 'tis Roderigo!

Gratiano. What, of Venice?

Iago. Even he, sir. Did you know him?

Gratiano.   Know him? Ay.

Iago. Signior Gratiano? I cry your gentle pardon.
  These bloody accidents must excuse my manners
  That so neglected you.

95 *Gratiano.*   I am glad to see you.

Iago. How do you, Cassio?—O, a chair, a chair!

Gratiano. Roderigo?

Iago. He, he, 'tis he! [*A chair brought in.*] O, that's
  well said;° the chair.
  Some good man bear him carefully from hence.
  I'll fetch the general's surgeon. [*To Bianca*] For you,
100 mistress,
  Save you your labor. [*To Cassio*] He that lies slain
  here, Cassio,
  Was my dear friend. What malice was between you?

Cassio. None in the world; nor do I know the man.

Iago. What, look you pale?—O, bear him out o' th'
  air.   [*Cassio is carried off.*]
  Stay you, good gentlemen.—Look you pale, mis-
105 tress?
  Do you perceive the gastness° of her eye?
  Nay, if you stare, we shall hear more anon.
  Behold her well; I pray you look upon her.

⁹⁸ *well said* well done ¹⁰⁶ *gastness* terror

Do you see, gentlemen? Nay, guiltiness will speak,
Though tongues were out of use.°   110

[*Enter Emilia.*]

Emilia. Alas, what is the matter? What is the matter,
   husband?

Iago. Cassio hath here been set on in the dark
   By Roderigo and fellows that are scaped.
   He's almost slain, and Roderigo quite dead.

Emilia. Alas, good gentleman! Alas, good Cassio!   115

Iago. This is the fruits of whoring. Prithee, Emilia,
   Go know of Cassio where he supped tonight.
   [*To Bianca*] What, do you shake at that?

Bianca. He supped at my house; but I therefore shake
   not.

Iago. O, did he so? I charge° you go with me.   120

Emilia. Oh fie upon thee, strumpet!

Bianca. I am no strumpet, but of life as honest
   As you that thus abuse me.

Emilia.   As I? Fie upon thee!

Iago. Kind gentlemen, let's go see poor Cassio
   dressed.°
   [*To Bianca*] Come, mistress, you must tell's another
   tale.   125
   Emilia, run you to the citadel
   And tell my lord and lady what hath happed.
                                   [*Exit Emilia.*]
   Will you go on afore?   *Exeunt [all but Iago].*
                   This is the night
   That either makes me or fordoes me quite.° [*Exit.*]

---

110 *tongues were out of use* men no longer spoke   120 *charge* command
124 *dressed* bandaged   129 *fordoes me quite* completely ruins me

Scene II. [*Desdemona's chamber.*]

Enter Othello [with a light]; and Desdemona
in her bed.

Othello. It is the cause, it is the cause, my soul.
    Let me not name it to you, you chaste stars.
    It is the cause. Yet I'll not shed her blood,
    Nor scar that whiter skin of hers than snow,
5   And smooth as monumental alabaster.
    Yet she must die, else she'll betray more men.
    Put out the light, and then put out the light.
    If I quench thee, thou flaming minister,°
    I can again thy former light restore,
10 Should I repent me; but once put out thy light,
    Thou cunning'st° pattern of excelling nature,
    I know not where is that Promethean heat°
    That can thy light relume.° When I have plucked
        the rose,
    I cannot give it vital° growth again;
15 It needs must wither. I'll smell thee on the tree.
                                        [*He kisses her.*]
    O balmy breath, that dost almost persuade
    Justice to break her sword. One more, one more!
    Be thus when thou art dead, and I will kill thee,
    And love thee after. One more, and that's the last!
20 So sweet was ne'er so fatal. I must weep,
    But they are cruel tears. This sorrow's heavenly;
    It strikes where it doth love. She wakes.

Desdemona. Who's there? Othello?

Othello.   Ay, Desdemona.

V.ii.⁸ *minister* worker, servant   ¹¹ *cunning'st* most intricate and skill-
fully wrought (by nature excelling itself)   ¹² *Promethean heat* divine
fire (Prometheus is the Titan who stole fire from heaven and gave it to
man)   ¹³ *relume* relight   ¹⁴ *vital* living

Desdemona. Will you come to bed, my lord?

Othello. Have you prayed tonight, Desdemon?

Desdemona.   Ay, my lord.   25

Othello. If you bethink yourself of any crime
Unreconciled as yet to heaven and grace,
Solicit for it straight.

Desdemona. Alack, my lord, what may you mean by
that?

Othello. Well, do it, and be brief; I will walk by.°   30
I would not kill thy unprepared spirit.
No, heavens forfend! I would not kill thy soul.

Desdemona. Talk you of killing?

Othello.   Ay, I do.

Desdemona.   Then heaven
Have mercy on me!

Othello.   Amen, with all my heart.

Desdemona. If you say so, I hope you will not kill me.   35

Othello. Humh.

Desdemona. And yet I fear you; for you're fatal then
When your eyes roll so. Why I should fear I know
not,
Since guiltiness I know not; but yet I feel I fear.

Othello. Think on thy sins.

Desdemona.   They are loves I bear to you.   40

Othello. Ay, and for that thou diest.

Desdemona. That death's unnatural that kills for
loving.
Alas, why gnaw you so your nether lip?
Some bloody passion shakes your very frame.
These are portents; but yet I hope, I hope,   45
They do not point on me.

Othello.   Peace and be still.

30 *by* nearby

Desdemona. I will so. What's the matter?

Othello. That handkerchief which I so loved and gave thee,
Thou gav'st to Cassio.

Desdemona.   No, by my life and soul!
Send for the man and ask him.

50 *Othello.*   Sweet soul, take heed,
Take heed of perjury; thou art on thy deathbed.

Desdemona. Ay, but not yet to die.

Othello.   Presently.°
Therefore confess thee freely of thy sin,
For to deny each article° with oath
55 Cannot remove nor choke the strong conception
That I do groan withal. Thou art to die.

Desdemona. Then Lord have mercy on me.

Othello.   I say, amen.

Desdemona. And have you mercy too. I never did
Offend you in my life; never loved Cassio
60 But with such general warranty° of heaven
As I might love. I never gave him token.

Othello. By heaven, I saw my handkerchief in's hand!
O perjured woman! thou dost stone° my heart,
And mak'st me call what I intend to do
65 A murder, which I thought a sacrifice.
I saw the handkerchief.

Desdemona.   He found it then.
I never gave it him. Send for him hither.
Let him confess a truth.

Othello.   He hath confessed.

Desdemona. What, my lord?

Othello. That he hath used thee.

Desdemona.   How? Unlawfully?

---

52 *Presently* immediately   54 *article* item (of the charge of adultery. Othello makes heavy use of legal terms in this scene)   60 *warranty* allowance   63 *stone* turn to stone

Othello.   Ay.   70

Desdemona. He will not say so.

Othello.   No, his mouth is stopped.
  Honest Iago hath ta'en order for't.°

Desdemona. O, my fear interprets. What, is he dead?

Othello. Had all his hairs been lives, my great revenge
  Had stomach° for them all.   75

Desdemona. Alas, he is betrayed, and I undone!

Othello. Out, strumpet! Weep'st thou for him to my
  face?

Desdemona. O, banish me, my lord, but kill me not!

Othello. Down, strumpet!

Desdemona. Kill me tomorrow; let me live tonight!   80

Othello. Nay, if you strive——

Desdemona. But half an hour!

Othello.   Being done, there is no pause.

Desdemona. But while I say one prayer!

Othello.   It is too late.
                              Smothers her.

            Emilia at the door.

Emilia. [*Calls within.*] My lord, my lord! What, ho, my
  lord, my lord!

Othello. What noise is this? Not dead? Not yet quite
  dead?   85
  I that am cruel am yet merciful;
  I would not have thee linger in thy pain.
  So, so.

Emilia. [*Within*] What, ho! My lord, my lord!

Othello.   Who   ?

Emilia. [*Within*] O, good my lord, I would speak a
  word with you.

---

⁷² *ta'en order for't* made sure of it   ⁷⁵ *stomach* appetite

90   *Othello.* Yes, 'tis Emilia.—By and by.—She's dead.—
     'Tis like she comes to speak of Cassio's death.
     The noise was high.° Ha! No more moving?
     Still as the grave.—Shall she come in? Were't
       good?—
     I think she stirs again. No.— What's best to do?
95   If she come in, she'll sure speak to my wife.
     My wife! My wife! What wife? I have no wife.
     O, insupportable! O heavy hour!
     Methinks it should be now a huge eclipse
     Of sun and moon, and that th' affrighted globe
     Should yawn° at alteration.

100 *Emilia.*   [*Within*] I do beseech you
     That I may speak with you, O good my lord!

     Othello. I had forgot thee. O, come in, Emilia.
     Soft, by and by.—Let me the curtains draw.—
     [*Draws the bed hangings and then opens the door.*]
     Where art thou?

              Enter Emilia.

            What's the matter with thee now?

105 *Emilia.* O my good lord, yonder's foul murders done!

     Othello. What? Now?

     Emilia. But now, my lord.

     Othello. It is the very error° of the moon.
     She comes more nearer earth than she was wont
110   And makes men mad.

     Emilia. Cassio, my lord, hath killed a young Venetian
     Called Roderigo.

     Othello.   Roderigo killed?
     And Cassio killed?

---

⁹² *high* loud (Q1 reads "here")   ⁹⁸⁻¹⁰⁰ *Methinks . . . alteration* (the
Elizabethans believed that great changes in human affairs were reflected
by disorders in nature)   ¹⁰⁰ *yawn* gape open (as in an earthquake)
¹⁰⁸ *error* wandering out of regular course (disorders in the heavens
were believed by some to cause disorders on earth, as well as vice
versa)

Emilia. No, Cassio is not killed.

Othello. Not Cassio killed? Then murder's out of tune,
And sweet revenge grows harsh. 115

Desdemona. O, falsely, falsely murdered!

Emilia. O Lord! What cry is that?

Othello. That? What?

Emilia. Out and alas! that was my lady's voice.
Help! Help, ho! Help! O lady, speak again!
Sweet Desdemona! O sweet mistress, speak! 120

Desdemona. A guiltless death I die.

Emilia. O, who hath done this deed?

Desdemona. Nobody—I myself. Farewell.
Commend me to my kind lord. O, farewell!
[*She dies.*]

Othello. Why, how should she be murd'red?

Emilia. Alas, who knows? 125

Othello. You heard her say herself, it was not I.

Emilia. She said so. I must needs report the truth.

Othello. She's like a liar gone to burning hell!
'Twas I that killed her.

Emilia. O, the more angel she,
And you the blacker devil! 130

Othello. She turned to folly, and she was a whore.

Emilia. Thou dost belie her, and thou art a devil.

Othello. She was false as water.

Emilia. Thou art rash as fire to say
That she was false. O, she was heavenly true!

Othello. Cassio did top her. Ask thy husband else. 135
O, I were damned beneath all depth in hell
But that I did proceed upon just grounds
To this extremity. Thy husband knew it all.

Emilia. My husband?

Othello. Thy husband.

Emilia.   That she was false to wedlock?

140 *Othello.* Ay, with Cassio. Had she been true,
    If heaven would make me such another world
    Of one entire and perfect chrysolite,°
    I'd not have sold her for it.

Emilia.   My husband?

Othello. Ay, 'twas he that told me on her first.
145   An honest man he is, and hates the slime
    That sticks on filthy deeds.

Emilia.   My husband?

Othello. What needs this iterance? Woman, I say thy
    husband.

Emilia. O mistress, villainy hath made mocks with
    love!
    My husband say she was false?

Othello.   He, woman.
150   I say, thy husband. Dost understand the word?
    My friend, thy husband; honest, honest Iago.

Emilia. If he say so, may his pernicious soul
    Rot half a grain a day! He lies to th' heart.
    She was too fond of her most filthy bargain.

155 *Othello.* Hah?

Emilia. Do thy worst.
    This deed of thine is no more worthy heaven
    Than thou wast worthy her.

Othello.   Peace, you were best.°

Emilia. Thou hast not half that pow'r to do me harm
160   As I have to be hurt. O gull! O dolt!
    As ignorant as dirt! Thou hast done a deed—
                    [*Othello moves to draw his sword.*]
    I care not for thy sword; I'll make thee known,
    Though I lost twenty lives. Help! Help! Ho! Help!
    The Moor hath killed my mistress! Murder! murder!

142 *chrysolite* topaz   158 *Peace, you were best* i.e., you had better be
silent

Enter Montano, Gratiano, and Iago [and Others].

Montano. What is the matter? How now, general? 165

Emilia. O, are you come, Iago? You have done well,
  That men must lay their murders on your neck.

Gratiano. What is the matter?

Emilia. Disprove this villain, if thou be'st a man.
  He says thou told'st him that his wife was false. 170
  I know thou didst not; thou'rt not such a villain.
  Speak, for my heart is full.

Iago. I told him what I thought, and told no more
  Than what he found himself was apt and true.

Emilia. But did you ever tell him she was false? 175

Iago. I did.

Emilia. You told a lie, an odious damnèd lie!
  Upon my soul, a lie! A wicked lie!
  She false with Cassio? Did you say with Cassio?

Iago. With Cassio, mistress. Go to, charm° your
  tongue. 180

Emilia. I will not charm my tongue; I am bound to
  speak:
  My mistress here lies murdered in her bed.

All. O heavens forfend!

Emilia. And your reports have set the murder on.

Othello. Nay, stare not, masters. It is true indeed. 185

Gratiano. 'Tis a strange truth.

Montano. O monstrous act!

Emilia.   Villainy, villainy, villainy!
  I think upon't—I think I smell't!—O villainy!
  I thought so then.—I'll kill myself for grief.—
  O villainy, villainy! 190

Iago. What, are you mad? I charge you get you home.

Emilia. Good gentlemen, let me have leave to speak.

180 *charm* control

'Tis proper I obey him, but not now.
Perchance, Iago, I will ne'er go home.

Othello. O! O! O!   [*Falls on the bed.*

195 *Emilia.*   Nay, lay thee down and roar,
For thou hast killed the sweetest innocent
That e'er did lift up eye.

Othello.   O, she was foul!   [*Rises.*
I scarce did know you, uncle. There lies your niece,
Whose breath, indeed, these hands have newly
    stopped.
200 I know this act shows horrible and grim.

Gratiano. Poor Desdemon! I am glad thy father's dead.
Thy match was mortal to him, and pure grief
Shore his old thread in twain. Did he live now,
This sight would make him do a desperate turn;
205 Yea, curse his better angel from his side,
And fall to reprobation.°

Othello. 'Tis pitiful; but yet Iago knows
That she with Cassio hath the act of shame
A thousand times committed. Cassio confessed it;
210 And she did gratify his amorous works
With that recognizance and pledge of love,
Which I first gave her. I saw it in his hand.
It was a handkerchief, an antique token
My father gave my mother.

215 *Emilia.* O God! O heavenly God!

Iago. Zounds, hold your peace!

Emilia.   'Twill out, 'twill out! I peace?
No, I will speak as liberal as the north.°
Let heaven and men and devils, let them all,
All, all, cry shame against me, yet I'll speak.

Iago. Be wise, and get you home.

220 *Emilia.*   I will not.
                    [*Iago draws and threatens Emilia.*]

---

²⁰⁶ *reprobation* damnation   ²¹⁷ *liberal as the north* freely (and bitingly)
as the north wind blows

Gratiano. Fie! Your sword upon a woman?

Emilia. O thou dull Moor, that handkerchief thou speak'st of
 I found by fortune, and did give my husband;
 For often with a solemn earnestness—
 More than indeed belonged to such a trifle— 225
 He begged of me to steal't.

Iago.   Villainous whore!

Emilia. She give it Cassio? No, alas, I found it,
 And I did give't my husband.

Iago.   Filth, thou liest!

Emilia. By heaven, I do not, I do not, gentlemen.
 O murd'rous coxcomb! What should such a fool 230
 Do with so good a wife?

Othello.   Are there no stones° in heaven
 But what serves for the thunder? Precious villain!
 [*The Moor runs at Iago, but is disarmed by Montano.*
        Iago kills his wife.]

Gratiano. The woman falls. Sure he hath killed his wife.

Emilia. Ay, ay. O, lay me by my mistress' side.
           [*Exit Iago.*]

Gratiano. He's gone, but his wife's killed.   235

Montano. 'Tis a notorious° villain. Take you this weapon,
 Which I have recovered from the Moor.
 Come, guard the door without. Let him not pass,
 But kill him rather. I'll after that same villain,
 For 'tis a damnèd slave.
    Exit [*with all but Othello and Emilia*].

Othello.   I am not valiant neither; 240
 But every puny whipster° gets my sword.
 But why should honor outlive honesty?
 Let it go all.

---

231 *stones* thunderbolts 236 *notorious* out-and-out 241 *puny whipster* small top-whipping boy (?)

Emilia.　　　　What did thy song bode, lady?
　　　Hark, canst thou hear me? I will play the swan,
245　And die in music. [*Sings*] "Willow, willow, willow."
　　　Moor, she was chaste. She loved thee, cruel Moor,
　　　So come my soul to bliss as I speak true.
　　　So speaking as I think, alas, I die.　　　[*She dies.*]

Othello. I have another weapon in this chamber;
250　It was a sword of Spain, the ice-brook's temper.
　　　O, here it is.—Uncle, I must come forth.

Gratiano. [*Within*] If thou attempt it, it will cost thee
　　　　dear.
　　　Thou hast no weapon, and perforce must suffer.

Othello. Look in upon me then and speak with me,
255　Or, naked as I am, I will assault thee.

　　　　　　　[*Enter Gratiano.*]

Gratiano. What is the matter?

Othello.　　　　　　　Behold, I have a weapon;
　　　A better never did itself sustain
　　　Upon a soldier's thigh. I have seen the day
　　　That with this little arm and this good sword
260　I have made my way through more impediments
　　　Than twenty times your stop. But O vain boast!
　　　Who can control his fate? 'Tis not so now.
　　　Be not afraid, though you do see me weaponed.
　　　Here is my journey's end, here is my butt,°
265　And very seamark of my utmost sail.°
　　　Do you go back dismayed? 'Tis a lost fear.
　　　Man but a rush° against Othello's breast,
　　　And he retires. Where should Othello go?
　　　Now, how dost thou look now? O ill-starred wench!
270　Pale as thy smock! When we shall meet at compt,°
　　　This look of thine will hurl my soul from heaven,
　　　And fiends will snatch at it. Cold, cold, my girl?
　　　Even like thy chastity.
　　　O cursèd, cursèd slave! Whip me, ye devils,

²⁶⁴ *butt* target, stopping place　²⁶⁵ *seamark of my utmost sail* marker
of my farthest journey　²⁶⁷ *Man but a rush* attack with only a reed
²⁷⁰ *compt* Judgment Day

From the possession of° this heavenly sight!   275
Blow me about in winds! roast me in sulfur!
Wash me in steep-down gulfs of liquid fire!
O Desdemon! Dead Desdemon; dead. O! O!

Enter Lodovico, Cassio, Montano, and Iago
[as prisoner,] with Officers.

Lodovico. Where is this rash and most unfortunate
man?

Othello. That's he that was Othello? Here I am.   280

Lodovico. Where is that viper? Bring the villain forth.

Othello. I look down towards his feet°——but that's a
fable.
If that thou be'st a devil, I cannot kill thee.
                                    [*Wounds Iago.*]

Lodovico. Wrench his sword from him.
                            [*Othello is disarmed.*]

Iago.   I bleed, sir, but not killed.

Othello. I am not sorry neither. I'd have thee live; 285
For in my sense, 'tis happiness to die.

Lodovico. O thou Othello that was once so good,
Fall'n in the practice° of a cursèd slave,
What shall be said to thee?

Othello.   Why, anything:
An honorable murderer, if you will;   290
For naught I did in hate, but all in honor.

Lodovico. This wretch hath part confessed his villainy.
Did you and he consent in Cassio's death?

Othello. Ay.

Cassio. Dear general, I never gave you cause.   295

Othello. I do believe it, and I ask your pardon.
Will you, I pray, demand that demi-devil
Why he hath thus ensnared my soul and body?

---

²⁷⁵ *the possession of* being possessed by   ²⁸² *towards his feet* i.e., for
his cloven hoofs   ²⁸⁸ *practice* plotting

Iago. Demand me nothing. What you know, you know.
300 From this time forth I never will speak word.

Lodovico. What, not to pray?

Gratiano.   Torments will ope your lips.

Othello. Well, thou dost best.

Lodovico. Sir, you shall understand what hath befall'n,
Which, as I think, you know not. Here is a letter
305 Found in the pocket of the slain Roderigo;
And here another. The one of them imports
The death of Cassio to be undertook
By Roderigo.

Othello. O villain!

Cassio.   Most heathenish and most gross!

310 *Lodovico.* Now here's another discontented paper
Found in his pocket too; and this, it seems,
Roderigo meant t' have sent this damnèd villain;
But that, belike, Iago in the interim
Came in and satisfied him.

Othello.   O thou pernicious caitiff!
315 How came you, Cassio, by that handkerchief
That was my wife's?

Cassio.   I found it in my chamber;
And he himself confessed it but even now
That there he dropped it for a special purpose
Which wrought to his desire.

Othello.   O fool! Fool! Fool!

320 *Cassio.* There is besides in Roderigo's letter,
How he upbraids Iago that he made him
Brave me upon the watch; whereon it came
That I was cast; and even but now he spake,
After long seeming dead—Iago hurt him,
325 Iago set him on.

Lodovico. You must forsake this room and go with
    us.
Your power and your command is taken off,
And Cassio rules in Cyprus. For this slave,

If there be any cunning cruelty
That can torment him much and hold him long,   830
It shall be his. You shall close prisoner rest
Till that the nature of your fault be known
To the Venetian state. Come, bring away.

Othello. Soft you, a word or two before you go.
I have done the state some service, and they know't.   835
No more of that. I pray you, in your letters,
When you shall these unlucky deeds relate,
Speak of me as I am. Nothing extenuate,
Nor set down aught in malice. Then must you speak
Of one that loved not wisely, but too well;   840
Of one not easily jealous, but, being wrought,
Perplexed in the extreme; of one whose hand,
Like the base Judean,° threw a pearl away
Richer than all his tribe; of one whose subdued
     eyes,
Albeit unusèd to the melting mood,   845
Drops tears as fast as the Arabian trees
Their med'cinable gum. Set you down this.
And say besides that in Aleppo once,
Where a malignant and a turbaned Turk
Beat a Venetian and traduced the state,   850
I took by th' throat the circumcisèd dog
And smote him—thus.   [*He stabs himself.*]

Lodovico. O bloody period!°

Gratiano.   All that is spoke is marred.

Othello. I kissed thee ere I killed thee. No way but this,
Killing myself, to die upon a kiss.   855
          [*He falls over Desdemona and dies.*]

Cassio. This did I fear, but thought he had no weapon;
For he was great of heart.

Lodovico.   [*To Iago*] O Spartan dog,
More fell° than anguish, hunger, or the sea!

---

³⁴³ *Judean* (most editors use the Q1 reading, "Indian," here, but F is
clear; both readings point toward the infidel, the unbeliever)   ³⁵³ *period*
end   ³⁵⁸ *fell* cruel

Look on the tragic loading of this bed.
360   This is thy work. The object poisons sight;
Let it be hid.   [*Bed curtains drawn.*]
           Gratiano, keep° the house,
And seize upon the fortunes of the Moor,
For they succeed on you. To you, lord governor,
Remains the censure of this hellish villain,
365   The time, the place, the torture. O, enforce it!
Myself will straight aboard, and to the state
This heavy act with heavy heart relate.   *Exeunt.*

FINIS

[361] *keep* remain in

Textual Note

Othello contains some of the most difficult editorial problems of any Shakespearean play. The play was entered in *The Stationer's Register* on 6 October, 1621, and printed in a quarto edition, Q1, by Thomas Walkley in 1622, some eighteen or nineteen years after it was first staged. More curiously, at the time that Walkley printed his quarto edition, the plans for printing the folio edition of Shakespeare's collected works were completed and printing was well along. The Folio, F, appeared in late 1623, and the text of *Othello* included in it differs considerably from Q1. A second quarto, Q2, was printed from F in 1630. The chief differences between the two major texts, Q1 and F, are: (1) There are 160 lines in F that are not in Q1; some of these omissions affect the sense in Q1, but others seem to be either intentional cuts in Q1 or additions in F. (2) There are a number of oaths in Q1 that are not in F; this fact can be interpreted in a number of ways, but all arguments go back to the prohibition in 1606 of swearing on stage—but apparently not in printed editions. (3) The stage directions in Q1 are much fuller than in F. (4) There are a large number of variant readings in the two texts, in single words, in phrases, and in lineation; where Q1, for example, reads "toged" (i.e., wearing a toga), F reads "tongued"; where Q1 reads "Worships," F reads "Moorships."

These may seem petty problems, but they present an editor with a series of most difficult questions about what to print at any given point where the two texts are in disagreement. The usual solution in the past has been for the editor to include all material in F and Q1, and where the two texts are in disagreement to select the reading he prefers. The result is what is known as an eclectic text. But modern bibliographical studies have demonstrated that it is possible to proceed, in some cases at least, in a more precise manner by examining the conflicting texts carefully in order to arrive at something like a reasonable judgment about their relative authority. Shakespearean bibliography has become a most elaborate affair, however, and in most cases it has become necessary to take the word of specialists on these matters. Unfortunately, in the case of *Othello* the experts are not in agreement, and none of their arguments has the ring of certainty. Here is, however, the most general opinion of how the two different texts came into being and how they are related.

After Shakespeare wrote the play, his original draft, usually termed "foul papers," was copied, around 1604, by a scribe and made into what is known as the "prompt-book," the official copy of the play used in the theater as the basis for production. This promptbook was the property of the players' company, the King's Men in this case, and remained in their possession to be used, and perhaps revised, whenever they produced *Othello*. Being a repertory company they would present a play for a few performances, then drop it for a time, and then present it again when conditions seemed favorable. At some time around 1620, another copy was made of the original foul papers, or some later copy of them, and this served as the basis for the 1622 Quarto. Later, when the publishers of the Folio got around to printing *Othello,* they took a copy of Q1 and corrected it by the original prompt-book, and this corrected copy was then given to the compositors who were setting type for F. There are genuine objections to this theory, the most telling raised by the most recent editor of the play, M. R. Ridley, in *The Arden Shakespeare* edition of *Othello;* but the theory does explain certain difficult facts, and most bibliographers seem to accept some version of it.

The end of this line of argument is to establish fairly

reasonably the authority of the F text as being the closest either to what Shakespeare wrote originally or to the play as he finally left it after playhouse revisions. This agrees with what most scholars find in reading the two texts. Sir Walter Greg puts this common belief in the superiority of F in the strongest terms: "In the great majority of cases there can be no doubt that F has preserved the more Shakespearean reading." (*The Shakespeare First Folio,* Oxford, 1955, p. 365.) For practical purposes what this means is that where an F reading makes sense, then an editor has no choice but to accept it—even though he "likes" the Q reading better and would have used it if he had *written,* instead of only edited, the play. But while an editor may be aided and comforted by the bibliographers' decision that F is more authoritative than Q1, his problems are by no means solved. There are places where F does not make sense but Q1 does, places where F is deficient in some way and Q is clear and complete, and places where both fail to make sense or seem to point to a common failure to transcribe correctly their original. When this occurs an editor must try to understand how the trouble occurred and then fall back on his judgment. This will force him to try to reconstruct the original manuscript from which we are told Q and F both derive, and he must attempt to deduce the original reading which both scribes mangled or which the typesetters in the different printing houses misread or made a mistake in setting.

This editorial process is endlessly complicated, but the general basis of this edition is as follows: F is taken for the copy text and its readings are preserved wherever they make sense. Oaths and stage directions are, however, taken from Q1, since they were presumably part of the original manuscript, but were deleted by the promptbook transcriber to comply with the prohibition against swearing on stage and because the prompt copy did not require such elaborate stage directions as a reading version—somewhat contrary to common sense, this last, but the bibliographers insist upon it. Where mislineation occurs in F, but Q1 has it correctly, the Q1 lineation is used on the theory that it has a better chance of being the original than any hypo-

thetical reconstruction of my own. Finally, where F and
Q1 both produce nonsense, changes, based on the above
theory about the transmission of the text and on the work
of previous editors, have been made.

Where F is deficient, the reading adopted and printed in
this text is given below first in italics; unless otherwise
stated it is taken from Q1. The original F reading that has
been changed follows in roman. Obvious typographical
errors in F, expansions of abbreviations, spelling variants
("murder," "murther"), and changes in punctuation and
lineation are not noted. The act and scene divisions are
translated from Latin, and the division at II.iii is from the
Globe edition rather than from F; otherwise the divisions
of F and the Globe edition are identical. "The Names of
the Actors," here printed at the beginning of the play, in
F follows the play.

I.i.1 *Tush! Never* Never   4 *'Sblood, but* But   26 *other* others
27 *Christian* Christen'd   30 *God bless* blesse   63 *full* fall *thick-
lips* Thicks-lips   83 *Zounds, sir* Sir   105 *Zounds, sir* Sir   111 *germans* Germaines   143 *produced* producted   151 *hell pains* (emendation) hell apines [hells paines Q1]

I.ii.33 *Duke* Dukes   37 *Even* enen   49 *carack* (emendation) Car-
ract [Carrick Q1]   50 *he's made* he' made   57 *Come* Cme
67 *darlings* Deareling   74 *weaken* weakens   83 *Whither* Whether
86 *if I do* if do

I.iii.53 *nor* hor   74 *your* yonr   99 *maimed* main'd   106 *Duke* [F
omits]   107 *overt test* oer Test   110 *First Senator* Sen.   122 *till*
tell   138 *travel's* trauellours   140 *rocks, and hills* Rocks, Hills
heads head   142 *other* others   146 *thence* hence   154 *intentively*
instinctively   203 *preserved* presern'd   227 *couch* (emendation)
Coach [Cooch Q1]   229 *alacrity* Alacartie   259 *me* my [F and Q1]
273 *First Senator* Sen.   286 *First Senator* Sen.   321–22 *balance*
braine   328 *scion* (emendation) Seyen [seyen Q1]   376 *snipe* snpe
379 *H'as* She ha's

II.i.9 *mortise* (emendation) morties [morties Q1]   33 *prays* praye
40 *Third Gentleman* Gent.   53 *First Gentleman* Gent.   56 *Second
Gentleman* Gent.   59 *Second Gentleman* Gent.   65 *ingener* In-
geniuer   66 *Second Gentleman* Gent.   94 *Second Gentleman*
Gent.   168 *gyve* (emendation) giue [catch Q1]   173 *an* and
175 *clyster* cluster   212 *hither* thither   242 *has* he's   261 *mutualities* mutabilities   299 *wife* wist   307 *nightcap* Night-Cape

II.iii.39 *unfortunate* infortunate 57 *to* put put to 61 *God* heauen 72 *God* Heauen 77 *Englishman* Englishmen 93 *thine* thy 95 *'Fore God* Why 99 *God's* heauen's 108 *God forgive* Forgiue 141 *Within . . . help* [F omits; Q1 reads "Helpe, helpe, within"] 142 *Zounds, you* You 156 *God's will* Alas 160 *God's will* Fie, fie 162 *Zounds, I* I 217 *leagued* (emendation) [league F and Q1] 260 *God* Heauen 274 *to* ro 288 *O God* Oh 343 *were 't* were to 362 *enmesh* en-mash 378 *By the mass* In troth

III.i.1s.d. [F includes the Clown] 20 *Exeunt Musicians* Exit Mu. 25 *general's wife* Generall 30 *Cassio* [no speech ascription in F]

III.ii.6 *We'll* Well

III.iii.74 *By'r Lady* Trust me 94 *you* he 106 *By heaven* Alas 135 *free to* free 136 *vile* vild 139 *But some* Wherein 148 *Shape* (emendation) Shapes 162 *By heaven I'll* Ile 170 *fondly* (emendation) soundly [strongly Q1] 175 *God* heauen 182 *exsufflicate* (emendation) exufflicate (F and Q1) 217 *my* your 222 *vile* vilde 248 *hold him* him 258 *qualities* Quantities 259 *human* humane 281 *to* too 335 *of* in 347 *make* makes 372 *b' wi'* buy 392 *supervisor* supervision 437 *that was* (Malone's emendation) it was [F and Q1]

III.iv.77 *God* Heauen 81 *Heaven* Blesse 97 *I'faith* In sooth 170 *I'faith* Indeed 186 *by my faith* in good troth

IV.i.21 *infected* infectious 37 *Zounds, that's* that's 79 *unsuiting* resulting 103 *conster* conserue 109 *power* dowre 113 *i'faith* indeed 124 *win* winnes 132 *beckons* becomes 164 *Faith, I* I 218 *God save* Save 248 *an obedient* obedient

IV.ii.16 *requite* requit 30 *Nay* May 48 *kinds* kind 154 *in* [Q2] or 168 *stay* stays

IV.iii.14 *bade* bid 51 *hie* high

V.i.1 *bulk* Barke 22 *hear* heard 34 *hies* highes 35 *Forth* For 50 *heaven's* heaven 104 *out o' th'* o' th'

V.ii.13 *the rose* thy Rose 35 *say so* say 57 *Then Lord* O Heauen 100 *Should* Did 116 *O Lord* Alas 126 *heard* heare 206 *reprobation* Reprobance 215 *O God! O heavenly God* O Heauen! Oh heauenly powres 216 *Zounds* Come

The Source of Othello

Shakespeare's play is based on a story in Giraldi Cinthio's *Hecatommithi* (III, 7), a collection of a hundred tales printed in Italy in the sixteenth century. So far as is known, there was no English translation of the source story in Shakespeare's time, and while he may have read it in a French translation of Gabriel Chappuys, it seems probable that he read the original Italian. For a discussion of the evidence for this view and a good comparison of the story and the play, see Kenneth Muir, *Shakespeare's Sources* (London, 1957), Vol. I, "Comedies and Tragedies," pp. 122–23. The translation reprinted here is that of J. E. Taylor, done in 1855.

Selection from Giraldi Cinthio
Hecatommithi

There once lived in Venice a Moor, who was very valiant and of a handsome person; and having given proofs in war of great skill and prudence, he was highly esteemed by the Signoria of the Republic, who in rewarding deeds of valor advanced the interests of the state.

It happened that a virtuous lady of marvelous beauty, named Disdemona, fell in love with the Moor, moved thereto by his valor; and he, vanquished by the beauty and the noble character of Disdemona, returned her love; and their affection was so mutual that, although the parents of the lady strove all they could to induce her to take another husband, she consented to marry the Moor; and they lived in such harmony and peace in Venice that no word ever passed between them that was not affectionate and kind.

Now it happened at this time that the Signoria of Venice made a change in the troops whom they used to maintain in Cyprus, and they appointed the Moor commander of the soldiers whom they dispatched thither. Joyful as was the Moor at the honor proffered him, such dignity being only conferred on men of noble rank and well-tried faith, and who had displayed bravery in arms—yet his pleasure was lessened when he reflected on the length and dangers of the voyage, fearing that Disdemona would be pained at his absence. But Disdemona, who had no other happiness in the world than the Moor, and who rejoiced to witness the testimony of his valor her husband had received from so powerful and noble a republic, was all impatient that he should embark with his troops, and longed to accompany him to so honorable a post. And all the more it vexed her to see the Moor so troubled; and not knowing what could be the reason, one day, when they were at dinner, she said to him, "How is it, O Moor, that when so honorable a post has been conferred on you by the Signoria, you are thus melancholy?"

The Moor answered Disdemona, "My pleasure at the honor I have received is disturbed by the love I bear you; for I see that of necessity one of two things must happen—either that I take you with me to encounter the perils of the sea, or, to save you from this danger, I must leave you here in Venice. The first could not be otherwise than serious to me, for all the toil you would have to bear and every danger that might befall you would cause me extreme anxiety and pain, yet, were I to leave you behind me, I should be hateful to myself, since in parting from you I should part from my own life."

Disdemona, on hearing this, replied: "My husband, what thoughts are these that wander through your mind? Why let such things disturb you? I will accompany you whithersoe'er you go, were it to pass through fire, as now to cross the water in a safe and well-provided ship; if indeed there are toils and perils to encounter, I will share them with you. And in truth I should think you loved me little were you to leave me here in Venice, denying me to bear you company, or could believe that I would liefer bide in safety here than share the dangers that await you. Prepare then for the voyage with all the readiness which the dignity of the post you hold deserves."

The Moor, in the fullness of his joy, threw his arms around his wife's neck, and with an affectionate and tender kiss exclaimed, "God keep you long in such love, dear wife!" Then speedily donning his armor, and having prepared everything for his expedition, he embarked on board the galley with his wife and all his troops, and, setting sail, they pursued their voyage, and with a perfectly tranquil sea arrived safely at Cyprus.

Now amongst the soldiery there was an Ensign, a man of handsome figure, but of the most depraved nature in the world. This man was in great favor with the Moor, who had not the slightest idea of his wickedness; for, despite the malice lurking in his heart, he cloaked with proud and valorous speech and with a specious presence the villainy of his soul with such art that he was to all outward show another Hector or Achilles. This man had likewise taken with him his wife to Cyprus, a young, and fair, and virtuous lady; and being of Italian birth she was much loved by Disdemona, who spent the greater part of every day with her.

In the same Company there was a certain Captain of a troop, to whom the Moor was much affectioned. And Disdemona, for this cause, knowing how much her husband valued him, showed him proofs of the greatest kindness, which was all very grateful to the Moor. Now the wicked Ensign, regardless of the faith that he had pledged his wife, no less than of the friendship, fidelity, and obligation which he owed the Moor, fell passionately in love with Disdemona, and bent all his thoughts to achieve his conquest; yet he dared not to declare his passion openly, fearing that, should the Moor perceive it, he would at once kill him. He therefore sought in various ways, and with secret guile, to betray his passion to the lady; but she, whose every wish was centered in the Moor, had no thought for this Ensign more than for any other man; and all the means he tried to gain her love had no more effect than if he had not tried them. But the Ensign imagined that the cause of his ill success was that Disdemona loved the Captain of the troop; and he pondered how to remove him from her sight. The love which he had borne the lady now changed into the bitterest hate, and, having failed in his purposes, he devoted all his thoughts to plot the death of the Captain of the troop and to divert the affection of the Moor from Disdemona. After revolving in his mind various schemes, all alike wicked, he at length resolved to accuse her of unfaithfulness to her husband, and to represent the Captain as her paramour. But knowing the singular love the Moor bore to Disdemona, and the friendship which he had for the Captain, he was well aware that, unless he practiced an artful fraud upon the Moor, it were impossible to make him give ear to either accusation; wherefore he resolved to wait until time and circumstance should open a path for him to engage in his foul project.

Not long afterwards it happened that the Captain, having drawn his sword upon a soldier of the guard, and struck him, the Moor deprived him of his rank; whereat Disdemona was deeply grieved, and endeavored again and again to reconcile her husband to the man. This the Moor told to the wicked Ensign, and how his wife importuned him so much about the Captain that he feared he should be forced at last to receive him back to service. Upon this hint the Ensign resolved to act, and began to work his web of intrigue. "Perchance," said he, "the lady Disdemona may have good reason to look kindly on him."

"And wherefore?" said the Moor.

"Nay, I would not step 'twixt man and wife," replied the Ensign, "but let your eyes be witness to themselves."

In vain the Moor went on to question the officer—he

would proceed no further; nevertheless, his words left a sharp, stinging thorn in the Moor's heart, who could think of nothing else, trying to guess their meaning and lost in melancholy. And one day, when his wife had been endeavoring to pacify his anger toward the Captain, and praying him not to be unmindful of ancient services and friendship for one small fault, especially since peace had been made between the Captain and the soldier he had struck, the Moor was angered, and exclaimed, "Great cause have you, Disdemona, to care so anxiously about this man! Is he a brother, or your kinsman, that he should be so near your heart?"

The lady, with all gentleness and humility, replied, "Be not angered, my dear lord; I have no other cause to bid me speak than sorrow that I see you lose so dear a friend as, by your own words, this Captain has been to you; nor has he done so grave a fault that you should bear him so much enmity. Nay, but you Moors are of so hot a nature that every little trifle moves you to anger and revenge."

Still more enraged at these words, the Moor replied, "I could bring proofs—by heaven it mocks belief! but for the wrongs I have endured revenge must satisfy my wrath."

Disdemona, in astonishment and fright, seeing her husband's anger kindled against her, so contrary to his wont, said humbly and with timidness, "None save a good intent has led me thus to speak with you, my lord; but to give cause no longer for offense, I'll never speak a word more on the subject."

The Moor, observing the earnestness with which his wife again pleaded for the Captain, began to guess the meaning of the Ensign's words; and in deep melancholy he went to seek that villain and induce him to speak more openly of what he knew. Then the Ensign, who was bent upon injuring the unhappy lady, after feigning at first great reluctance to say aught that might displease the Moor, at length pretended to yield to his entreaties, and said, "I can't deny it pains me to the soul to be thus forced to say what needs must be more hard to hear than any other grief; but since you will it so, and that the regard I owe your honor compels me to confess the truth, I will no longer refuse to satisfy your questions and my duty. Know, then, that for no other reason is your lady vexed to see the Captain in disfavor than the pleasure that she has in his company whenever he comes to your house, and all the more since she has taken an aversion to your blackness."

These words went straight to the Moor's heart; but in order to hear more (now that he believed true all that the Ensign had told him) he replied, with a fierce glance, "By heavens, I scarce can hold this hand from plucking out that tongue of thine, so bold, which dares to speak such slander of my wife!"

"Captain," replied the Ensign, "I looked for such reward for these my faithful officers—none else; but since my duty, and the jealous care I bear your honor, have carried me thus far, I do repeat, so stands the truth, as you have heard it from these lips; and if the lady Disdemona hath, with a false show of love for you, blinded your eyes to what you should have seen, this is no argument but that I speak the truth. Nay, this same Captain told it me himself, like one whose happiness is incomplete until he can declare it to another; and, but that I feared your anger, I should have given him, when he told it me, his merited reward, and slain him. But since informing you of what concerns you more than any other man brings me so undeserved a recompense, would I had held my peace, since silence might have spared me your displeasure."

Then the Moor, burning with indignation and anguish, said, "Make thou these eyes self-witnesses of what thou tell'st, or on thy life I'll make thee wish thou hadst been born without a tongue."

"An easy task it would have been," replied the villain, "when he was used to visit at your house; but now that you have banished him, not for just cause, but for mere frivolous pretext, it will be hard to prove the truth. Still, I do not forgo the hope to make you witness of that which you will not credit from my lips."

Thus they parted. The wretched Moor, struck to the heart as by a barbed dart, returned to his home, and awaited the day when the Ensign should disclose to him the truth which was to make him miserable to the end of his days. But the evil-minded Ensign was, on his part, not less troubled by the chastity which he knew the lady Disdemona observed inviolate; and it seemed to him impossible to discover a means of making the Moor believe what he had falsely told him; and, turning the matter over in his thoughts in various ways, the villain resolved on a new deed of guilt.

Disdemona often used to go, as I have already said, to visit the Ensign's wife, and remained with her a good part of the day. Now, the Ensign observed that she carried about with her a handkerchief, which he knew the Moor had given her, finely embroidered in the Moorish fashion, and which was precious to Disdemona, nor less so to the Moor. Then he conceived the plan of taking this kerchief from her secretly, and thus laying the snare for her final ruin. The Ensign had a little daughter, a child three years of age, who was much loved by Disdemona, and one day, when the unhappy lady had gone to pay a visit at the house of this vile man, he took the little child up in his arms and carried her to Disdemona, who took her and pressed her to her bosom; whilst at the same instant this traitor, who had extreme dexterity of hand, drew the kerchief from her sash so cunningly that she did not notice him, and overjoyed he took his leave of her.

Disdemona, ignorant of what had happened, returned home, and, busy with other thoughts, forgot the handkerchief. But a few days afterwards, looking for it and not finding it, she was in alarm, lest the Moor should ask her for it, as he oft was wont to do. Meanwhile, the wicked Ensign, seizing a fit opportunity, went to the Captain of the troop, and with crafty malice left the handkerchief at the head of his bed without his discovering the trick, until the following morning, when, on his getting out of bed, the handkerchief fell upon the floor, and he set his foot upon it. And not being able to imagine how it had come to his house, knowing that it belonged to Disdemona, he resolved to give it to her; and waiting until the Moor had gone from home, he went to the back door and knocked. It seemed as if fate conspired with the Ensign to work the death of the unhappy Disdemona. Just at that time the

Moor returned home, and hearing a knocking at the back
door, he went to the window, and in a rage exclaimed,
"Who knocks there?" The Captain, hearing the Moor's
voice, and fearing lest he should come downstairs and
attack him, took to flight without answering a word. The
Moor went down, and opening the door hastened into the
street and looked about, but in vain. Then, returning into
the house in great anger, he demanded of his wife who it
was that had knocked at the door. Disdemona replied, as
was true, that she did not know; but the Moor said, "It
seemed to me the Captain."

"I know not," answered Disdemona, "whether it was he
or another person."

The Moor restrained his fury, great as it was, wishing to
do nothing before consulting the Ensign, to whom he
hastened instantly, and told him all that had passed, praying him to gather from the Captain all he could respecting
the affair. The Ensign, overjoyed at the occurrence, promised the Moor to do as he requested, and one day he took
occasion to speak with the Captain when the Moor was so
placed that he could see and hear them as they conversed.
And whilst talking to him of every other subject than of
Disdemona, he kept laughing all the time aloud, and feigning astonishment, he made various movements with his
head and hands, as if listening to some tale of marvel. As
soon as the Moor saw the Captain depart, he went up to
the Ensign to hear what he had said to him. And the Ensign,
after long entreaty, at length said, "He has hidden from me
nothing, and has told me that he has been used to visit your
wife whenever you went from home, and that on the last
occasion she gave him this handkerchief which you presented to her when you married her."

The Moor thanked the Ensign, and it seemed now clear
to him that, should he find Disdemona not to have the
handkerchief, it was all true that the Ensign had told to
him. One day, therefore, after dinner, in conversation with
his wife on various subjects, he asked her for the kerchief.
The unhappy lady, who had been in great fear of this, grew
red as fire at this demand; and to hide the scarlet of her
cheeks, which was closely noted by the Moor, she ran to

a chest and pretended to seek the handkerchief, and after hunting for it a long time, she said, "I know not how it is—I cannot find it; can you, perchance, have taken it?"

"If I had taken it," said the Moor, "why should I ask it of you? but you will look better another time."

On leaving the room, the Moor fell to meditating how he should put his wife to death, and likewise the Captain of the troop, so that their deaths should not be laid to his charge. And as he ruminated over this day and night, he could not prevent his wife's observing that he was not the same towards her as he had been wont; and she said to him again and again, "What is the matter? What troubles you? How comes it that you, who were the most light-hearted man in the world, are now so melancholy?"

The Moor feigned various reasons in reply to his wife's questioning, but she was not satisfied, and, although conscious that she had given the Moor no cause, by act or deed, to be so troubled, yet she feared that he might have grown wearied of her; and she would say to the Ensign's wife, "I know not what to say of the Moor; he used to be all love towards me; but within these few days he has become another man; and much I fear that I shall prove a warning to young girls not to marry against the wishes of their parents, and that the Italian ladies may learn from me not to wed a man whom nature and habitude of life estrange from us. But as I know the Moor is on such terms of friendship with your husband, and communicates to him all his affairs, I pray you, if you have heard from him aught that you may tell me of, fail not to befriend me." And as she said this, she wept bitterly.

The Ensign's wife, who knew the whole truth (her husband wishing to make use of her to compass the death of Disdemona), but could never consent to such a project, dared not, from fear of her husband, disclose a single circumstance: all she said was, "Beware lest you give any cause of suspicion to your husband, and show to him by every means your fidelity and love."—"Indeed I do so," replied Disdemona, "but it is all of no avail."

Meanwhile the Moor sought in every way to convince himself of what he fain would have found untrue, and he

prayed the Ensign to contrive that he might see the handkerchief in the possession of the Captain. This was a difficult matter to the wicked Ensign; nevertheless, he promised
to use every means to satisfy the Moor of the truth of what
he said.

Now, the Captain had a wife at home who worked the
most marvelous embroidery upon lawn, and seeing the
handkerchief, which belonged to the Moor's wife, she resolved, before it was returned to her, to work one like it.
As she was engaged in this task, the Ensign observed her
standing at a window, where she could be seen by all the
passers-by in the street, and he pointed her out to the Moor,
who was now perfectly convinced of his wife's guilt. Then
he arranged with the Ensign to slay Disdemona and the
Captain of the troop, treating them as it seemed they both
deserved. And the Moor prayed the Ensign that he would
kill the Captain, promising eternal gratitude to him. But
the Ensign at first refused to undertake so dangerous a
task, the Captain being a man of equal skill and courage;
until at length, after much entreating and being richly paid,
the Moor prevailed on him to promise to attempt the deed.

Having formed this resolution, the Ensign, going out
one dark night, sword in hand, met the Captain on his way
to visit a courtesan, and struck him a blow on his right
thigh, which cut off his leg and felled him to the earth.
Then the Ensign was on the point of putting an end to his
life, when the Captain, who was a courageous man and
used to the sight of blood and death, drew his sword, and,
wounded as he was, kept on his defense, exclaiming with
a loud voice, "I'm murdered!" Thereupon the Ensign,
hearing the people come running up, with some of the
soldiers who were lodged thereabouts, took to his heels to
escape being caught; then turning about again, he joined
the crowd, pretending to have been attracted by the noise.
And when he saw the Captain's leg cut off, he judged that,
if not already dead, the blow must, at all events, end his
life; and whilst in his heart he was rejoiced at this, he yet
feigned to compassionate the Captain as he had been his
brother.

The next morning the tidings of this affair spread through

the whole city, and reached the ears of Disdemona; whereat she, who was kindhearted and little dreamed that any ill would betide her, evinced the greatest grief at the calamity. This served but to confirm the Moor's suspicions, and he went to seek for the Ensign, and said to him, "Do you know that my wife is in such grief at the Captain's accident that she is well nigh gone mad."

"And what could you expect, seeing he is her very soul?" replied the Ensign.

"Ay, soul forsooth!" exclaimed the Moor; "I'll draw the soul from out her body; call me no man if that I fail to shut the world upon this wretch."

Then they consulted of one means and another—poison and daggers—to kill poor Disdemona, but could resolve on nothing. At length the Ensign said, "A plan comes to my mind, which will give you satisfaction and raise cause for no suspicion. It is this: the house in which you live is very old, and the ceiling of your chamber has many cracks; I propose we take a stocking, filled with sand, and beat Disdemona with it till she dies; thus will her body bear no signs of violence. When she is dead we can pull down a portion of the ceiling, and thus make it seem as if a rafter falling on her head had killed the lady. Suspicion cannot rest on you, since all men will impute her death to accident."

This cruel counsel pleased the Moor, and he only waited for a fitting time to execute the plot. One night, when he and Disdemona had retired to bed, the Ensign, whom the Moor had concealed in a closet which opened into the chamber, raised a noise in the closet, according to a concerted plan; whereat the Moor said to his wife, "Did you not hear that noise?"

"Indeed I heard it," she replied.

"Rise," said the Moor, "and see what 'tis."

The unhappy Disdemona rose from bed, and the instant she approached the closet, out rushed the Ensign, and being strong and of stout nerve, he beat her cruelly with the bag of sand across her back; upon which Disdemona fell to the ground, scarce able to draw her breath; but with the little voice she had left, she called upon the Moor for aid.

But the Moor, leaping from bed, exclaimed, "Thou wicked-est of women, thus has thy falseness found its just reward, the recompense to wives who, counterfeiting love, place horns upon their husbands' brows."

The wretched lady, hearing these words, and feeling that she was near her end (for the Ensign had given her another blow), appealed to the justice of Heaven, since justice here had failed her, in proof of her fidelity and truth; and as she was thus calling Heaven to witness, the wicked Ensign in-flicted a third blow, under which she sank lifeless on the floor.

Then the Ensign and the Moor, laying Disdemona on the bed and wounding her head, pulled down part of the ceiling of the chamber, as they had arranged; whereupon the Moor began to call aloud for help, exclaiming that the house was falling. Hearing this uproar, the neighbors all came running up, and there found Disdemona lying dead beneath a rafter —a sight which, from the good life of that poor lady, did fill all hearts with sorrow.

On the following day Disdemona was buried, followed to the grave by the universal grief of the people. But Heaven, the just regarder of all hearts, willed not that so wicked a deed should go unpunished. Ere long the Moor, whom Disdemona had loved more than her own life, began to feel such sorrow at her loss that he went wandering about as one bereft of reason, searching in every part of the house. And reflecting in his thoughts that the Ensign had been the cause that he had lost, with Disdemona, all joy in life, he conceived so deep a hatred to that wicked man he could not bear to set eyes on him, and had it not been for his fear of the inviolable justice of the Signoria of Venice, he would have slain him openly. But being unable to do this with safety, he deprived him of his rank, and would not allow him to remain in his Company; whereat such an enmity arose between the two that no greater or more deadly can be imagined.

The Ensign, that wickedest of all bad men, now turned his thoughts to injuring the Moor; and seeking out the Captain, whose wound was by this time healed, and who went about with a wooden leg in place of the one that had been cut off, he said to him, " 'Tis time you should be avenged for your lost limb; and if you will come with me to Venice, I'll tell you who the malefactor is, whom I dare not mention to you here for many reasons; and I will bring you proofs."

The Captain of the troop, whose anger returned fiercely, but without knowing why, thanked the Ensign, and went with him to Venice. On arriving there the Ensign told him that it was the Moor who had cut off his leg, on account of the suspicion he had formed of Disdemona's conduct with him; and for that reason he had slain her, and then spread the report that the ceiling had fallen and killed her. Upon hearing which, the Captain accused the Moor to the Signoria, both of having cut off his leg and killed his wife, and called the Ensign to witness the truth of what he said. The Ensign declared both charges to be true, for that the Moor had disclosed to him the whole plot, and had tried to persuade him to perpetrate both crimes; and that, having afterwards killed his wife out of jealousy he had conceived, he had narrated to him the manner in which he had perpetrated her death.

The Signoria of Venice, when they heard of the cruelty inflicted by a barbarian upon a lady of their city, commanded that the Moor's arms should be pinioned in Cyprus, and he be brought to Venice, where, with many tortures, they sought to draw from him the truth. But the Moor, bearing with unyielding courage all the torment, denied the whole charge so resolutely that no confession could be drawn from him. But, although by his constancy and firmness he escaped death, he was, after being confined for several days in prison, condemned to perpetual banishment, in which he was eventually slain by the kinsfolk of Disdemona, as he merited. The Ensign returned to his own country, and, following up his wonted villainy, he accused one of his companions of having sought to persuade him to kill an enemy of his, who was a man of noble rank; whereupon this person was arrested and put to the torture; but when he denied the truth of what his accuser had declared, the Ensign himself was likewise tortured to make him prove the truth of his accusations; and he was tortured so that his body ruptured, upon which he was removed from prison and taken home, where he died a miserable death. Thus did Heaven avenge the innocence of Disdemona; and all these events were narrated by the Ensign's wife, who was privy to the whole, after his death, as I have told them here.

Commentaries

The four critical writings reprinted here give some idea of the range of *Othello* criticism and at the same time provide various insights into the play and critical guidelines for approaching it. Thomas Rymer's discussion of *Othello* from his *A Short View of Tragedy* (1693), is a famous attack on the play by a determined neoclassicist and realist. Rymer's smugness and lack of understanding of the nature of dramatic poetry are ridiculous, but his absurd, and at times infuriating, misinterpretations force a reader to formulate and thus become conscious of his own assumptions about the nature of poetry and drama. The Romantic movement in literature had as one of its by-products a great revival of interest in and a new approach to Shakespeare, and Samuel Taylor Coleridge, besides being a great poet, was the first modern Shakespearean critic. Keats, Byron, Lamb, Hazlitt, and Coleridge were all particularly fascinated by the plays, but it was Coleridge who in several series of public lectures brought Romantic theories of art to bear on Shakespeare and began to create that enthusiasm for the plays so characteristic of the nineteenth century. Coleridge never wrote a book on Shakespeare and his lectures were never printed, but notes and newspaper reports of them have survived, and these along with various marginalia from his books and reports of his "table talk" make it possible to put together at least the outline of his views. Modern criticism grows out of Romantic criticism, though it differs in many of its assumptions about the nature of poetry and in its working techniques. The two pieces of modern criticism here reprinted are distinguished interpretations of *Othello* which offer two different, but complementary, critical approaches. Maynard Mack's "The Jacobean Shakespeare" explores the individual tragedies by defining the "vertebrate characteristics" they share with other Shakespearean tragedies. Mack seeks the common constituent elements and the basic patterns of development of Shakespearean tragedy. Heilman, in contrast, narrows his focus to *Othello* alone and searches for the meaning of the play in certain recurring words, images, and ideas.

Thomas Rymer

From *A Short View of Tragedy*

THE FABLE

Othello, a blackamoor captain, by talking of his prowess and feats of war, makes Desdemona, a senator's daughter, to be in love with him; and to be married to him without her parents' knowledge; and having preferred Cassio to be his lieutenant (a place which his ensign Iago sued for), Iago, in revenge, works the Moor into a jealousy that Cassio cuckolds him: which he effects by stealing and conveying a certain handkerchief, which had, at the wedding, been by the Moor presented to his bride. Hereupon, Othello and Iago plot the deaths of Desdemona and Cassio, Othello murders her, and soon after is convinced of her innocence. And as he is about to be carried to prison in order to be punished for the murder, he kills himself.

Whatever rubs or difficulty may stick on the bark, the moral, sure, of this fable is very instructive.

1. First, this may be a caution to all maidens of quality how, without their parents' consent, they run away with blackamoors. . . .

Secondly, this may be a warning to all good wives that they look well to their linen.

Thirdly, this may be a lesson to husbands, that before their jealousy be tragical, the proofs may be mathematical. . . .

Nothing is more odious in nature than an improbable

lie; and, certainly, never was any play fraught, like this of *Othello*, with improbabilities.

The characters, or manners, which are the second part in a tragedy, are not less unnatural and improper than the fable was improbable and absurd.

Othello is made a Venetian general. We see nothing done by him nor related concerning him that comports with the condition of a general or, indeed, of a man, unless the killing himself to avoid a death the law was about to inflict upon him. When his jealousy had wrought him up to a resolution of's taking revenge for the supposed injury, he sets Iago to the fighting part, to kill Cassio; and chooses himself to murder the silly woman, his wife, that was like to make no resistance.

His love and his jealousy are no part of a soldier's character, unless for comedy.

But what is most intolerable is Iago. He is no black-amoor soldier, so we may be sure he should be like other soldiers of our acquaintance; yet never in tragedy, nor in comedy, nor in nature was a soldier with his character; take it in the author's own words;

> *Emilia.* . . . some eternal villain,
>   Some busy, and insinuating rogue,
>   Some cogging, cozening slave, to get some office.

Horace describes a soldier otherwise:

> *impiger, iracundus, inexorabilis, acer.*[1]

Shakespeare knew his character of Iago was inconsistent. In this very play he pronounces,

> If thou dost deliver more or less than truth,
>   Thou art no soldier. . . .

This he knew, but to entertain the audience with something new and surprising, against common sense and nature, he would pass upon us a close, dissembling, false, insinuating rascal instead of an openhearted, frank, plain-

---

[1] "Active, irascible, unyielding, fierce." From Horace's *Art of Poetry.* [*Editor's note.*]

dealing soldier, a character constantly worn by them for some thousands of years in the world. . . .

Nor is our poet more discreet in his Desdemona: he had chosen a soldier for his knave, and a Venetian lady is to be the fool.

This senator's daughter runs away to (a carrier's inn) the Sagittary with a blackamoor: is no sooner wedded to him, but the very night she beds him, is importuning and teasing him for a young smockfaced lieutenant, Cassio. And though she perceives the Moor jealous of Cassio, yet will she not forbear, but still rings Cassio, Cassio in both his ears.

Roderigo is the cully of Iago, brought in to be murdered by Iago, that Iago's hands might be the more in blood, and be yet the more abominable villain: who without that was too wicked on all conscience; and had more to answer for than any tragedy or furies could inflict upon him. So there can be nothing in the characters, either for the profit or to delight an audience.

The third thing to be considered is the thoughts. But from such characters we need not expect many that are either true, or fine, or noble.

And without these, that is, without sense or meaning, the fourth part of tragedy, which is the expression, can hardly deserve to be treated on distinctly. The verses rumbling in our ears are of good use to help off the action.

In the neighing of an horse or in the growling of a mastiff there is a meaning, there is as lively expression, and, may I say, more humanity than many times in the tragical flights of Shakespeare.

Step then amongst the scenes to observe the conduct in this tragedy.

The first we see are Iago and Roderigo, by night in the streets of Venice. After growling a long time together, they resolve to tell Brabantio that his daughter is run away with the blackamoor. Iago and Roderigo were not of quality to be familiar with Brabantio, nor had any provocation from him to deserve a rude thing at their hands. Brabantio was a noble Venetian, one of the sovereign lords and principal persons in the government, peer to the most

serene Doge, one attended with more state, ceremony and
punctilio than any English duke or nobleman in the government will pretend to. This misfortune in his daughter
is so prodigious, so tender a point, as might puzzle the
finest wit of the most supersubtle Venetian to touch upon
it, or break the discovery to her father. See then how deli-
cately Shakespeare minces the matter:

> *Roderigo.* What ho, Brabantio, Signior Brabantio, ho.
>
> *Iago.* Awake, what ho, Brabantio,
>   Thieves, thieves, thieves:
>   Look to your house, your daughter, and your bags.
>   Thieves, thieves.
>
>   *Brabantio at a window.*
>
> *Brabantio.* What is the reason of this terrible summons?
>   What is the matter there?
>
> *Roderigo.* Signior, is all your family within?
>
> *Iago.* Are your doors locked?
>
> *Brabantio.* Why, wherefore ask you this?
>
> *Iago.* Sir, you are robbed, for shame put on your gown,
>   Your heart is burst, you have lost half your soul
>   Even now, very now, an old black ram
>   Is tupping your white ewe: arise, arise,
>   Awake the snorting citizens with the bell,
>   Or else the devil will make a grandsire of you, arise
>   I say.

. . . But besides the manners to a magnifico, humanity
cannot bear that an old gentleman in his misfortune should
be insulted over with such a rabble of scoundrel language,
when no cause or provocation. Yet thus it is on our stage,
this is our school of good manners, and the speculum vitae.

But our magnifico is here in the dark, nor are yet his
robes on: attend him to the Senate house and there see
the difference, see the effects of purple.

So, by and by, we find the Duke of Venice with his
senators in council, at midnight, upon advice that the
Turks, or Ottamites, or both together, were ready in

transport ships, put to sea, in order to make a descent
upon Cyprus. This is the posture, when we see Brabantio
and Othello join them. By their conduct and manner of
talk, a body must strain hard to fancy the scene at Venice;
and not rather in some of our Cinq-ports, where the baily
and his fishermen are knocking their heads together on
account of some whale; or some terrible broil upon the
coast. But to show them true Venetians, the maritime
affairs stick not long on their hand; the public may sink or
swim. They will sit up all night to hear a doctors commons,
matrimonial cause. And have the merits of the cause at
large laid open at 'em, that they may decide it before they
stir. What can be pleaded to keep awake their attention so
wonderfully?

Never, sure, was form of pleading so tedious and so
heavy as this whole scene and midnight entertainment.
Take his own words: says the respondent.

> *Othello.* Most potent, grave, and reverend signiors,
>   My very noble, and approved good masters:
>   That I have tane away this old man's daughter;
>   It is most true: true, I have married her,
>   The very front and head of my offending,
>   Hath this extent, no more: rude I am in my speech.
>   And little blest with the set phrase of peace,
>   For since these arms of mine had seven years' pith,
>   Till now some nine moons wasted, they have used
>   Their dearest action in the tented field:
>   And little of this great world can I speak,
>   More than pertains to broils and battail,
>   And therefore little shall I grace my cause,
>   In speaking of myself; yet by your gracious patience
>   I would a round unvarnished tale deliver,
>   Of my whole course of love, what drugs, what
>   charms,
>   What conjuration, and what mighty magic,
>   (For such proceedings am I charged withal)
>   I won his daughter.

. . . One might rather think the novelty and strangeness
of the case prevailed upon them: no, the senators do not

reckon it strange at all. Instead of starting at the prodigy, everyone is familiar with Desdemona, as he were her own natural father, rejoice in her good fortune, and wish their own several daughters as hopefully married. Should the poet have provided such a husband for an only daughter of any noble peer in England, the blackamoor must have changed his skin, to look our House of Lords in the face. . . .

In the beginning of this second act, before they had lain together, Desdemona was said to be our captain's captain; now they are no sooner in bed together, but Iago is advising Cassio in these words.

> *Iago.* . . . Our general's wife is now the general, I may say so in this respect, for that he hath devoted, and given up himself to the contemplation, mark, and devotement of her parts and graces. Confess yourself freely to her, importune her; she'll help to put you in your place again: she is so free, so kind, so apt, so blessed a disposition, that she holds it a vice in her goodness, not to do more than she is requested. This broken joint between you and her husband, intreat her to splinter . . .

And he says afterwards.

> *Iago.* . . . 'Tis most easy
> The inclining Desdemona to subdue,
> In any honest suit. She's framed as fruitful,
> As the free elements: and then for her
> To win the Moor, were't to renounce his baptism,
> All seals and symbols of redeemed sin,
> His soul is so enfettered to her love,
> That she may make, unmake, do what she list:
> Even as her appetite shall play the God
> With his weak function . . .

This kind of discourse implies an experience and long conversation, the honeymoon over, and a marriage of some standing. Would any man, in his wits, talk thus of a bridegroom and bride the first night of their coming together?

Yet this is necessary for our poet; it would not otherwise serve his turn. This is the source, the foundation of his plot; hence is the spring and occasion for all the jealousy and bluster that ensues.

Nor are we in better circumstances for Roderigo. The last thing said by him in the former act was,

> *Roderigo.* . . . I'll go sell all my land.

A fair estate is sold to put money in his purse for this adventure. And lo here, the next day.

> *Roderigo.* I do follow here in the chase, not like a hound that hunts, but one that fills up the cry: my money is almost spent. I have been tonight exceedingly well cudgeled. I think the issue will be, I shall have so much experience for my pains, and so no money at all, and with a little more wit return to Venice.

The Venetian squire had a good riddance for his acres. The poet allows him just time to be once drunk, a very conscionable reckoning! . . .

What we have seen, that there needs no great cunning, no great poetry and address to make the Moor jealous. Such impatience, such a rout for a handsome young fellow, the very morning after her marriage must make him either to be jealous, or to take her for a changeling, below his jealousy. After this scene, it might strain the poet's skill to reconcile the couple and allay the jealousy. Iago now can only *actum agere,* and vex the audience with a nauseous repetition.

Whence comes it then, that this is the top scene, the scene that raises *Othello* above all other tragedies on our theaters? It is purely from the action; from the mops and the mows, the grimaces, the grins and gesticulation. Such scenes as this have made all the world run after Harlequin and Scaramuccio. . . .

Othello, the night of his arrival at Cyprus, is to consummate with Desdemona; they go to bed. Both are raised and run into the town amidst the soldiers that were a fighting: then go to bed again; that morning he sees Cassio with her; she importunes him to restore Cassio. Othello shows nothing of the soldier's mettle: but like a tedious, drawling, tame goose is gaping after any paltry insinuation, laboring to be jealous; and catching at every blown surmise.

Iago. My lord, I see you are moved.

Othello. No, not much moved.
 I do not think but Desdemona is honest.

Iago. Long live she so, and long live you to think so.

Othello. And yet how nature erring from itself—

Iago. Ay, there's the point: as to be bold with you,
 Not to affect many proposed matches
 Of her own clime, complexion, and degree,
 Wherein we see, in all things, nature tends,
 Fye, we may smell in such a will most rank,
 Foul disproportion, thoughts unnatural . . .

The poet here is certainly in the right, and by consequence the foundation of the play must be concluded to be monstrous; and the constitution, all over, to be most rank,

Foul disproportion, thoughts unnatural.

Which instead of moving pity, or any passion tragical and reasonable, can produce nothing but horror and aversion, and what is odious and grievous to an audience. After this fair morning's work, the bride enters, drops a curtsy.

Desdemona. How now, my dear Othello,
 Your dinner, and the generous islanders
 By you invited, do attend your presence.

Othello. I am to blame.

Desdemona. Why is your speech so faint? Are you not well?

Othello. I have a pain upon my forehead, dear.

Michael Cassio came not from Venice in the ship with Desdemona, nor till this morning could be suspected of an opportunity with her. And 'tis now but dinner time; yet the Moor complains of his forehead. He might have set a guard on Cassio, or have locked up Desdemona, or have observed their carriage a day or two longer. He is on other occasions phlegmatic enough: this is very hasty. But after dinner we have a wonderful flight:

> *Othello.* What sense had I of her stolen hours of lust?
>   I saw't not, thought it not, it harmed not me:
>   I slept the next night well, was free and merry,
>   I found not Cassio's kisses on her lips . . .

A little after this, says he,

> *Othello.* Give me a living reason that she's disloyal.
>
> *Iago.* . . . I lay with Cassio lately,
>   And being troubled with a raging tooth, I could not
>   sleep;
>   There are a kind of men so loose of soul,
>   That in their sleeps will mutter their affairs,
>   One of this kind is Cassio:
>   In sleep I heard him say: sweet Desdemona,
>   Let us be wary, let us hide our loves:
>   And then, Sir, would he grip, and wring my hand,
>   Cry out, sweet creature; and then kiss me hard,
>   As if he plucked up kisses by the roots,
>   That grew upon my lips, then laid his leg
>   Over my thigh, and sighed, and kissed, and then
>   Cried, cursed fate, that gave thee to the Moor.

By the rapture of Othello one might think that he raves, is not of sound memory, forgets that he has not yet been two nights in the matrimonial bed with his Desdemona. But we find Iago, who should have a better memory, forging his lies after the very same model. The very night of their marriage at Venice, the Moor, and also Cassio, were sent away to Cyprus. In the second act, Othello and his bride go the first time to bed; the third

act opens the next morning. The parties have been in
view to this moment. We saw the opportunity which was
given for Cassio to speak his bosom to her; once, indeed,
might go a great way with a Venetian. But once will not
do the poet's business; the audience must suppose a great
many bouts, to make the plot operate. They must deny their
senses, to reconcile it to common sense: or make it any
way consistent, and hang together. . . .

Iago had some pretense to be discontent with Othello
and Cassio: and what passed hitherto was the operation
of revenge. Desdemona had never done him harm, always
kind to him, and to his wife; was his countrywoman, a
dame of quality; for him to abet her murder shows nothing
of a soldier, nothing of a man, nothing of nature in it.
The Ordinary of Newgate never had the like monster to
pass under his examination. Can it be any diversion to see
a rogue beyond what the Devil ever finished? Or would
it be any instruction to an audience? Iago could desire no
better than to set Cassio and Othello, his two enemies,
by the ears together; so he might have been revenged on
them both at once: and choosing for his own share the
murder of Desdemona, he had the opportunity to play
booty and save the poor harmless wretch. But the poet
must do everything by contraries: to surprise the audience
still with something horrible and prodigious, beyond any
human imagination. At this rate he must out-do the Devil
to be a poet in the rank with Shakespeare.

Soon after this, arrives from Venice Lodovico, a noble
cousin of Desdemona; presently she is at him also, on
the behalf of Cassio.

> *Desdemona.* Cousin there's fallen between him and
>   my Lord
>   An unkind breach, but you shall make all well.
>
> *Lodovico.* Is there division 'twixt my Lord and Cassio.
>
> *Desdemona.* A most unhappy one, I would do much
>   To atone them, for the love I bear to Cassio.

By this time, we are to believe the couple have been
a week or two married: and Othello's jealousy, that had

raged so loudly and had been so uneasy to himself, must have reached her knowledge. The audience have all heard him more plain with her than was needful to a Venetian capacity: and yet she must still be impertinent in her suit for Cassio, well, this magnifico comes from the Doge, and senators, to displace Othello.

Lodovico. . . . Deputing Cassio in his government.

Desdemona. Trust me, I am glad on't.

Othello. Indeed.

Desdemona. My lord.

Othello. I am glad to see you mad.

Desdemona. How, sweet Othello.

Othello. Devil.

Desdemona. I have not deserved this.

Othello. O Devil, Devil . . .
    Out of my sight.

Desdemona. I will not stay to offend you.

Lodovico. Truly, an obedient lady.
    I do beseech your lordship call her back.

Othello. Mistress.

Desdemona. My lord.

Othello. What would you with her, sir?

Lodovico. Who, I, my lord?

Othello. Ay, you did wish that I would make her turn.
    Sir, she can turn, and turn, and yet go on,
    And turn again, and she can weep, sir, weep.
    And she is obedient, as you say, obedient:
    Very obedient . . .

Lodovico. What strike your wife?

Of what flesh and blood does our poet make these noble Venetians? the men without gall; the women without either brains or sense? A senator's daughter runs away with this blackamoor; the government employs this Moor to defend them against the Turks, so resent not the Moor's marriage at present, but the danger over, her father gets the Moor cashiered, sends his kinsman, Signior Lodovico, to Cyprus with the commission for a new general; who, at his arrival, finds the Moor calling the lady, his kinswoman, whore and strumpet, and kicking her: what says the magnifico?

> *Lodovico.* My Lord this would not be believed in Venice,
> Tho' I should swear I saw't, 'tis very much;
> Make her amends: she weeps.

The Moor has nobody to take his part, nobody of his color: Lodovico has the new governor, Cassio, and all his countrymen Venetians about him. What poet would give a villainous blackamoor this ascendant? What tramontain could fancy the Venetians so low, so despicable, or so patient? This outrage to an injured lady, the divine Desdemona, might in a colder climate have provoked somebody to be her champion: but the Italians may well conclude we have a strange genius for poetry. In the next scene Othello is examining the supposed bawd: then follows another storm of horror and outrage against the poor chicken, his wife. Some drayman or drunken tinker might possibly treat his drab at this sort of rate, and mean no harm by it; but for his excellency, a my lord general, to serenade a senator's daughter with such a volley of scoundrel filthy language, is sure the most absurd maggot that ever bred from any poet's addle brain. . . .

Yet to make all worse, her murder, and the manner of it, had before been resolved upon and concerted. But nothing is to provoke a Venetian; she takes all in good part; had the scene lain in Russia, what could we have expected more? With us a tinker's trull would be nettled, would repartee with more spirit, and not appear so void of spleen.

> *Desdemona.* O good Iago,
> What shall I do to win my lord again?

No woman bred out of a pigsty, could talk so meanly. After this she is called to supper with Othello, Lodovico,

&c. after that comes a filthy sort of pastoral scene, where the wedding sheets, and song of willow, and her mother's maid, poor Barbara, are not the least moving things in this entertainment. . . .

The last act begins with Iago and Roderigo, who a little before had been upon the huff:

> *Roderigo*. I say it is not very well: I will make myself known to Desdemona; if she will return me my jewels, I will give over my suit, and repent my unlawful solicitation, if not, assure yourself, I'll seek satisfaction of you.

Roderigo, a noble Venetian, had sought Desdemona in marriage, is troubled to find the Moor had got her from him, advises with Iago, who wheedles him to sell his estate and go over the sea to Cyprus in expectation to cuckold Othello; there having cheated Roderigo of all his money and jewels, on pretense of presenting them to Desdemona, our gallant grows angry and would have satisfaction from Iago, who sets all right by telling him Cassio is to be governor, Othello is going with Desdemona into Mauritania: to prevent this, you are to murder Cassio, and then all may be well. . . .

Had Roderigo been one of the banditti, he might not much stick at the murder. But why Roderigo should take this for payment, and risk his person where the prospect of advantage is so very uncertain and remote, nobody can imagine. It had need be a supersubtle Venetian that this plot will pass upon. Then after a little spurt of villainy and murder, we are brought to the most lamentable that ever appeared on any stage. A noble Venetian lady is to be murdered by our poet: in sober sadness, purely for being a fool. No pagan poet but would have found some machine for her deliverance. Pegasus would have strained hard to have brought old Perseus on his back, time enough, to rescue this Andromeda from so foul a monster. Has our Christian poetry no generosity, nor bowels? Ha, Sir Lancelot! ha St. George! Will no ghost leave the shades for us in extremity, to save a distressed damosel?

But for our comfort, however felonious is the heart, hear with what soft language he does approach her, with a candle in his hand:

> *Othello.* Put out the light and then put out the light;
>   If I quench thee, thou flaming minister,
>   I can again thy former light restore . . .

Who would call him a barbarian, monster, savage? Is this a blackamoor?

> *Soles occider & redire possunt . . .*[2]

The very soul and quintessence of Sir George Etheridge. One might think the general should not glory much in this action, but make an hasty work on't, and have turned his eyes away from so unsoldierly an execution: yet is he all pause and deliberation: handles her as calmly: and is as careful of her soul's health, as it had been her father confessor. Have you prayed tonight, Desdemona? But the suspense is necessary, that he might have a convenient while so to roll his eyes, and so to gnaw his nether lip to the spectators. Besides the greater cruelty—*sub tam lentis maxillis.*[3]

But hark, a most tragical thing laid to her charge.

> *Othello.* That handkerchief, that I so loved, and gave thee,
>   Thou gav'st to Cassio.
>
> *Desdemona.* No by my life and soul:
>   Send for the man and ask him.
>
> *Othello.* . . . By heaven, I saw my handkerchief in his hand . . .
>   . . . I saw the handkerchief.

So much ado, so much stress, so much passion and repetition about an handkerchief? Why was not this called

---

[2] "Suns may set and rise again." From a lyric by Catullus. [*Editor's Note.*]

[3] Suetonius reports that under Tiberius the Romans were said to be ground "by jaws that crunch slowly." [*Editor's Note.*]

the *Tragedy of the Handkerchief?* What can be more
absurd than (as Quintilian expresses it) *in parvis litibus has
Tragœdias movere?* [4] We have heard of Fortunatus his
purse, and of the invisible cloak, long ago worn thread-
bare, and stowed up in the wardrobe of obsolete romances:
one might think that were a fitter place for this handkerchief than that it, at this time of day, be worn on the
stage, to raise everywhere all this clutter and turmoil. Had
it been Desdemona's garter, the sagacious Moor might
have smelled a rat: but the handkerchief is so remote a
trifle, no booby, on this side Mauritania, could make
any consequence from it.

We may learn here that a woman never loses her tongue,
even though after she is stifled.

Desdemona. O falsely, falsely murdered.

Emilia. Sweet Desdemona, O sweet Mistress, speak.

Desdemona. A guiltless death I die.

Emilia. O who has done the deed?

Desdemona. Nobody, I myself, farewell.
   Commend me to my kind lord, O farewell.

. . . But hark what follows:

Othello. . . . O heavy hour!
   Methinks it should be now a huge eclipse
   Of sun and moon, and that the affrighted globe
   Should yawn at alteration.

This is wonderful. Here is poetry to elevate and amuse.
Here is sound all-sufficient. It would be uncivil to ask
Flamstead [first royal astronomer], if the sun and moon
can both together be so hugely eclipsed, in any heavy
hour whatsoever. Nor must the spectators consult Gresham
College, whether a body is naturally frighted till he yawn
again. The fortune of Greece is not concerned with these
matters. These are physical circumstances a poet may be
ignorant in, without any harm to the public. These slips

[4] "To make tragedies out of trivial subjects." [*Editor's Note.*]

have no influence on our manners and good life, which are the poet's province.

Rather may we ask here what unnatural crime Desdemona or her parents had committed to bring this judgment down upon her; to wed a blackamoor, and innocent to be thus cruelly murdered by him. What instruction can we make out of this catastrophe? Or whither must our reflection lead us? Is not this to envenom and sour our spirits, to make us repine and grumble at providence and the government of the world? If this be our end, what boots it to be virtuous?

Desdemona dropped the handkerchief and missed it that very day after her marriage; it might have been rumpled up with her wedding sheets: and this night that she lay in her wedding sheets, the fairy napkin (whilst Othello was stifling her) might have started up to disarm his fury and stop his ungracious mouth. Then might she (in a trance for fear) have lain as dead. Then might he, believing her dead, touched with remorse, have honestly cut his own throat, by the good leave, and with the applause of all the spectators. Who might thereupon have gone home with a quiet mind, admiring the beauty of providence, fairly and truly represented on the theater. . . .

But from this scene to the end of the play we meet with nothing but blood and butchery, described much-what to the style of the last speeches and confessions of the persons executed at Tyburn: with this difference, that there we have the fact, and the due course of justice, whereas our poet, against all justice and reason, against all law, humanity and nature, in a barbarous arbitrary way, executes and makes havoc of his subjects, hab-nab, as they come to hand. Desdemona dropped her handkerchief; therefore she must be stifled. Othello, by law to be broken on the wheel, by the poet's cunning escapes with cutting his own throat. Cassio, for I know not what, comes off with a broken shin. Iago murders his benefactor Roderigo, as this were poetical gratitude. Iago is not yet killed, because there never yet was such a villain alive. The devil, if once he brings a man to be dipped in a deadly sin, lets him alone, to take his course: and now when the foul fiend has done with him, our wise authors take the sinner into their poetical service, there to accomplish him, and do the devil's drudgery.

Philosophy tells us it is a principle in the nature of man to be grateful.

History may tell us that John an Oaks, John a Stiles, or Iago were ungrateful; poetry is to follow nature; philosophy must be his guide: history and fact in particular cases of John an Oaks, or John of Stiles, are no warrant or direction for a poet. Therefore Aristotle is always telling us that poetry is . . . more general and abstracted, is led more by the philosophy, the reason and nature of things, than history: which only records things higgledy-piggledy, right or wrong, as they happen. History might without any preamble or difficulty say that Iago was ungrateful. Philosophy then calls him unnatural; but the poet is not, without huge labor and preparation to expose the monster; and after show the divine vengeance executed upon him. The poet is not to add willful murder to his ingratitude: he has not antidote enough for the poison: his hell and furies are not punishment sufficient for one single crime of that bulk and aggravation.

> *Emilia.* O thou dull Moor, that handkerchief thou
>   speakest on,
>   I found by fortune, and did give my husband:
>   For often with a solemn earnestness,
>   (More than indeed belonged to such a trifle)
>   He begged of me to steal it.

Here we see the meanest woman in the play takes this handkerchief for a trifle below her husband to trouble his head about it. Yet, we find, it entered into our poet's head to make a tragedy of this trifle.

Then for the unraveling of the plot, as they call it, never was old deputy recorder in a country town, with his spectacles in summoning up the evidence, at such a puzzle: so blundered, and bedoltified: as is our poet, to have a good riddance: and get the catastrophe off his hands.

What can remain with the audience to carry home with

them from this sort of poetry, for their use and edification? How can it work, unless (instead of settling the mind, and purging our passions) to delude our senses, disorder our thoughts, addle our brain, pervert our affections, hair our imaginations, corrupt our appetite, and fill our head with vanity, confusion, tintamarre, and jingle-jangle, beyond what all the parish clerks of London, with their Old Testament farces, and interludes, in Richard the Second's time could ever pretend to? Our only hopes, for the good of their souls, can be that these people go to the playhouse, as they do to church, to sit still, look on one another, make no reflection, nor mind the play more than they would a sermon.

There is in this play some burlesque, some humor and ramble of comical wit, some show, and some mimicry to divert the spectators: but the tragical part is, plainly, none other than a bloody farce, without salt or savor.

Samuel Taylor Coleridge

[Comments on *Othello*]

The admirable preparation, so characteristic of Shakespeare, in the introduction of Roderigo as the dupe on whom Iago first exercises his art, and in so doing displays his own character. Roderigo is already fitted and predisposed [to be a dupe] by his own passions—without any fixed principle or strength of character (the want of character and the power of the passions—like the wind loudest in empty houses—form his character)—but yet not without the moral notions and sympathies with honor which his rank, connections, had hung upon him. The very three first lines happily state the nature and foundation of the friendship—the purse—as well as the contrast of Roderigo's intemperance of mind with Iago's coolness, the coolness of a preconceiving experimenter. The mere language of protestation in

> If ever I did dream of such a matter,
> Abhor me—

which, fixing the associative link that determines Roderigo's continuation of complaint—

> Thou told'st me thou didst hold him in thy hate—

elicits a true feeling of Iago's—the dread of contempt habit[ual] to those who encourage in themselves and have

From *Shakespearean Criticism* by Samuel Taylor Coleridge. 2nd ed., ed. Thomas Middleton Raysor. New York: E. P. Dutton and Company, Inc., 1960; London: J. M. Dent & Sons, Ltd., 1961. 2 vols.

their keenest pleasure in the feeling and expression of contempt for others. His high self-opinion—and how a wicked man employs his real feelings as well as assumes those most alien from his own, as instruments of his purpose.

> *Iago.* Virtue! a fig! 'tis in ourselves that we are thus or thus.

Iago's passionless character, all will in intellect; therefore a bold partisan here of a truth, but yet of a truth converted into falsehood by absence of all the modifications by the frail nature of man. And the last sentiment—

> . . . our raging motions, our carnal stings, our unbitted lusts; whereof I take this, that you call love, to be a sect or scion—

There lies the Iagoism of how many! And the repétition, "Go make money!"—a pride in it, of an anticipated dupe, stronger than the love of lucre.

> *Iago.* Go to, farewell, put money enough in your purse:
> Thus do I ever make my fool my purse.

The triumph! Again, "put money," after the effect has been fully produced. The last speech [Iago's soliloquy], the motive-hunting of motiveless malignity—how awful! In itself fiendish; while yet he was allowed to bear the divine image, too fiendish for his own steady view. A being next to devil, only not quite devil—and this Shakespeare has attempted—executed—without disgust, without scandal!

[V. ii. 349–51. Othello's death-speech.]

> . . . of one whose hand,
> Like the base Indian, threw a pearl away
> Richer than all his tribe.

Following, in part, a suggestion of the scholar Warburton, Theobald, in his edition of the play, defends the reading of the first Folio, *Iudean,* which he alters to *Judian.*

Thus it is for no-poets to comment on the greatest of poets! To make Othello say that he, who had killed his wife, was like Herod, who had killed his! Oh, how many beauties in this one line were impenetrable by the *thought*-swarming, ever *idea*less Warburton! Othello wishes to excuse himself—to excuse himself by accusing. This struggle of feeling is finely conveyed in the word "base," which is applied to the *rude* Indian not in his own character, but as the momentary representative of Othello. "Indian" means American or Carib, a savage *in genere.* Othello's *belief* is not caused by jealousy; it is forced upon him by Iago, and is such as any man would and must feel who had believed in Iago as Othello did. His great mistake is that *we* know Iago for a villain from the first moment.

Maynard Mack

The Jacobean Shakespeare:

Some Observations on the Construction of the Tragedies

This chapter aims at being a modest supplement (I cannot too much stress the adjective) to A. C. Bradley's pioneering analysis of the construction of Shakespearean tragedy, the second of his famous lectures, published some fifty-five years ago. Bradley's concern was with what would probably today be called the clearer outlines of Shakespearean practice—the management of exposition, conflict, crisis, catastrophe; the contrasts of pace and scene; the over-all patterns of rise-and-fall, variously modulated; the slackened tension after the crisis and Shakespeare's devices for countering this; and the faults.

Bradley is quite detailed about the faults. Sometimes, he says, there are too rapid shiftings of scene and *dramatis personae,* as in the middle section of *Antony and Cleopatra.* Sometimes there is extraneous matter, not required for plot or character development, like the player's speech in *Hamlet* about the murder of Priam, or Hamlet's advice later to the same player on speaking in the theater. Sometimes there are soliloquies too obviously expositional, as when Edgar disguises to become Poor Tom in *King*

From *Stratford-upon-Avon Studies: Jacobean Theatre* (Vol. I), ed. John Russell Brown and Bernard Harris. London: Edward Arnold (Publishers) Ltd., 1960; New York: St. Martin's Press, Inc., 1961. © Edward Arnold (Publishers) Ltd., 1960. Reprinted by permission of the publishers.

Lear. Or there is contradiction and inconsistency, as the double time in *Othello.* Or flatulent writing: "obscure, inflated, tasteless," or "pestered with metaphors." Or "gnomic" insertions, like the Duke's couplet interchange with Brabantio in *Othello,* used "more freely than, I suppose, a good playwright now would care to do." And finally, to make an end, there is too often sacrificing of dramatic appropriateness to get something said that the author wants said. Thus the comments of the Player King and Claudius on the instability of human purpose arise because Shakespeare "wishes in part simply to write poetry, and partly to impress on the audience thoughts which will help them to understand, not the player-king nor yet King Claudius, but Hamlet himself." These failings, Bradley concludes, belong to an art of drama imperfectly developed, which Shakespeare inherited from his predecessors and acquiesced in, on occasion, from "indifference or want of care."

Though Bradley's analysis is still the best account we have of the outward shape of Shakespearean tragedy, a glance at his list of faults and, especially, his examples reminds us that a vast deal of water has got itself under the critical bridges since 1904. It is not simply that most of the faults he enumerates would no longer be regarded as such, but would, instead, be numbered among the characteristic practices of Shakespearean dramaturgy, even at its most triumphant. Still more striking is the extent to which our conception of the "construction" of the tragedies has itself changed. The matters Bradley described have not ceased to be important—far from it: several of our current interpreters, one feels, would benefit if, like Bottom of Master Mustardseed, they were to desire him "of more acquaintance." Still, it is impossible not to feel that Bradley missed something—that there is another kind of construction in Shakespeare's tragedies than the one he designates, more inward, more difficult to define, but not less significant. This other structure is not, like his, generated entirely by the interplay of plot and character. Nor is it, on the other hand, though it is fashionable nowadays to suppose so, ultimately a verbal matter. It is poetic, but it goes well beyond what in certain quarters today is called (with something like a lump in the throat) "the poetry." Some of its elements arise from the playwright's visualizing imagination, the consciousness of groupings, gestures, entrances, exits. Others may even be prior to language, in the sense that they appear to belong to a paradigm of tragic "form" that was consciously or unconsciously part of Shakespeare's inheritance and intuition as he worked.

At any rate, it is into this comparatively untraveled and uncharted territory of inward structure that I should like to launch a few tentative explorations. I shall occasionally look backward as far as *Julius Caesar* (1599), *Richard II* (1595–1600), and even *Romeo and Juliet* (1595–6); but in the main I shall be concerned with the tragedies of Shakespeare's prime, from *Hamlet* (1600–1) to *Coriolanus* (1607–8). In these seven or eight years, Shakespeare's golden period, he consolidated a species of tragic structure that for suggestiveness and flexibility has never been matched.[1] I do not anticipate being able to return with a map of this obscure terrain. I hope only to convince better travelers that there is something out there to be known.

First, the hero. The Shakespearean tragic hero, as everybody knows, is an overstater. His individual accent will vary with his personality, but there is always a residue of hyperbole. This, it would seem, is for Shakespeare the authentic tragic music, mark of a world where a man's reach must always exceed his grasp and everything costs not less than everything.

> Wert thou as far
> As that vast shore wash'd with the farthest sea,
> I would adventure for such merchandise.
>
> (*Romeo*, II.ii.82)

[1] The flexibility of the structure is witnessed by the amazing differences between the tragedies, of which it is, however, the lowest common multiple. In my discussion, I shall necessarily take the differences between the tragedies for granted and stress simply the vertebrate characteristics they share.

'Swounds, show me what thou'lt do:
Woo't weep? woo't fight? woo't fast? woo't tear thyself?
Woo't drink up eisel? eat a crocodile
I'll do't.   (*Hamlet*, V.i.297)

                  Nay, had she been true,
If heaven would make me such another world
Of one entire and perfect chrysolite,
I'ld not have sold her for it.   (*Othello*, V.ii.140)

Death, traitor! nothing could have subdued nature
To such a lowness but his unkind daughters.
                          (*Lear*, III.iv.72)

Will all great Neptune's ocean wash this blood
Clean from my hand?   (*Macbeth*, II.ii.60)

                     I, that with my sword
Quarter'd the world, and o'er green Neptune's back
With ships made cities, . . .   (*Antony*, IV.xiv.57)

               I go alone,
Like to a lonely dragon, that his fen
Makes fear'd and talk'd of more than seen.
                   (*Coriolanus*, IV.i.29)

    This idiom is not, of course, used by the hero only. It
is the language he is dressed in by all who love him, and
often by those who do not:

This was the noblest Roman of them all: . . .
His life was gentle, and the elements
So mix'd in him that Nature might stand up
And say to all the world "This was a man!"
                     (*Caesar*, V.v.68)

The courtier's, soldier's, scholar's, eye, tongue, sword;
The expectancy and rose of the fair state,
The glass of fashion and the mold of form,
The observed of all observers, . . .
                  (*Hamlet*, III.i.159)

Can he be angry? I have seen the cannon,
When it hath blown his ranks into the air,
And, like the devil, from his very arm
Puff'd his own brother:—and can he be angry?

                                    (*Othello*, III.iv.134)

On the Alps
It is reported thou didst eat strange flesh,
Which some did die to look on.

                                    (*Antony*, I.iv.66)

Let me twine
Mine arms about that body, where against
My grainèd ash an hundred times hath broke,
And scarr'd the moon with splinters.

                                    (*Coriolanus*, IV.v.112)

But by whomever used, it is a language that depends
for its vindication—for the redemption of its paper
promises into gold—upon the hero, and any who stand,
heroically, where he does. It is the mark of his, and their,
commitment to something beyond "the vast waters Of
the petrel and the porpoise," as Mr. Eliot has it in *East
Coker,* a commitment to something—not merely death—
which shackles accidents and bolts up change and palates
no dung whatever.

Thus the hyperbole of tragedy stands at the opposite
end of a tonal scale from the hyperbole of comedy, which
springs from and nourishes detachment:

When I was about thy years, Hal, I was not an eagle's
talon in the waist; I could have crept into any alderman's thumb-ring.   (*I Henry IV*, II.iv.362)

O, she misused me past the endurance of a block! an
oak but with one green leaf on it would have answered
her; my very visor began to assume life, and scold with
her.   (*Much Ado*, II.i.246)

He has a son, who shall be flayed alive; then 'nointed
over with honey, set on the head of a wasp's nest; then

stand till he be three quarters and a dram dead; then
recovered again with aqua-vitae or some other hot in-
fusion; then, raw as he is, and in the hottest day prog-
nostication proclaims, shall he be set against a brick-wall,
the sun looking with a southward eye upon him, where
he is to behold him with flies blown to death.

(*Winter's Tale,* IV.iv.811)

Comic overstatement aims at being preposterous. Until
it becomes so, it remains flat. Tragic overstatement, on
the other hand, aspires to be believed, and unless in some
sense it is so, remains bombast.

Besides the hyperbolist, in Shakespeare's scheme of
things, there is always the opposing voice, which belongs
to the hero's foil. As the night the day, the idiom of
absoluteness demands a vocabulary of a different intensity,
a different rhetorical and moral wave length, to set it off.
This other idiom is not necessarily understatement, though
it often takes the form of a deflating accent and very often
involves colloquialism—or perhaps merely a middling sort
of speech—expressive of a suppler outlook than the hero's,
and of other and less upsetting ways of encountering
experience than his hyperbolic, not to say intransigent,
rigorism. " 'Twere to consider too curiously to consider
so," says Horatio of Hamlet's equation between the dust
of Alexander and a bunghole, and this enunciates perfectly
the foil's role. There is no tragedy in him because he does
not consider "curiously"; there are always more things
in earth and heaven than are dreamt of in his philosophy.

Each of the Shakespearean tragedies contains at least
one personage to speak this part, which is regularly assigned to someone in the hero's immediate entourage—
servitor, wife, friend. In *Romeo and Juliet,* it is of course
Mercutio, with his witty resolution of all love into sex.
In *Julius Caesar,* it is Cassius, whose restless urgent
rhythms, full of flashing images, swirl about Brutus's
rounder and abstracter speech, like dogs that bay the
moon:

> *Brutus.* I do believe that these applauses are
>   For some new honors that are heap'd on Caesar.

> *Cassius.* Why, man, he doth bestride the narrow world
> Like a Colossus, and we petty men
> Walk under his huge legs and peep about
> To find ourselves dishonorable graves. (I.ii.133)

In the famous forum speeches, this second voice is taken over temporarily by Antony, and there emerges a similar but yet more powerful contrast between them. Brutus's prose—in which the actuality of the assassination is intellectualized and held at bay by the strict patterns of an obtrusively formal rhetoric, almost as though corporal death were transubstantiated to "a ballet of bloodless categories"—gives way to Antony's sinewy verse about the "honorable men," which draws the deed, and its consequence the dead Caesar, ever closer till his own vengeful emotions are kindled in the mob.

In *Hamlet,* the relation of foil to hero undergoes an unusual adaptation. Here, since the raciest idiom of the play belongs to the hero himself, the foil, Horatio, is given a quite conventional speech, and, to make the contrast sharper (Hamlet being of all the heroes the most voluble), as little speech as may be. Like his stoicism, like his "blood and judgment"—

> so well commingled,
> That they are not a pipe for fortune's finger
> To sound what stop she please—   (III.ii.74)

Horatio's "Here, sweet lord," "O, my dear lord," "Well, my lord" are, presumably (as the gentleman in *Lear* says of Cordelia's tears), "a better way" than Hamlet's self-lacerating virtuosities and verbosities. But of course we do not believe this and are not meant to: who would be Horatio if he could be Hamlet?

Plainly, this is one of the two questions that all the tragic foils exist to make us ask (the other we shall come to presently). Who, for instance, would be Enobarbus, clear-sighted as he is, in preference to Antony? His brilliant sardonic speech, so useful while he can hold his own career and all about him in the comic focus of detachment, withers in the face of his engagement to ultimate issues, and he dies speaking with imagery, accent, and feeling which are surely meant to identify him at the last with the absoluteness of the heroic world, the more so since his last syllables anticipate Cleopatra's:

> Throw my heart
> Against the flint and hardness of my fault;
> Which, being dried with grief, will break to powder,
> And finish all foul thoughts. O Antony,
> Nobler than my revolt is infamous,
> Forgive me in thine own particular;
> But let the world rank me in register
> A master-leaver and a fugitive:
> O Antony! O Antony!   (IV.ix.15)

Such unequivocal judgments are a change indeed on the part of one who could earlier rally cynically with Menas about "two thieves kissing" when their hands meet.

King Lear is given two foils. The primary one is obviously the Fool, whose rhymes and riddles and jets of humor in the first two acts set off both the old king's brooding silences and his massively articulated longer speeches when aroused. But in the storm scenes, and occasionally elsewhere, one is almost as keenly conscious of the relief into which Lear's outrageous imprecations are thrown by the mute devoted patience of his servant Kent. For both foils—and this of course is their most prominent function as representatives of the opposing voice—the storm itself is only a storm, to be stoically endured, in the one case, and, in the other, if his master would but hear reason, eschewed:

> O nuncle, court holy-water in a dry house is better than this rainwater out o' door. Good nuncle, in, ask thy daughters' blessing: . . .   (III.ii.10)

Doubtless the Fool does not wish to be taken quite *au pied de la lettre* in this—his talk is always in the vein of the false daughters', his action quite other. But neither for him nor for Kent does facing the thunder have any kind of transcendent meaning. In Lear's case, it has; the thunder he hears is like the thunder heard over Himavant in *The Waste Land*; it has what the anthropologists call "mana"; and his (and our) consuming questions are what it means—and if it means—and whose side it is on.

In my view, the most interesting uses of the opposing voice occur in *Macbeth* and *Othello*. In *Macbeth,* Shakespeare gives it to Lady Macbeth, and there was never, I think, a more thrilling tragic counterpoint set down for the stage than that in the scene following the murder of Duncan, when her purely physical reading of what has happened to them both is met by his metaphysical intuitions. His "noise" to her is just the owl screaming and the crickets' cry. The voice of one crying "sleep no more" is only his "brain-sickly" fear. The blood on his hands is what "a little water clears us of." "Consider it not so deeply," she says at one point, with an echo of Horatio in the graveyard. "These deeds must not be thought After these ways." But in the tragic world, which always opens on transcendence, they must; and this she herself finds before she dies, a prisoner to the deed, endlessly washing the damned spot that will not out. "What's done cannot be undone" is a language that like Enobarbus she has to learn.

Othello's foil of course is Iago, about whose imagery and speech there hangs, as recent commentators have pointed out, a constructed air, an ingenious, hyperconscious generalizing air, essentially suited to one who, as W. H. Clemen has said, "seeks to poison . . . others with his images" (*The Development of Shakespeare's Imagery,* p. 122). Yet Iago's poison does not work more powerfully through his images than through a corrosive habit of abstraction applied in those unique relations of love and faith where abstraction is most irrelevant and most destructive. Iago has learned to "sickly o'er" the central and irreducible individual with the pale cast of class and kind:

Blessed fig's end! The wine she drinks is made of
grapes. . . .   (II.i.251)

These Moors are changeable in their wills. . . . If
sanctimony and a frail vow betwixt an erring barbarian
and a supersubtle Venetian be not too hard for my
wits . . .   (I.iii.342–43, 350–53)

Come on, come on; you are pictures out of doors,
Bells in your parlors, wildcats in your kitchens,
Saints in your injuries, devils being offended,
Players in your housewifery, and housewives in your
    beds.   (II.i.108)

    I know our country disposition well;
    In Venice they do let heaven see the pranks
    They dare not show their husbands.   (III.iii.201)

Othello's downfall is signaled quite as clearly when he
drifts into this rationalized dimension—

                        O curse of marriage,
    That we can call these delicate creatures ours,
    And not their appetites—   (III.iii.267)

leaving behind his true vernacular, the idiom of "My life
upon her faith!", as when his mind fills with Iago's copula-
tive imagery. Shakespeare seems to have been well aware
that love (especially such love as can be reflected only in
the union of a black man with a white woman, East with
West) is the mutual knowing of uniqueness:

            Reason, in itself confounded,
            Saw division grow together,
            To themselves yet either neither,
            Simple were so well compounded,

            That it cried, How true a twain
            Seemeth this concordant one!
            Love hath reason, reason none,
            If what parts can so remain.

            Whereupon it made this threne
            To the phoenix and the dove,

> Go-supremes and stars of love,
> As chorus to their tragic scene.
>> (*The Phoenix and the Turtle*, 41)

And also that there are areas of experience where, as a great saint once said, one must first believe in order that one may know.

To one who should ask why these paired voices seem to be essential ingredients of Shakespearean tragedy, no single answer can, I think, be given. They occur partly, no doubt, because of their structural utility, the value of complementary personalities in a work of fiction being roughly analogous to the value of thesis and antithesis in a discursive work. Partly too, no doubt, because in stage performance, the antiphonal effects of the two main vocabularies, strengthened by diversity in manner, costume, placing on the stage, supply variety of mood and gratify the eye and ear. But these are superficial considerations. Perhaps we come to something more satisfactory when we consider that these two voices apparently answer to reverberations which reach far back in the human past. *Mutatis mutandis,* Coriolanus and Menenius, Antony and Enobarbus, Macbeth and Lady Macbeth, Lear and his Fool, Othello and Iago, Hamlet and Horatio, Brutus and Cassius, Romeo and Mercutio exhibit a kind of duality that is also exhibited in Oedipus and Jocasta (as well as Creon), Antigone and Ismene, Prometheus and Oceanus, Phaedra and her nurse —and also, in many instances in Greek tragedy, by the protagonist and the chorus.

If it is true, as can be argued, that the Greek chorus functions in large measure as spokesman for the values of the community, and the first actor, in large measure, for the passionate life of the individual, we can perhaps see a philosophical basis for the long succession of opposing voices. What matters to the community is obviously accommodation—all those adjustments and resiliences that enable it to survive; whereas what matters to the individual, at least in his heroic mood, is just as obviously integrity—all that enables him to remain an *individual,* one thing not many.

The confrontation of these two outlooks is therefore a confrontation of two of our most cherished instincts, the instinct to be resolute, autonomous, free, and the instinct to be "realistic," adaptable, secure. If it is also true, as I think most of us believe, that tragic drama is in one way or other a record of man's affair with transcendence (whether this be defined as gods, God, or, as by Malraux, the human "fate," which men must "question" even if they cannot control), we can see further why the hero must have an idiom—such as hyperbole—that establishes him as moving to measures played above, or outside, our normal space and time. For the *reductio ad absurdum* of the tragic confrontation is the comic one, exemplified in Don Quixote and his Sancho, where the comedy arises precisely from the fact that the hero only *imagines* he moves to measures above and outside our normal world; and where, to the extent that we come to identify with his faith, the comedy slides towards pathos and even the tragic absolute.

These considerations, however, remain speculative. What is not in doubt is that dramaturgically the antiphony of two voices and two vocabularies serves Shakespeare well, and in one of its extensions gives rise to a phenomenon as peculiar and personal to him as his signature. Towards the close of a tragic play, or if not towards the close, at the climax, will normally appear a short scene or episode (sometimes more than one) of spiritual cross purposes: a scene in which the line of tragic speech and feeling generated by commitment is crossed by an alien speech and feeling very much detached. Bradley, noting such of these episodes as are "humorous or semi-humorous," places them among Shakespeare's devices for sustaining interest after the crisis, since their introduction "affords variety and relief, and also heightens by contrast the tragic feelings." Another perceptive critic has noted that though such scenes afford "relief," it is not by laughter. "We return for a moment to simple people, a gravedigger, a porter, a countryman, and to the goings on of every day, the feeling for bread and cheese, and when we go back to the high tragic mood we do so with a heightened sense that we are moving in a world fully realized" (F. P. Wilson, *Eliza-*

bethan and Jacobean, p. 122). To such comments, we must add another. For the whole effect of these episodes does not come simply from variety, or from the juxtaposition of bread and cheese with the high tragic mood, though these elements are certainly present in it.

It arises, in the main, I think, from the fact that Shakespeare here lays open to us, in an especially poignant form, what I take to be the central dialogue of tragic experience. It is a dialogue of which the Greek dialogue of individual with community, the seventeenth-century dialogue of soul with body, the twentieth-century dialogue of self with soul are perhaps all versions in their different ways: a dialogue in which each party makes its case in its own tongue, incapable of wholly comprehending what the other means. And Shakespeare objectifies it for us on his stage by the encounter of those by whom, "changed, changed utterly," a terrible beauty has been born, with those who are still players in life's casual comedy. Hamlet and the gravediggers, Desdemona and Emilia, Cleopatra and the clown afford particularly fine examples of Shakespeare's technique in this respect.

In the first instance, the mixture of profoundly imaginative feelings contained in Hamlet's epitaph for Yorick—

> I knew him, Horatio: a fellow of infinite jest, of most excellent fancy; he hath borne me on his back a thousand times; and now, how abhorred in my imagination it is! my gorge rises at it. Here hung those lips that I have kissed I know not how oft. Where be your gibes now? your gambols? your songs? your flashes of merriment, that were wont to set the table on a roar? Not one now, to mock your own grinning? quite chap-fallen? Now get you to my lady's chamber, and tell her, let her paint an inch thick, to this favor she must come; make her laugh at that—   (V.i.203)

is weighed over against the buffoon literalism of the clown—

> *Hamlet.* What man dost thou dig it for?
>
> *First Clown.* For no man, sir.

Hamlet. What woman, then?

First Clown. For none, neither.

Hamlet. Who is to be buried in 't?

First Clown. One that was a woman, sir; but, rest her
    soul, she's dead—   (V.i.141)

and against his uncompromising factualism too, his hard
dry vocabulary of detachment, without overtones, by which
he cuts his métier down to a size that can be lived with:

I'faith, if he be not rotten before he die, . . . he will
last you some eight year or nine year: a tanner will last
you nine year.   (V.i.180)

But in this scene Hamlet's macabre thoughts are not
allowed to outweigh the clown. A case is made for factualism and literalism. Horatio is seen to have a point in saying
it is to consider too curiously to consider as Hamlet does.
A man must come to terms with the graveyard; but how
long may he linger in it with impunity, or allow it to linger
in him? Such reckonings the opposing voice, whether
spoken by the primary foil or by another, is calculated to
awake in us: this is the second kind of question that it
exists to make us ask.

In a sense, then, the implicit subject of all these episodes
is the predicament of being human. They bring before us
the grandeur of man's nature, which contains, potentially,
both voices, both ends of the moral and psychic spectrum.
They bring before us the necessity of his choice, because
it is rarely given to him to go through any door without
closing the rest. And they bring before us the sadness, the
infinite sadness of his lot, because, short of the "certain
certainties" that tragedy does not deal with, he has no
sublunar way of knowing whether defiant "heroism" is
really more to be desired than suppler "wisdom." The alabaster innocence of Desdemona's world shines out beside
the crumpled bedsitters of Emilia's—

Desdemona. Wouldst thou do such a deed for all the
　　world?

Emilia. Why, would not you?

Desdemona. 　　　　　　　No, by this heavenly light!

Emilia. Nor I neither by this heavenly light;
　　I might do't as well i' the dark.

Desdemona. Wouldst thou do such a deed for all the
　　world?

Emilia. The world's a huge thing: it is a great price
　　For a small vice.

Desdemona. In troth, I think thou wouldst not.

Emilia. In troth, I think I should . . . who would not
　　make her husband a cuckold to make him a mon-
　　arch? I should venture purgatory for 't.

Desdemona. Beshrew me, if I would do such a wrong
　　For the whole world.

Emilia. Why, the wrong is but a wrong i' the world;
　　and having the world for your labor, 'tis a wrong in
　　your own world, and you might quickly make it
　　right.

Desdemona. I do not think there is any such woman—
　　　　　　　　　　　　　　　　　(IV.iii.65)

but the two languages never, essentially, commune—and,
for this reason, the dialogue they hold can never be finally
adjudicated.

The same effect may be noted in Cleopatra's scene with
the countryman who brings her the asps. Her exultation
casts a glow over the whole scene of her death. But her
language when the countryman has gone would not have
the tragic resonance it has, if we could not hear echoing
between the lines the gritty accents of the opposing voice:

　Give me my robe, put on my crown; I have
　Immortal longings in me.

Truly, I have him: but I would not be the party that
should desire you to touch him, for his biting is
immortal; those that do die of it do seldom or never
recover.

The stroke of death is as a lover's pinch,
Which hurts, and is desired.

I heard of one of them no longer than yesterday: a
very honest woman, but something given to lie; as a
woman should not do, but in the way of honesty: how
she died of the biting of it, what pain she felt.

                              Peace, peace!
Dost thou not see my baby at my breast,
That sucks the nurse asleep?
                              (V.ii.283–313)

Give it nothing, I pray you, for it is not worth the
    feeding.   (V.ii.245–71)

The "worm"—or "my baby"; the Antony Demetrius and
Philo see—or the Antony whose face is as the heavens;
the "small vice" of Emilia—or the deed one would not do
for the whole world; the skull knocked about the mazzard
by a sexton's spade—or the skull which "had a tongue in
it and could sing once": these are incommensurables,
which human nature nevertheless must somehow measure,
reconcile, and enclose.

We move now from "character" to "action," and to the
question: what happens in a Shakespearean tragedy? Bradley's traditional categories—exposition, conflict, crisis,
catastrophe, etc.—give us one side of this, but, as we
noticed earlier, largely the external side, and are in any
case rather too clumsy for the job we try to do with them.
They apply as well to potboilers of the commercial theater
as to serious works of art, to prose as well as poetic drama.
What is worse, they are unable to register the unique capac-

ity of Shakespearean dramaturgy to hint, evoke, imply, and, in short, by indirections find directions out. The nature of some of Shakespeare's "indirections" is a topic we must explore before we can hope to confront the question posed above with other terms than Bradley's.

To clarify what I mean by indirection, let me cite an instance from *King Lear*. Everybody has noticed, no doubt, that Lear's Fool (apart from being the King's primary foil) gives voice during the first two acts to notations of topsi-turviness that are not, one feels, simply his own responses to the inversions of order that have occurred in family and state, but a reflection of the King's; or, to put the matter another way, the situation is so arranged by Shakespeare that we are invited to apply the Fool's comments to Lear's inner experience, and I suspect that most of us do so. The Fool thus serves, to some extent, as a screen on which Shakespeare flashes, as it were, readings from the psychic life of the protagonist, possibly even his subconscious life, which could not otherwise be conveyed in drama at all. Likewise, the Fool's *idée fixe* in this matter, his apparent obsession with one idea (often a clinical symptom of in-cipient insanity) is perhaps dramatic shorthand, and even sleight-of-hand, for goings-on in the King's brain that only occasionally bubble to the surface in the form of conscious apprehensions: "O let me not be mad, not mad sweet heaven." "O fool, I shall go mad." Conceivably, there may even be significance in the circumstance that the Fool does not enter the play as a speaking character till after King Lear has behaved like a fool, and leaves it before he is cured.

Whatever the truth of this last point, the example of the Fool in Lear introduces us to devices of play construc-tion and ways of recording the progress of inward "action," which, though the traditional categories say nothing about them, are a basic resource of Shakespeare's playwriting, and nowhere more so than in the tragedies. We may now consider a few of them in turn.

First, there are the figures, like the Fool, some part of whose consciousness, as conveyed to us at particular mo-ments, seems to be doing double duty, filling our minds with impressions analogous to those which we may presume to be occupying the conscious or unconscious mind of the hero, whether he is before us on the stage or not. A possible example may be Lady Macbeth's sleepwalking scene. Macbeth is absent at this juncture, has gone "into the field"—has not in fact been visible during two long scenes and will not be visible again till the next scene after this. In the interval, the slaying at Macduff's castle and the conversations between Malcolm and Macduff keep him before us in his capacity as tyrant, murderer, "Hell-kite," seen from the outside. But Lady Macbeth's sleepwalking is, I think, Shakespeare's device for keeping him before us in his capacity as tragic hero and sufferer. The "great perturbation in nature" of which the doctor whispers ("to receive at once the benefit of sleep, and do the effects of watching"), the "slumbery agitation," the "thick-coming fancies That keep her from her rest": these, by a kind of poetical displacement, we may apply to him as well as to her; and we are invited to do so by the fact that from the moment of the first murder all the play's references to sleep, and its destruction, have had reference to Macbeth himself. We are, of course, conscious as we watch the scene, that this is Lady Macbeth suffering the metaphysical aspects of murder that she did not believe in; we may also be conscious that the remorse pictured here tends to distinguish her from her husband, who for some time has been giving his "initiate fear" the "hard use" he said it lacked, with dehumanizing consequences. Yet in some way the pity of this situation suffuses him as well as her, the more so because in every word she utters his presence beside her is supposed; and if we allow this to be true, not only will Menteith's comment in the following scene—

> Who then shall blame
> His pester'd senses to recoil and start,
> When all that is within him does condemn
> Itself for being there—   (V.ii.22)

evoke an image of suffering as well as retribution, but we shall better understand Macbeth's striking expression, at his next appearance, in words that we are almost bound to feel have some reference to himself, of corrosive griefs haunting below the conscious levels of the mind:

> Canst thou not minister to a mind diseased,
> Pluck from the memory a rooted sorrow,
> Raze out the written troubles of the brain
> And with some sweet oblivious antidote
> Cleanse the stuff'd bosom of that perilous stuff
> Which weighs upon the heart?   (V.iii.40)

Such speeches as this, and as Lady Macbeth's while sleepwalking—which we might call umbrella speeches, since more than one consciousness may shelter under them—are not uncommon in Shakespeare's dramaturgy, as many critics have pointed out. *Lear* affords the classic examples: in the Fool, as we have seen, and also in Edgar. Edgar's speech during the storm scenes projects in part his role of Poor Tom, the eternal outcast; in part, Edmund (and also Oswald), the vicious servant, self-seeking, with heart set on lust and proud array; possibly in part, Gloucester, whose arrival with a torch the Fool appropriately announces (without knowing it) in terms related to Edgar's themes: "Now a little fire in a wide field were like an old lecher's heart"; and surely, in some part too, the King, for the chips and tag-ends of Edgar's speech reflect, as if from Lear's own mind, not simply mental disintegration, but a strong sense of a fragmented moral order: "Obey thy parents; keep thy word justly; swear not; commit not with man's sworn spouse. . . ."

But in my view, the most interesting of all the umbrella speeches in the tragedies is Enobarbus's famous description of Cleopatra in her barge. The triumvirs have gone offstage, Antony to have his first view of Octavia. When we see him again, his union with Octavia will have been agreed on all parts (though not yet celebrated), and he will be saying to her, with what can hardly be supposed to be insincerity:

> My Octavia,
> Read not my blemishes in the world's report:

I have not kept my square; but that to come
Shall all be done by the rule. Good night, dear lady.
(II.iii.4)

Then the soothsayer appears, reminds Antony that his
guardian angel will always be overpowered when Caesar's
is by, urges him to return to Egypt; and Antony, left alone
after the soothsayer has gone, meditates a moment on the
truth of the pronouncement and then says abruptly:

I will to Egypt:
And though I make this marriage for my peace,
I' the east my pleasure lies.   (II.iii.38)

There is plainly a piece of prestidigitation here. It is
performed in part by means of the soothsayer's entry, which
is evidently a kind of visual surrogate for Antony's own
personal intuition. ("I see it in my motion, have it not in
my tongue," the soothsayer says, when asked for the
reasons he wishes Antony to return; and that is presumably
the way Antony sees it too: in his "motion," i.e., involun-
tarily, intuitively.) But a larger part is played by Enobarbus's account of Cleopatra. Between the exit of the
triumvirs and the reappearance of Antony making unsolic-
ited promises to Octavia, this is the one thing that inter-
venes. And it is the only thing that needs to. Shakespeare
has made it so powerful, so colored our imaginations with
it, that we understand the promises of Antony, not in the
light in which he understands them as he makes them, but
in the riotous brilliance of Enobarbus's evocation of Cleopatra. The psychic gap, in Antony, between "My Octavia"
and "Good night, dear lady," on the one hand, and "I will
to Egypt," on the other, is filled by a vision, given to us, of
irresistible and indeed quasi-unearthly power, of which
the soothsayer's intuition is simply a more abstract formu-
lation. Here again, by indirection, Shakespeare finds direction out.

Not all mirror situations in the tragedies involve reflection of another consciousness. Some, as is well known, em-
phasize the outlines of an action by recapitulating it, as
when Edgar's descent to Poor Tom and subsequent gradual

re-ascent to support the gored state echoes the downward
and upward movement in the lives of both King Lear and
Gloucester; or as when Enobarbus's defection to, and again
from, the bidding of his practical reason repeats that which
Antony has already experienced, and Cleopatra will experience (at least in one way of understanding Act V) between
Antony's death and her own. *Hamlet,* complex in all respects, offers an unusually complex form of this. The three
sons, who are, in various senses, all avengers of dead
fathers, are all deflected, temporarily, from their designs
by the maneuvers of an elder (Claudius for Laertes and
Hamlet; the King of Norway, inspired by Claudius, for
Fortinbras), who in two cases is the young man's uncle.
There are of course important differences between these
three young men which we are not to forget; but with respect to structure, the images in the mirror are chiefly
likenesses. Hamlet, outmaneuvered by Claudius, off to England to be executed, crosses the path of Fortinbras, who
has also been outmaneuvered by Claudius (working through
his uncle), and is off to Poland to make mouths at the
invisible event, while at the same moment Laertes, clam-
oring for immediate satisfaction in the King's palace, is
outmaneuvered in his turn. Likewise, at the play's end, all
three young men are "victorious," in ways they could hardly
have foreseen. The return of Fortinbras, having achieved
his objective in Poland, to find his "rights" in Denmark
achieved without a blow, is timed to coincide with Hamlet's
achieving his objective in exposing and killing the King,
and Laertes' achieving his objective of avenging his father's
death on Hamlet. When this episode is played before us in
the theater, there is little question, to my way of thinking,
but that something of the glow and martial upsurge dramatized in Fortinbras's entrance associates itself to Hamlet,
even as Fortinbras's words associate Hamlet to a soldier's
death. Meantime, Laertes, who has been trapped by the
King and has paid with his life for it, gives us an alterna-
tive reflection of the Prince, which is equally a part of the
truth.

Fortinbras's arrival at the close of *Hamlet* is an instance of an especially interesting type of mirroring to be found everywhere in Shakespeare's work—the emblematic entrance, and exit. Sometimes such exits occur by death, as the death of Gaunt, who takes a sacramental view of kingship and nation, in *Richard II*, at the instant when Richard has destroyed, by his personal conduct and by "farming" his realm, the sacramental relationships which make such a view possible to maintain. Gaunt has to die, we might say, before a usurpation like his son's can even be imagined; and it is, I take it, not without significance that the first word of Bolingbroke's return comes a few seconds after we have heard (from the same speaker, Northumberland) that Gaunt's tongue "is now a stringless instrument." Something similar, it seems clear, occurs with the death of Mamillius in *The Winter's Tale*. Sickening with his father's sickening mind, Mamillius dies in the instant that his father repudiates the message of the oracle; and though, in the end, all else is restored to Leontes, Mamillius is not.

In the tragedies, emblematic entrances and exits assume a variety of forms, ranging from those whose significance is obvious to those where it is uncertain, controversial, and perhaps simply a mirage. One entrance whose significance is unmistakable occurs in the first act of *Macbeth*, when Duncan, speaking of the traitor Cawdor, whom he has slain, laments that there is no art to find the mind's construction in the face, just as the new Cawdor, traitor-to-be, appears before him. Equally unmistakable is the significance of the King's exit, in the first scene of *Lear*, with the man who like himself has put externals first. "Come, noble Burgundy," he says, and in a pairing that can be made profoundly moving on the stage, the two men go out together.

But what are we to say of Antony's freedman Eros, who enters for the first time (at least by name) just before his master's suicide and kills himself rather than kill Antony. This is all from his source, Plutarch's life of Antony; but why did Shakespeare include it? Did Eros's name mean something to him? Are we to see here a shadowing of the other deaths for love, or not? And the carrying off of Lepidus, drunk, from the feast aboard Pompey's galley.

Does this anticipate his subsequent fate? and if it does, what does the intoxication signify which in this scene all the great men are subject to in their degree. Is it ordinary drunkenness; or is it, like the drunkenness that afflicts Caliban, Trinculo, and Stephano in *The Tempest,* a species of self-intoxication, Shakespeare's subdued comment on the thrust to worldly power? Or again, what of the arrival of the players in *Hamlet?* Granted their role in the plot, does Shakespeare make no other profit from them? Are such matters as the speech on Priam's murder and the advice on acting interesting excrescences, as Bradley thought, or does each mirror something that we are to appropriate to our understanding of the play: in the first instance, the strange confederacy of passion and paralysis in the hero's mind,[2] in the second, the question that tolls on all sides through the castle at Elsinore: when is an act not an "act"? [3]

These are questions to which it is not always easy to give a sound answer. The ground becomes somewhat firmer underfoot, I think, if we turn for a concluding instance to Bianca's pat appearances in *Othello.* R. B. Heilman suggests that in rushing to the scene of the night assault on Cassio, when she might have stayed safely within doors, and so exposing herself to vilification as a "notable strumpet," Bianca acts in a manner "thematically relevant, because Othello has just been attacking Desdemona as a strumpet"—both "strumpets," in other words, are faithful (*Magic in the Web,* p. 180). Whether this is true or not, Bianca makes two very striking entrances earlier, when in each case she may be thought to supply in living form on the stage the prostitute figure that Desdemona has become in Othello's mind. Her second entrance is notably expressive. Othello here is partially overhearing while Iago rallies Cassio about Bianca, Othello being under the delusion that the talk is of Desdemona. At the point when, in Othello's mental imagery, Desdemona becomes the soliciting whore

[2] See an important comment on this by H. Levin, in *Kenyon Review* (1950), pp. 273–96.

[3] I have touched on this point in *Tragic Themes in Western Literature,* ed. C. Brooks (1953).

—"she tells him how she plucked him to my chamber"—
Bianca enters in the flesh, and not only enters, but flour-
ishes the magic handkerchief, now degenerated, like the
love it was to ensure, to some "minx's," some "hobbyhorse's" token, the subject of jealous bickering. In the
theater, the emblematic effect of this can hardly be ignored.[4]

Further types of mirroring will spring to every reader's
mind. The recapitulation of a motif, for instance, as in the
poisoning episodes in *Hamlet*. *Hamlet* criticism has too
much ignored, I think, the fact that a story of poisoning
forms the climax of the first act, a mime and "play" of
poisoning the climax of the third, and actual poisoning, on
a wide scale, the climax of the fifth. Surely this repetition
was calculated to keep steady for Shakespeare's Elizabethan audiences the political and moral bearings of the play?
We may say what we like about Hamlet's frailties, which
are real, but we can hardly ignore the fact that in each of
the poisoning episodes the poisoner is the King. The King,
who ought to be like the sun, giving warmth, radiance, and
fertility to his kingdom, is actually its destroyer. The "leper-
ous distilment" he pours into Hamlet's father's ear, which
courses through his body with such despatch, has coursed
just as swiftly through the body politic, and what we see in
Denmark as a result is a poisoned kingdom, containing one
corruption upon another of Renaissance ideals: the "wise
councilor," who is instead a tedious windbag; the young
"man of honor," who has no trust in another's honor, as
his advice to his sister shows, and none of his own, as his
own treachery to Hamlet shows; the "friends," who are not
friends but spies; the loved one, the "mistress," who proves
disloyal (a decoy, however reluctant, for villainy), and
goes mad—through poison also, "the poison of deep grief";
the mother and Queen, who instead of being the guardian
of the kingdom's matronly virtues has set a harlot's blister
on love's forehead and made marriage vows "as false as
dicers' oaths"; and the Prince, the "ideal courtier," the

---

[4] Another emblematic entrance is the first entrance of the soothsayer
in *Julius Caesar;* see "The Teaching of Drama," *Essays on the Teaching
of English,* ed. E. J. Gordon and E. S. Noyes (1960).

Renaissance man—once active, energetic, now reduced to anguished introspection; a glass of fashion, now a sloven in antic disarray; a noble mind, now partly unhinged, in fact as well as seeming; the observed of all observers, now observed in a more sinister sense; the mold of form, now capable of obscenities, cruelty, even treachery, mining below the mines of his school friends to hoist them with their own petard. All this, in one way or another, is the poison of the King, and in the last scene, lest we miss the point, we are made to see the spiritual poison become literal and seize on all those whom it has not already destroyed.

> a Prince's Court
> Is like a common Fountaine, whence should flow
> Pure silver-droppes in generall: But if't chance
> Some curs'd example poyson't neere the head,
> Death, and diseases through the whole land spread.

The lines are Webster's, but they state with precision one of the themes of Shakespeare's play.

Finally, in the tragedies as elsewhere in Shakespeare, we have the kinds of replication that have been specifically called "mirror scenes," [5] or (more in Ercles' vein) scenes of "analogical probability." [6] The most impressive examples here are frequently the opening scenes and episodes. The witches of *Macbeth,* whose "foul is fair" and battle that is "won *and* lost" anticipate so much to come. The "great debate" in *Antony and Cleopatra,* initiated in the comments of Philo and the posturings of the lovers, and reverberating thereafter within, as well as around, the lovers till they die. The watchmen on the platform in *Hamlet,* feeling out a mystery—an image that will re-form in our minds again and again as we watch almost every member of the *dramatis personae* engage in similar activity later on. The technique of manipulation established at the outset of *Othello,* the persuading of someone to believe something

---

[5] By H. T. Price, in *Joseph Quincy Adams Memorial Studies,* ed. J. McManaway (1948), pp. 101 ff.

[6] See P. J. Aldus, *Shakespeare Quarterly* (1955), pp. 397 ff. Aldus deals suggestively with the opening scene of *Julius Caesar.*

he is reluctant to believe and which is not true in the sense presented—exemplified in Iago's management of both Roderigo and Brabantio, and prefiguring later developments even to the detail that the manipulator operates by preference through an instrument.

Lear offers perhaps the best of all these instances. Here the "Nature" of which the play is to make so much, ambiguous, double-barreled, is represented in its normative aspect in the hierarchies on the stage before us—a whole political society from its *primum mobile,* the great King, down to lowliest attendant, a whole family society from father down through married daughters and sons-in-law to a third daughter with her wooers—and, in its appetitive aspect, which Edmund will formulate in a few moments, in the overt self-will of the old King and the hidden self-will, the "plighted cunning," of the false daughters. As the scene progresses, in fact, we can see these hierarchies of the normative nature, which at first looked so formidable and solid, crumble away in the repudiation of Cordelia, the banishment of Kent, the exit of Lear and Burgundy, till nothing is left standing on the stage but Nature red in tooth and claw as the false daughters lay their heads together.

I have dwelt a little on these effects of "indirection" in the tragedies because I believe that most of us as playgoers are keenly conscious of their presence. I have perhaps described them badly, in some instances possibly misconceived them; but they are not my invention; this kind of thing has been pointed to more and more widely during the past fifty years by reputable observers. In short, these effects, in some important sense, are "there." And if they are, the question we must ask is, Why? What are they for? How are they used?

I return then to the query with which this section began: what *does* happen in a Shakespearean tragedy? Is it possible to formulate an answer that will, while not repudiating the traditional categories so far as they are useful, take into account the matters we have been examining? In the present state of our knowledge I am not convinced that this is possible: we have been too much concerned in this century with the verbal, which is only part of the picture.

Nevertheless, I should like to make a few exploratory gestures.

Obviously the most important thing that happens in a Shakespearean tragedy is that the hero follows a cycle of change, which is, in part, psychic change. And this seems generally to be constituted in three phases. During the first phase, corresponding roughly to Bradley's exposition, the hero is delineated. Among other things, he is placed in positions that enable him to sound the particular timbre of his tragic music:

> Not so, my lord; I am too much i' the sun.
> (Hamlet, I.ii.67)

> Seems, madam! nay, it is; I know not "seems."
> (I.ii.76)

> My father's brother, but no more like my father
> Than I to Hercules.   (I.ii.152)

>   My fate cries out,
> And makes each petty artery in this body
> As hardy as the Nemean lion's nerve.   (I.iv.81)

Chiming against this we are also permitted to hear the particular timbre of the opposing voice, spoken by the foil as well as others:

>   If it be,
> Why seems it so particular with thee?
>
> (I.ii.74)

> For what we know must be and is as common
> As any the most vulgar thing to sense,
> Why should we in our peevish opposition
> Take it to heart?   (I.ii.98)

> What if it tempt you toward the flood, my lord,
> Or to the dreadful summit of the cliff
> That beetles o'er his base into the sea,
> And there assume some other horrible form,
> Which might deprive your sovereignty of reason
> And draw you into madness?   (I.iv.69)

From now on, as we saw, these are the differing attitudes towards experience that will supply the essential dialogue of the play.

The second phase is much more comprehensive. It contains the conflict, crisis, and falling action—in short, the heart of the matter. Here several interesting developments occur. The one certain over-all development in this phase is that the hero tends to become his own antithesis. We touched on this earlier in the case of Hamlet, in whom "the courtier's, soldier's, scholar's, eye, tongue, sword" suffer some rather savage violations before the play is done. Likewise, Othello the unshakable, whose original composure under the most trying insults and misrepresentations almost takes the breath away, breaks in this phase into furies, grovels on the floor in a trance, strikes his wife publicly. King Lear, "the great image of authority" both by temperament and position, becomes a helpless crazed old man crying in a storm, destitute of everything but one servant and his Fool. Macbeth, who would have "holily" what he would have "highly," who is too full of the milk of human kindness to catch the nearest way, whose whole being revolts with every step he takes in his own revolt— his hair standing on end, his imagination filling with angels "trumpet-tongued," his hands (after the deed) threatening to pluck out his own eyes—turns into the numbed usurper, "supped full with horrors," who is hardly capable of responding even to his wife's death. The development is equally plain in Antony and Coriolanus. "The greatest prince o' th' world, The noblest," finds his greatness slipped from him, and his nobility debased to the ignominy of having helpless emissaries whipped. The proud and upright Coriolanus, patriot soldier, truckles in the market place for votes, revolts to the enemy he has vanquished, carries war against his own flesh and blood.

This manner of delineating tragic "action," though it may be traced here and there in other drama, seems to be on the whole a property of the Elizabethans and Jacobeans. Possibly it springs from their concern with "whole" personalities on the tragic stage, rather than as so often with the ancients and Racine, just those aspects of personality that guarantee the *dénouement*. In any case, it seems to have become a consistent feature of Shakespeare's dramaturgy, and beautifully defines the sense of psychological alienation and uprootedness that tragic experience in the Elizabethan and Jacobean theater generally seems to embrace. Its distinctively tragic implications stand out the more when we reflect that psychic change in comedy (if indeed comedy can be said to concern itself with psychic change at all) consists in making—or in showing—the protagonist to be more and more what he always was.[7]

In this second phase too, either as an outward manifestation of inward change, or as a shorthand indication that such change is about to begin or end, belong the tragic journeys. Romeo is off to Mantua, Brutus to the Eastern end of the Roman world, Hamlet to England, Othello to Cyprus, Lear and Gloucester to Dover, Timon to the cave, Macbeth to the heath to revisit the witches, Antony to Rome and Athens, Coriolanus to Antium.[8] Such journeys, we rightly say, are called for by the plots. But perhaps we should not be wrong if we added that Shakespearean plotting tends to call for journeys, conceivably for discernible reasons. For one thing, journeys can enhance our impression that psychological changes are taking place, either by emphasizing a lapse of time, or by taking us to new settings, or by both. I suspect we register such effects subconsciously more often than we think.

Furthermore, though it would be foolish to assign to any of the journeys in Shakespeare's tragedies a precise symbolic meaning, several of them have vaguely symbolic overtones—serving as surrogates either for what can never be exhibited on the stage, as the mysterious processes leading to psychic change, which cannot be articulated into speech, even soliloquy, without losing their formless instinctive character; or for the processes of self-discovery, the learning processes—a function journeys fulfill in many of the world's best-known stories (the *Aeneid,* the *Divine Com-*

---

[7] I have elaborated this point in an introduction to Fielding's *Joseph Andrews* (1948).

[8] These are merely samples; other journeys occur that I have not named here.

edy, Tom Jones, etc.) and in some of Shakespeare's comedies. Hamlet's abortive journey to England is possibly an instance of the first category. After his return, and particularly after what he tells us of his actions while at sea, we are not surprised if he appears, spiritually, a changed man. Lear's and Gloucester's journey to Dover is perhaps an instance of the second category, leading as it does through suffering to insight and reconciliation.

During the hero's journey, or at any rate during his over-all progress in the second phase, he will normally pass through a variety of mirroring situations of the sort formerly discussed (though it will be by us and not him that the likeness in the mirror is seen). In some of these, the hero will be confronted, so to speak, with a version of his own situation, and his failure to recognize it may be a measure of the nature of the disaster to ensue. Coriolanus, revolted from Rome and now its enemy, meets himself in Aufidius's embrace in Antium. Hamlet meets himself in Fortinbras as the latter marches to Poland, but does not see the likeness—only the differences. Lear goes to Goneril's and there meets, as everyone remembers, images of his own behavior to Cordelia. Thrust into the night, he meets his own defenselessness in Edgar, and is impelled to pray. Encountering in Dover fields, both Lear and Gloucester confront in each other an extension of their own experience: blindness that sees and madness that is wise. Macbeth revisits the witches on the heath and finds there (without recognizing them) not only the emblems of his death and downfall to come but his speciousness and duplicity. Antony encounters in Enobarbus's defection his own; and possibly, in Pompey, his own later muddled indecision between "honor" and *Realpolitik*. Othello hears the innocent Cassio set upon in the dark, then goes to re-enact that scene in a more figurative darkness in Desdemona's bedroom. Sometimes, alternatively or additionally, the hero's way will lie through quasi-symbolic settings or situations. The heath in both *Macbeth* and *King Lear* is infinitely suggestive, even if like all good symbols it refuses to dissipate its *Dinglichkeit* in meaning. The same is true of the dark castle platform in Hamlet, and the graveyard; of the cliff at Dover and Gloucester's leap; of the "monument," where both Antony and Cleopatra die; and of course, as many have pointed out, of the night scenes, the storm, the music, the changes of clothing, the banquets. So much in Shakespeare's tragedies stands on the brink of symbol that for this reason, if no other, the usual terms for describing their construction and mode of action need reinforcement.

After the hero has reached and passed through his own antithesis, there comes a third phase in his development that is extremely difficult to define. It represents a recovery of sorts; in some cases, perhaps even a species of synthesis. The once powerful, now powerless king, will have power again, but of another kind—the kind suggested in his reconciliation with Cordelia and his speech beginning "Come, let's away to prison"; and he will have sanity again, but in a mode not dreamed of at the beginning of the play. Or, to take Othello's case, it will be given the hero to recapture the faith he lost,[9] to learn that the pearl really was richer than all his tribe, and to execute quite another order of justice than the blinkered justice meted out to Cassio and the blind injustice meted out to Desdemona. Or again, to shift to Antony, the man who has so long been thrown into storms of rage and recrimination by the caprices of his unstable mistress receives the last of them without a murmur of reproach, though it has led directly to his death, and dies in greater unison with her than we have ever seen him live.

I believe that some mark of this nature is visible in all the tragedies. Coriolanus, "boy" though he is and in some ways remains, makes a triumphant choice (detract from his motives as we may), and he knows what it is likely to cost. Moreover, he refuses the way of escape that lies open if he should return now with Volumnia and Vergilia to Rome. "I'll not to Rome, I'll back with you," he tells Aufidius, "and pray you Stand to me in this cause." The young man who, after this, dies accused of treachery—by Aufidius's treachery, and the suggestibility of the crowd,

---

[9] This point is well made in Helen Gardner's *The Noble Moor* (1956).

as slippery in Corioli as Rome—cannot be thought identical in all respects with the young man who joined Menenius in the play's opening scene. He is that young man, but with the notable difference of his triumphant choice behind him; and there is bound to be more than a military association in our minds when the Second Lord of the Volscians, seeking to quell the mob, cries, "The man is noble, and his fame folds in This orb o' th' earth"; and again too when the First Lord exclaims over his body, "Let him be regarded As the most noble corse that ever herald Did follow to his urn." Even the monster Macbeth is so handled by Shakespeare, as has been often enough observed, that he seems to regain something at the close—if nothing more, at least some of that *élan* which made him the all-praised Bellona's bridegroom of the play's second scene; and everything Macbeth says, following Duncan's death, about the emptiness of the achievement, the lack of posterity, the sear, the yellow leaf, deprived of "that which should accompany old age, As honor, love, obedience, troops of friends," affords evidence that the meaning of his experience has not been lost on him.

To say this, I wish to make it clear, is not to say that the Shakespearean tragic hero undergoes an "illumination," or, to use the third term of K. Burke's sequence, a Mathema or perception.[10] This is a terminology that seems to me not very useful to the discussion of tragedy as Shakespeare presents it. It is sufficient for my purposes to say simply that the phase in which we are conscious of the hero as approaching his opposite is followed by a final phase in which we are conscious of him as exhibiting one or more aspects of his original, or—since these may not coincide—his better self: as in the case of Antony's final reunion with Cleopatra, and Coriolanus's decision not to sack Rome. Whether we then go on to give this phenomenon a specific spiritual significance, seeing in it the objective correlative of "perception" or "illumination," is a question that depends, obviously, on a great many factors, more of them perhaps situated in our own individual philos-

10 *A Grammar of Motives* (1945), pp. 38 ff.

ophies than in the text, and, so, likely to lead us away
from Shakespeare rather than towards him. Clearly if
Shakespeare wished us to engage in this activity, he was
remiss in the provision of clues. Even in *King Lear*, the one
play where some sort of regeneration or new insight in the
hero has been universally acknowledged, the man before
us in the last scene—who sweeps Kent aside, rakes all who
have helped him with grapeshot ("A plague upon you,
murderers, traitors all. I might have saved her . . ."),
exults in the revenge he has exacted for Cordelia's death,
and dies self-deceived in the thought she still lives—this
man is one of the most profoundly human figures ever
created in a play; but he is not, certainly, the Platonic idea
laid up in heaven, or in critical schemes, of regenerate man.

I have kept to the end, and out of proper order, the
most interesting of all the symbolic elements in the hero's
second phase. This is his experience of madness. One dis-
covers with some surprise, I think, how many of Shakespeare's heroes are associated with this disease. Only Titus,
Hamlet, Lear, and Timon, in various senses, actually go
mad; but Iago boasts that he will make Othello mad, and
in a way succeeds; Antony, after the second defeat at sea,
is said by Cleopatra to be

> more mad,
> Than Telamon for his shield; the boar of Thessaly
> Was never so emboss'd;   (IV.xiii.2)

Caithness in *Macbeth* tells us that some say the king is mad,
while "others, that lesser hate him, Do call it valiant fury";
Romeo, rather oddly, enjoins Paris at Juliet's tomb to

> be gone; live, and hereafter say,
> A madman's mercy bade thee run away.
>   (V.iii.66)

Even Brutus, by the Antony of *Antony and Cleopatra*, is
said to have been "mad."
What (if anything), one wonders, may this mean?

Doubtless a sort of explanation can be found in Elizabethan psychological lore, which held that the excess of any passion approached madness, and in the general prevalence, through Seneca and other sources, of the adage: *Quos vult perdere Jupiter dementat prius.*[11] Furthermore, madness, when actually exhibited, was dramatically useful, as Kyd had shown. It was arresting in itself, and it allowed the combination in a single figure of tragic hero and buffoon, to whom could be accorded the license of the allowed fool in speech and action.

Just possibly, however, there was yet more to it than this, if we may judge by Shakespeare's sketches of madness in Hamlet and King Lear. In both these, madness is to some degree a punishment or doom, corresponding to the adage. Lear prays to the heavens that he may not suffer madness, and Hamlet asks Laertes, in his apology before the duel, to overlook his conduct, since "you must needs have heard, how I am punish'd With a sore distraction." It is equally obvious, however, that in both instances the madness has a further dimension, as insight, and this is true also of Ophelia. Ophelia, mad, is able to make awards of flowers to the King and Queen which are appropriate to frailties of which she cannot be supposed to have conscious knowledge. For the same reason, I suspect we do not need Dover Wilson's radical displacement of Hamlet's entry in II. ii, so as to enable him to overhear Polonius.[12] It is enough that Hamlet wears, even if it is for the moment self-assumed, the guise of the madman. As such, he can be presumed to have intuitive unformulated awarenesses that reach the surface in free (yet relevant) associations, like those of Polonius with a fishmonger, Ophelia with carrion. Lear likewise is allowed free yet relevant associations. His great speech in Dover fields on the lust of women derives from the designs of Goneril and Regan on Edmund, of which he consciously knows nothing. Moreover, both he and Hamlet can be privileged in madness to say things— Hamlet about the corruption of human nature, and Lear

---

[11] "Whom God wishes to destroy he first makes mad." [*Editor's note.*]

[12] *What Happens in "Hamlet"* (1935), pp. 103 ff.

about the corruption of the Jacobean social system (and
by extension about all social systems whatever), which
Shakespeare could hardly have risked apart from this
license. Doubtless one of the anguishes of being a great
artist is that you cannot tell people what they and you and
your common institutions are really like—when viewed
absolutely—without being dismissed as insane. To commu-
nicate at all, you must acknowledge the opposing voice; for
there always is an opposing voice, and it is as deeply rooted
in your own nature as in your audience's.

Just possibly, therefore, the meaning of tragic madness
for Shakespeare approximated the meaning that the legen-
dary figure of Cassandra (whom Shakespeare had in fact
put briefly on his stage in the second act of *Troilus and
Cressida*) has held for so many artists since his time.
Cassandra's madness, like Lear's and Hamlet's—possibly,
also, like the madness *verbally* assigned to other Shakespearean tragic heroes—contains both punishment and
insight. She is doomed to know, by a consciousness that
moves to measures outside our normal space and time; she
is doomed never to be believed, because those to whom she
speaks can hear only the opposing voice. With the language of the god Apollo sounding in her brain, and the
incredulity of her fellow mortals ringing in her ears, she
makes an ideal emblem of the predicament of the Shakespearean tragic hero, caught as he is between the absolute
and the expedient. And by the same token, of the predicament of the artist—Shakespeare himself, perhaps—who,
having been given the power to see the "truth," can convey
it only through poetry—what we commonly call a "fiction,"
and dismiss.

In all these matters, let me add in parenthesis, we would
do well to extend more generously our inferences about
Shakespeare to the Jacobean playwrights as a group. Some
of us have been overlong content with a view of Jacobean
tragedy as naïve as those formerly entertained of Restoration comedy, eighteenth-century literature, and modern
poetry. But a whole generation of writers does not become
obsessed by the sexual feuding of cavalier and citizen, or
rhetorical "rules" and social norms, or abrupt images and

catapulting rhythms, or outrageous stories of incest, madness, brutality, and lust, because the poetic imagination has suddenly gone "frivolous," or "cold," or "eccentric," or "corrupt." Such concerns respond to spiritual needs, however dimly apprehended, and one of the prime needs of Jacobean writers, as the intelligible and on the whole friendly universe of the Middle Ages failed around them, was quite evidently to face up to what men are or may be when stripped to their naked humanity and mortality, and torn loose from accustomed moorings. Flamineo's phrase in *The White Devil*—"this busy trade of life"—offered as a passing summary of the play's monstrous burden of blood and madness:

> This busy trade of life appears most vain,
> Since rest breeds rest, where all seek pain by pain—

is characteristically understated and ironic, like Iago's "Pleasure and action make the hours seem short." The creators of Iago and Flamineo, and all the responsible writers of Jacobean tragedy along with them, knew perfectly well that it was not in fact the "trade," or habitude, of life to which they held up art's mirror, but life "on the stretch," nature at its farthest reach of possibility. They were fascinated by violence because they were fascinated by the potencies of the human will: its weaknesses, triumphs, delusions, corruptions, its capacities for destruction and regeneration, its residual dignity when, all else removed, man stood at his being's limit; and because they knew that in violence lay the will's supreme test, for aggressor and sufferer alike.

Whatever the themes of individual plays, therefore, the one pervasive Jacobean theme tends to be the undertaking and working out of acts of will, and especially (in that strongly Calvinistic age) of acts of self-will. This is surely the reason why, in Clifford Leech's happy phrase, these writers know so little of heaven, so much of hell; and why, to one conversant with their work so many products of the century to come seem like fulfillments of ancient prophecy: Milton's Satan and his "God"—the philosophy embodied in *Leviathan*—even, perhaps, the clash of the Civil Wars and the cleavage in the English spirit reaching from Cavalier and Puritan to Jacobite and Whig and well beyond. At the very beginning of the century, these writers had got hold of the theme that was to exercise it in all departments, political, economic, religious, cultural, till past its close, the problem of anarchic will; and so decisive, so many-sided is their treatment of this problem that even in Milton's massive recapitulation of it in *Paradise Lost* the issue seems sometimes to be losing in vitality what it has gained in clarity, to be fossilizing and becoming formula. The utterances of *his* white devil have more resonance but less complexity and immediacy of feeling than those of Vittoria Corombona, Bosola, Macbeth, or Beatrice Vermandero; and some of them bear a perilous resemblance to the posturings of Restoration heroic tragedy, where the old agonies are heard from still, but now clogged, and put through paces like captive giants in a raree show.

However this may be, I return at the end to the proposition I set out with: there is a lot about the construction of a Shakespearean tragic "action" that we still do not know. My own attempts to get towards it in this chapter are fumbling and may be preposterous: even to myself they sound a little like Bottom's dream. But the interesting thing about Bottom's dream, from my point of view, is that, though he found he was an ass all right, the Titania he tried to tell about was real.

Robert B. Heilman

Wit and Witchcraft:

An Approach to *Othello*

The critic who proposes a reading of *Othello* may hope for
it that it will appear at least to illuminate some of the parts
and at most to contribute to the understanding of the sum of
the parts. If *Othello* is not the most complex of the tragedies,
the problem of its over-all form is still a large one, and he
who aspires to a full account of the creative relationship of
all the parts [1] must be content if he seems generally to be
moving in the right direction. The theory of the whole that
proceeds from an examination of the parts will at best be
a distant cousin of the drama; such wit as the critic may
have can but follow the witchcraft of the dramatist (to take
Iago's words out of context) from afar. But the cousin may
help identify the drama, the wit tell how the witchcraft has
gone. At the same time the critic, whatever he imparts,
must at many points duplicate and parallel his predecessors while essaying to be himself; so he runs the double
risk of not encompassing the novelty which will absolve

From *The Sewanee Review*, Vol. 64, No. 1, Winter 1956, copyright
© 1956 by The University of the South, pp. 1–4, 8–10, and *Arizona
Quarterly*, Spring 1956, pp. 5–16. Reprinted by permission of the
author and the editors, with new transitional material supplied by the
author in *Shakespeare*, ed. Leonard F. Dean. New York: Oxford University Press, Inc., 1957. Copyright © 1957 by Oxford University Press,
Inc. The ideas in this essay are among those developed by Mr. Heilman
in *Magic in the Web: Action and Language in* Othello, copyright 1956
by the University of Kentucky Press. Used with permission.

him of the suspicion of merely repeating what oft was thought, or of falling into innovations which in other quarters will seem dubious because such things were never thought.

The parts which make up the whole are numerous and diverse. Othello is a part. Iago is a part. Iago's deception of Roderigo is a part. Iago's remarks on reputation, Desdemona's incredulity at the sexual misbehavior of wives, Emilia's revulsion against Iago, Cassio's drunken babbling are parts. All recognitions and reversals, all thoughts and feelings of characters are parts. The nighttime in which most of the major actions occur is a part. Iago's use of *honesty* is a part. All the uses of *honesty* are a part. All the metaphors of medicine and disease, the images from army life, the language of light and dark are parts.

The point is to keep the idea of the part flexible and inclusive, as a step toward adequate freedom in the description of structure. A view of the parts begotten of a preoccupation with gross anatomy will yield a coarse and constricted account of structure. On the other hand, compiling an unlimited serial list of parts would be futile. The main thing is to be aware of a part in all its relational possibilities.[2] Othello's farewell to arms (III.iii.346 ff.) is relevant to the specific situation of the moment, to Othello's personality generally, to Shakespeare's conception of the modes of response to disaster possible to human beings. Emilia's picking up the handkerchief helps advance the action by contributing to Iago's deception of Othello, but it is also relevant to her character and to Shakespeare's conception of the modes of wifely devotion and marital relationship (not to mention its relations by contrast with actions of Desdemona and Bianca and of Emilia herself later). The theories of sex which Iago advances to Roderigo are relevant to his purpose of controlling Roderigo, to his modes of thought generally, and to Shakespeare's awareness of the whole realm of philosophies of love.

For working criticism, the broad categories of the parts whose relatedness is to be observed are two: plot and poetry. We might again borrow Iago's words for metaphor and speak of the wit and witchcraft of the dramatist: the

conscious designing and articulating; and the mysterious
endowing of many parts—especially the poetic language—
with dramatic value and meaning far in excess of the
minimal logical requirements of the occasion: the magic in
the web. This is less a theory of composition than an effort
to suggest different aspects of the play that are only theo-
retically separable. Let us put it another way. If love is
what *Othello* is "about," *Othello* is not only a play about
love but a poem about love.[8] It has parts which interact in
the mode of "pure" drama—people having such and such
an effect on each other, irrespective of whether they com-
municate in verse, prose or pantomime; it also has parts
which interact in the manner of a poem. Again, this is a
theoretical separation: the characters have such and such
an effect by means of the words they speak; and conversely,
an analysis of the words they speak involves the student
regularly in a consideration of the "action" and inter-
action of the speakers. Yet when the dramatist has his
characters speak in poetic language, he vastly complicates
their communication with each other and with us. Figure,
rhythm, poetic order do not merely make "more vivid" or
"heighten" a literal prose statement that is otherwise un-
changed; they constitute a fundamentally different statement by the introduction of the nuance, overtone, feeling,
association, implication, and extension characteristic of
them; in other words, by subtly carrying us beyond the
finiteness, one-dimensionalism, and contextual restrictions
of the pure statement determined only by the strict logical
requirements of the immediate situation. When Othello
summons Desdemona and dismisses Emilia, "Leave procreants alone . . . ;/Cough or cry hem if anybody come./
Your mystery, your mystery! . . ." (IV.ii.28–30), he not
only dismisses Emilia, accuses Desdemona of infidelity,
and betrays his own insane bitterness, but he converts the
marriage into a brothel arrangement in which all three are
involved, and by so doing establishes imaginative lines of
connection with the role of Bianca and particularly with
the Iago philosophy of sexual conduct. If we take all the
lines of one character out of context and consider them as
a unit, we have always a useful body of information; but if,

when we study Iago's lines, we find that he consistently
describes himself in images of hunting and trapping, we
learn not only his plans of action but something of his
attitude to occasions, to his victims, and to himself; and
beyond that there is fixed for us an image of evil—one of
those by which the drama interprets the human situation.
When Othello says he threw away a "pearl," we recall that
Brabantio, in acceding to Desdemona's departure, called
her "jewel"; when Desdemona says she would rather have
lost her purse than the handkerchief, we recall that Iago,
who has stolen the handkerchief, has spoken of stealing a
purse; we spontaneously make these connections, and,
even if we go no further, our reading has brought forth
linkings that cannot be expunged; but we often do go
further, and seek out the formal order that is exemplified
in these images that leap out of their own contexts and
carry our imaginations into other parts of the play.[4] When
to these we add many other instances in which poetic language, functioning doubly or triply, takes us beyond
specific moments of action into others and on into general
areas of character, feeling, and thought, we find that we
have an immensely complicated verbal structure with which
we must come to terms—the "poem about love," as I have
called it. We are trying to describe what Traversi called
"a new kind of dramatic unity." [5]

In pursuit of this dramatic unity we must inevitably take
account of one notable characteristic of Shakespeare's verbal drama—its repetitiveness of images and likewise of abstract words. After Emilia has three times incredulously
asked, "My husband?" Othello demands, "What needs this
iterance, woman?" (V.ii.147). We all must play Othello to
Shakespeare's Emilia: "iterance" forces itself upon us as
a critical problem. The dramatist cannot conspicuously
repeat words and rely upon figures of the same class (e.g.,
clothes, military life) without catching our eye and raising
a question about what goes on. We are hardly likely to
attribute this recurrence to the artist's carelessness or
failing resourcefulness or to stop at description—an inert
lexicon of repetitions. When editors devotedly multiply
cross references to dictional or rhetorical echoes and antici-

pations, they act, one assumes, more from a sense of relationship than from a delight in coincidence. Speaking of *Antony and Cleopatra,* Professor Clemen uses a phrase that is valid for other plays: "this symbolical meaning of certain sequences of imagery." [6] As Paul Goodman puts it, Shakespeare's "profusion of images is so handled through a long play that it forms a systematic structure and is part of the plot." He elaborates on

> a method that is characteristically Shakespearean: this is to present a line of thought by an independent development of the system of imagery. Put formally: when several characters independently and throughout the play employ the same system of images, the diction becomes an independent part of the plot implying a thought, action, etc., whatever is the principle of the system. For it is not in character for different characters to use the same images. [7]

I suspect that it *may* be "in character for different characters to use the same images," which can be a device for suggesting similarities or even contrasts among them; or if the images belong dominantly to one character in one part of the play, and to another in another part, the change may be an important mark of dramatic progression, as when the almost pre-emptive use of animal imagery passes in mid-play from Iago to Othello. But beyond all its possible uses in characterization, recurrent diction has still other functions. Goodman's phrase "independent development" is the key. For though speeches are in one sense not separable from the characters, in another sense they do become disengaged from particular speakers and enter the general verbal fund of the play. (The more rich and profuse the language, the more this is likely to be true, just as the more rich and powerful the literary work, the more likely it is to become disengaged from its own times, however much these times may be needed for exegetic purposes, and to enter the general timeless fund of literary possessions.) Reiterative language is particularly prone to acquire a continuity of its own and to become "an independent part of the plot" [8] whose effect we can attempt to gauge. It may create "mood" or "atmosphere": the pervasiveness of images of injury, pain, and torture in *Othello* has a very strong impact that is not wholly determined by who uses the images. But most of all the "system of imagery" introduces thoughts, ideas, themes—elements of the meaning that is the author's final organization of all his materials.[9]

II

Before coming directly to the forming of the love-theme that differentiates *Othello* from other Shakespeare plays that utilize the same theme, I turn arbitrarily to Iago to inspect a distinguishing mark of his of which the relevance to thematic form in the play will appear a little later. When Iago with unperceived scoffing reminds Roderigo, who is drawn with merciless attraction to the unreachable Desdemona, that love effects an unwonted nobility in men, he states a doctrine which he "knows" is true but in which he may not "believe." Ennoblement by love is a real possibility in men, but Iago has to view it with bitterness and to try to undermine it. With his spontaneous antipathy to spiritual achievement, he must in principle deny the mysterious transformation of personality; instinctively he is the observer of all these habits that suggest infinite corruptibility as the comprehensive human truth. He is the believer in shrewd observation and in corruption in whose credo, which is not altogether unique, man is a union of lusting, folly, and plotting.

Good sense, hard sense, common sense, no nonsense, rationality—all these terms, we may suppose, are ones which Iago might consider as defining his perspective. As he plays against Othello with his game of honest and loving friend, he uses words that put him on that side of the fence. First he can't tell Othello his "thoughts" (about

Cassio) because of his "manhood, honesty," or *"wisdom"* [10] (III.iii.153–54); a little later he finds *"reason"* to tell them (193). Othello considers him *"wise"* (IV.i.76). While privately Iago may deny his love and kid his honesty, he takes his brains seriously. "Thus do I ever make my *fool* my purse," he boasts; to spend time with Roderigo otherwise, "Mine own gain'd *knowledge* should profane" (I.iii.374–75). Othello is to be treated like an *ass* (I.iii. 393; II.i.309). Iago applies the term *fool* successively to Roderigo (II.iii.48), Cassio (II.iii.353), Desdemona (IV.i.178), and Emilia (IV.ii.147), and condescends to fools "credulous" and "gross" (IV.i.47; III.iii.401). His view of himself as the clearheaded manipulator of gulls is significantly unchallenged despite the barrage of derogatory rhetoric eventually aimed at him. He remains the "smart man," apt in "deals," scornful of "suckers."

It is more fun for the smart man if his victim thinks he is using *his* head with especial acuteness. Early in the big deception scene (III.iii.93 ff.) on which all the subsequent action turns, Iago urges Othello "that your *wisdom* yet" should "take no notice" of Iago's "unsure observance" (148–51); later he repeats, "Nay, but be *wise*" (429). The idea that he is being sharp goes to Othello's head; he resolves to be *"cunning* in my patience" (IV.i.92), and he queries erring Desdemona, "Are you *wise?"* (IV.i.234). With his new wisdom he murders his unwise wife, and Emilia tells him what he has become: *"O gull! O dolt!/* As *ignorant* as dirt! . . . O thou *dull* Moor, . . . what should such a *fool/* Do with so good a wife?" (V.ii.160–231). How does Iago try to stop this confessional outburst which will ruin him? By commanding Emilia, "Be *wise,* and get you home" (220). Here he cannot induce that wisdom that serves his own end; the sharp-eyed engineer of folly in others now by necessity collapses into senseless abuse and violence. But Othello's reproach to himself, "O fool! fool! fool!" (319), inadequate a self-judgment as it is, acknowledges Emilia's indictment and, inadvertently, the success of Iago's plot to make him "egregiously an ass." After all this, Othello's "lov'd not wisely" is unconsciously an understatement.

Making a fool of someone else is an aesthetic demonstration of intellectual superiority. It is implicitly partial, temporary; a comic episode after which life goes on. Let this exploit in self-aggrandizement expand with the full pressure of passion, and the attack becomes an ultimate one against sanity: Iago's design to put Othello "into a jealousy so strong/That judgment cannot cure," driving him "even to madness" (II.i.301–02, 311). It is the extreme revenge possible to the man of "reason," a chaos that logically extends and completes the other modes of chaos which Iago instinctively seeks, in a variety of ways, at all stages of the action. Twice again he speaks of Othello's madness as a likelihood or as a formal objective (IV.i.56, 102), and his program works well enough to make Lodovico inquire about Othello's mental soundness (IV.i.269) and to make Othello express a doubt about his own sanity (V.ii.110). Madness spreads: Emilia fears lest Desdemona "run mad" (III.iii.315), Othello cries to her that he is "glad to see you mad" (IV.i.239), and she in turn fears his "fury" (IV.ii.32). But the planned madness eventually recoils upon its creator: "What, are you mad?" is Iago's response when Emilia tells the truth about what he has done (V.ii.191).

Such points in the auxiliary theme of madness (a slender anticipation of what will be done in *Lear*) mark the course of rational Iago. Insofar as he identifies rationality and wisdom with his own purposes, he is close enough to Everyman; but he is sharply individualized, and at the same time made the representative of a recognizable human class, when the drama reveals that his purposes require the irrationalizing of life for everyone else. Of the insights that create Iago, none is deeper than the recognition that a cool rationality may itself bring about or serve the irrational. Though Brabantio, awakened by the nocturnal outcries in front of his house, thinks that Iago has "lost" his "wits" and that Roderigo comes "in madness" (I.i.89,95), their universal technique of matching half-truths to latent fears makes him give up his sane conclusions and accept their distorted history of what has happened to Desdemona, so much so that he then attributes "a judgment maim'd and most imperfect" (I.iii.99), i.e., failure of mind, to anyone who takes a different view of the situation. Here Iago simply has to make Brabantio as irrational as possible; shortly he has to curb Roderigo's irrationality, or rather, to convert it from a less to a more serviceable form, from suicidal despair to the sexual pursuit of Desdemona. Now for the first step in this conversation Iago utilizes the traditional argument of the "authority of . . . our wills" and of "one scale of reason to poise another of sensuality"; "But we have reason to cool our raging motions, our carnal stings, our unbitted lusts; . . ." (I.iii.321–26). If in one sense this is the devil talking Scripture, in another it is Iago paying tribute to a faculty that he values deeply. He is the self-conscious possessor of assures him that his cause "hath . . . reason" (362–63) and critical utility of this passage is that it points to the distinction between the ostensible and the real functions that Iago assigns to reason. In no way does he press Roderigo really to apply reason to his emotional ailment, to diagnose it and moderate and perhaps cure it; on the contrary he assures him that his cause "hath . . . reason" (362–63) and encourages him to found his hopes on Desdemona's sharing in a universal unregeneracy which Iago quite evidently believes is subject to rational control by no one. But more than that we see that Iago has not the slightest thought of using reason to "cool" his own "raging motions," "carnal stings," and "unbitted lusts": reason is rather the agent of his unbitted lusts and of the raging motions of his hate. It is in their behalf that he reasons with Roderigo; his reason is instrumental, serving his own unreason by playing upon Roderigo's. When he mentions the rumor that his wife Emilia has been unfaithful with Othello, he hurries on to say, "I know not if't be true" (379); rather he intends to act on "mere suspicion," just to make sure. His mind is used not to determine the truth but to convert into action a feeling not founded in truth. This is a basic Shakespearean definition of evil: the sharp mind in the service of uncriticized passion. And the final irony, as Shakespeare sees it, is that the owner of the sharp mind is eventually destroyed by the passion his mind serves.

We see the innermost mechanism of this rational instrument when the Iago-Roderigo relationship comes to its last phase. Like several of the major characters, Roderigo is able at times to assess his own headwork: once he almost resolves to give up the lecherous pursuit of Desdemona and to return to Venice with "a little more wit" (II.iii.368); he is angrily aware that he has "foolishly suffer'd" and he suspects that he is "fopp'd" (IV.ii.178, 193). Iago retorts by praising Roderigo for both his brains (". . . your suspicion is not without *wit* and *judgment*") and his moral quality (210–214). The recurrent irony for Roderigo is that he cannot rely on his own good sense but falls back instead on Iago's version of what is good sense for him. Here comes the payoff. When once again Iago asserts that there is a way of sleeping with Desdemona, Roderigo's reply is, "Well, what it is? Is it within *reason* and compass?" (218–19). Is it "reasonably practical"? No other question, no other issue of sanction or value. How many philosophic frills are being got rid of, and how far down to positive bedrock this is getting, appears when Iago reveals the program: kill Cassio. Roderigo is still shockable. Iago soothes him, "Come, stand not amaz'd . . ." (239), and offers a cure for "amazement": "I will show you such a necessity in his death that you shall think yourself bound to put it on him" (240–41). To this promise of logical demonstration Roderigo responds in the same key: "I will hear further *reason* for this" (244). Iago makes good his promise, "And you shall be satisfied" (245), for when Roderigo is finally lying in wait to kill Cassio, he sums up the rationale of the project:

> I have no great devotion to the deed,
> And yet he hath given me satisfying *reasons*.
> 'Tis but a man gone.   (V.i.8–10)

Despite his moral hesitancy, Roderigo has found "satisfying reasons" for committing murder and thinking it a way to Desdemona's bed. In this climax of persuasion to evil, Iago's "reason" mediates between his own uncontrollable irrational drives and those of Roderigo. The rational serving one irrationality and appearing to serve another while playing selfishly upon it: this sums up, and sums up archetypally, the fundamental operating methods of the Iago way of life.

" 'Tis but a man gone" is pure Iago thought. It does away with every value or imperative or speculation that "man" or the death of man traditionally evokes, and it makes "a man" simply a neutral instance of a category, a statistical item, an object that can be acted on without moral responsibility. The philosophy " 'Tis but a man gone" (of which there are contemporary manifestations in whole political systems, in demagogic practices of our own, in some methods of business and advertising and even abstract thought, in propaganda) is consistent with Iago's reductive contention, which he develops at length, that love is no more than unstable sexual appetite; his declaration that "there is more sense" in a "bodily wound" than in "reputation," which he says is a chimera; his skepticism about "honor," which he implies is unreal because unseen; and even, in a slightly different way, with his contempt for Cassio's theoretical knowledge, "Mere prattle, without practice" (I.i.23). Theory of any kind may open the door to values that transcend the immediately utilitarian. "Iago's is a pragmatic world, and his imagery finds its authority in social usage," as Arthur Sewell has said. Iago says tacitly, "Let's get down to facts," that is, the tangible and the visible. (Seen from a slightly different perspective, he has affiliations with the antimetaphysical thinker, the extremist in semantics, the constitutional debunker.)

III

Reason as an ally of evil is a subject to which Shakespeare keeps returning, as if fascinated, but in different thematic forms as he explores different counter-forces. In *Macbeth* the rational effort to minimize the killings done for ambition's sake runs finally into the force of conscience. In *Lear*, rationalized self-seeking is counterbal anced by all the fidelities implied in *pietas*. And in *Othello*? Although Iago, as we saw, does not take seriously the ennobling power of love, he does not fail to let us know what he does take seriously. When, in his fake oath of loyalty to "wrong'd Othello," he vows "The execution of his wit, hands, heart" (III.iii.463), Iago's words give a clue to his truth: his heart is his malice, his hands literally wound Cassio and kill Roderigo, and his wit is the genius that creates all the strategy. How it enters into the dialectic of structure, or the thematic form, is made clear in one of Iago's promises to Roderigo that he shall have Desdemona: "if sanctimony and a frail vow betwixt an erring barbarian and a supersubtle Venetian be not too hard for my wits and all the tribe of hell, thou shalt enjoy her" (I.iii.350–354). "Tribe of hell" is somewhat rhetorical; the real antagonist is "my wits"—set against the rival power of love, which he cannot tolerate. But even beyond Iago's own conscious battle, his brains against a vow of love, there is a symbolic conflict in the heart of the drama. And for this symbolic conflict Iago, again assuaging the pain of Roderigo, gives us a name by the words he chooses:

> Thou know'st we work by wit, and not by witchcraft;
> And wit depends on dilatory time.   (II.iii.372–73)

Wit and *witchcraft:* in this antithesis is the symbolic structure, or the thematic form, of *Othello*. By *witchcraft,* of course, Iago means conjuring and spells to induce desired actions and states of being. But as a whole the play dramatically develops another meaning of *witchcraft* and forces upon us an awareness of that meaning: *witchcraft* is a metaphor for love. The "magic in the web" of the handkerchief, as Othello calls it (III.iv.69), extends into the fiber of the whole drama. Love is a magic bringer of harmony between those who are widely different (Othello and Desdemona), and it can be a magic transformer of personality; its ultimate power is fittingly marked by the miracle of Desdemona's voice speaking from beyond life, pronouncing forgiveness to the Othello who has murdered her (V.ii.123–4). Such events lie outside the realm of "wit"

—of the reason, cunning, and wisdom on which Iago rests—and this wit must be hostile to them. Wit must always strive to conquer witchcraft, and there is an obvious sense in which it should conquer; but there is another sense in which, though it try, it should not and cannot succeed; that, we may say, is what *Othello* is "about." Whatever disasters it causes, wit fails in the end: it cuts itself off in a demonic silence before death (Iago's "last words" are "I will never speak word"—(V.ii.300), while witchcraft—love—speaks after death (Desdemona's last farewell).

Between the poles of wit and witchcraft, all the major characters in the play find their orientation. Emilia looks at a good deal of life through the Iago wit, but yields to the love for Desdemona which transforms her into a sacrificial figure. Under the influence of the Iago wit, Cassio, acting through Desdemona's friendly love, tries to high-pressure Othello into a charity (a revocation of his dismissal) that could come only spontaneously. Roderigo falls under the witchcraft of love, but, instead of letting it take effect as it might, to bring him death or renunciation, chooses Iago's wit game and plays for what he cannot have. Emilia and Desdemona, dying, are not creatures of wit: what we have called witchcraft has led them to a trans-rational achievement of spirit.

The conflict of Desdemona and Iago for Othello can be called the conflict of love and hate, or the conflict of two different potentialities in the soul where both reside. It may also be called the conflict of wit and witchcraft for Othello. Though Othello seems to be all the naïveté of Everyman, and Iago to be all his calculatingness and slyness, Othello gives himself more to wit than to witchcraft because he and Iago, though in different degrees, have much in common—a histrionic bent, an inadequate selfhood that crops up in self-pity and an eye for slights and injuries, an uncriticized instinct to soothe one's own feelings by punishing others (with an air of moral propriety), the need to possess in one's own terms or destroy, an incapacity for love that is the other side of self-love. All this is in another realm from that of witchcraft. When Othello decides to follow Iago and be "wise" and "cunning," he adopts a new code: he will "see" the facts, get the "evidence," "prove" his case against Desdemona, and execute "justice" upon her. This is the program of "wit." Now this is not only utterly inappropriate to the occasion on which, under Iago's tutelage, Othello elects to use it, nor is it simply one of several possible errors; rather he adopts an attitude or belief or style which is the direct antithesis of another mode of thought and feeling which is open to him. He makes that particular wrong choice which is the logical opposite of the right choice open to him. He essays to reason when reason is not relevant: he substitutes a disastrous wit for a saving witchcraft. He could reject Iago's "proof" against Desdemona "by an affirmation of faith," as Winifred Nowottny has put it, "which is beyond reason, by the act of choosing to believe in Desdemona." Othello, the prime beneficiary of witchcraft, might win all its gifts had he the faith that would open him to its action; but he is short on faith, is seduced by wit (the two actions are simply two faces of the same experience), and ruined. He knew the first miracle of love, the thing given without claim, but cut himself off from the greater miracle, the transformation of self into a giver. His final failure is that, though he comes to recognize that he has been witless, he is never capacious enough in spirit to know how fully he has failed or how much he has thrown away. He never sees the full Desdemona witchcraft.

In the light of Desdemona's spiritual wealth—the unfailing love that continues into forgiveness of her murderer—we can understand Iago as a spiritual have-not. Like the have-not in the realm of things who in a materially oriented culture suffers from envy and malice, the spiritual have-not lives in characteristic vices that Shakespeare has analyzed with many-angled perception. The analogy between the material and the spiritual have-not is confirmed by a line in *Lear*, Edmund's "Let me . . . have lands by wit," and by Iago's own addiction to actual theft (of Roderigo's gifts meant for Desdemona). If the analogy fails at one point—that the achievement of spiritual wealth depends on the individual and cannot be essentially helped by external accidents or blocked by external obstacles—that failure only underscores the failure of the spiritual have-not. His modes of action are exhaustively canvassed in Shakespeare's plot and in the poetry of the play. Wit is Iago's instrument to compensate for what he does not have. He perversely hates and yet lusts after what he does not have (Desdemona as a person, and as a symbol of love), and he undertakes to disparage it, minimize it, debunk it, and destroy it. Rule-or-ruin becomes rule-by-ruining. He must fashion the world after his own image: "And knowing what I am, I know what she shall be" (IV.i.75). So it pleases him to trap (he repeatedly uses the language of hunting and trapping) those who are unlike himself, by proclaiming virtues which he does not possess ("honest Iago," the friend of all), confusing the appearance of things seeming to act in one way (as light-bringer and physician during the two nocturnal brawls which he stirs up) while acting in another (making things "dark," wounding and killing). Noisiness and vulgarity of style become him, though as a skilled actor he can simulate the amiable, contained, and discreet adviser and consoler. His most far-reaching method is to seduce others philosophically—to woo them from assumptions in which their salvation might lie (faith in the spiritual quality of others), to baser assumptions that will destroy them (their freedom to act in the light of the accepted unregeneracy of all about them). Iago the moral agent is akin to Iago the philosopher: there is a common element in stealing purses, stealing good names, and stealing ideas needed for survival.

In sociological terms we might allegorize Iago as the criminal type, in political as the self-seeking divisive force or the patrioteer or the power-seeker who will pay any price, in cultural as the mass-mind, in psychological as all the impulses that lead to despair of human possibility, in moral as envy or hate or spiritual hardness (versions of pride), in mythical as The Enemy—the universal destroyer of ultimate values. Before all these, he is simply a human being, the apparent friend and lover of everybody. We think of these diverse tentative formulations only because he is so variously and richly set before us as the final outcome when certain potentialities of Everyman are freed to develop fully. There is no single way into this extraordinary characterization. As the spiritual have-not, Iago is universal, that is, many things at once, and of many times at once. He is our contemporary, and the special instances of his temper and style—as distinct from the Iagoism to which all men are liable—will be clear to whoever is alert to Shakespeare's abundant formulations. Seen in a limited and stereotyped form, he is the villain of all melodrama. He is Elizabethan—as Envy or Machiavel. And to go further back still, we see in how many parts of Dante's *Inferno* he might appear. He could be placed among the angry and violent. But his truer place is down among those who act in fraud and malice—the lowest category of sinner who on earth had least of spiritual substance and relied most on wit. Here we might put him on a higher level with the panders, but again it is when we reach the lower level that he is summoned more strongly, not once but by group after group: the hypocrites, the thieves, the evil counselors, the sowers of dissension, and, at the very bottom of the eighth circle, the impersonators and false witnesses. Finally, in the ninth and last circle, "damn'd beneath all depth in hell," come the treacherous. And here at last we go beyond time into our timeless myths of evil.

By an extraordinary composition of character Shakespeare has made Iago, literally or symbolically, share in all these modes of evil. And in Iago he has dramatized Dante's summary analysis: "For where the instrument of the mind is joined to evil will and potency, men can make no defense against it." But he has also dramatized the hidden springs of evil action, the urgency and passion and immediacy of it. He contemplates, too, the evildoer's "potency" and man's defenselessness: but these he interprets tragically by making them, not absolute, but partly dependent on the flaws or desire of the victims themselves. In the *Othello* world, Iago, seductive as he is, is not an inevitable teacher. Whoever would, could learn from Desdemona. He would have the choice of wit or witchcraft.

NOTES

1. One who is committed to a detailed study of the parts might seize protectively on Edward A. Armstrong's observation, "There is a strange psychological bias which tempts those interested in large issues to belittle detailed work," in *Shakespeare's Imagination* (London, 1946), p. 125n. Cf. G. Wilson Knight's preface to the 4th edition of *The Wheel of Fire* (London: Methuen, 1949), pp. vi–vii. In *Flaming Minister* (Durham: Duke University Press, 1953), G. R. Elliott makes a detailed commentary on individual passages and on their relationships.
2. Cf. L. C. Knights, *Explorations* (New York: Stewart, 1947), p. 31.
3. Cf. E. E. Stoll's phrase, "a tragedy which is also a poem, in which the parts 'mutually support and explain each other' . . ." This is in *Shakespeare and Other Masters* (Cambridge: Harvard University Press, 1940), p. 219. In *Poetry and Drama* (Cambridge: Harvard University Press, 1951), p. 43, T. S. Eliot speaks of the "perfection of verse drama, which would be a design of human action and of words, such as to present at once the two aspects of dramatic and musical order."
4. For numerous examples of images which link separated passages, see W. H. Clemen, *The Development of Shakespeare's Imagery* (Cambridge: Harvard University Press, 1951). Clemen makes a telling comment on the general sense of the interrelatedness of all parts which is created by the imagery (p. 224).
5. D. A. Traversi, *Approach to Shakespeare* (London, 1938), p. 14; and see his whole first chapter. Of *Othello* he says, "Plot and imagery, in fact, are fused as never before" (p. 86). Cf. his "Othello," *The Wind and the Rain,* vi (1950), 268–9. On the importance of the language spoken, the "wording," there are some relevant comments

by E. E. Stoll in *Poets and Playwrights* (Minneapolis: University of Minnesota Press, 1930), pp. 5 ff., 128.

6. Page 162.

7. *The Structure of Literature* (Chicago: University of Chicago Press, 1954), pp. 17, 64.

8. One might speak of an image-system as an inner organism—a part of the whole that could not exist without the whole and yet an entity having parts that function with respect to each other. This would be "a verbal drama" as distinct from "verbal drama" generally. As a created thing it does not "just happen"; nor yet, I believe, is it deliberately blueprinted and executed. One may surmise: a certain image or kind of image "comes up" for a speaker on a certain occasion; then it is felt consciously or semiconsciously to have some relevance to the import of the whole; and it continues to be used (with the varying degrees of consciousness presumably characteristic of the creative process) as a way of exploring character or mood or theme.

9. Cf. Price, *Construction in Shakespeare* (Michigan, 1951), pp. 24 and 35 ff., and George Rylands, "Shakespeare's Poetic Energy," *Proceedings of the British Academy*, xxxvii (1951), 99–119. Note his statement that the "repetition of a word in diverse contexts throughout the play, with its correlatives and associations, often gives the clue to the poetic thought, the *dianoia*, which informs the whole" (p. 102).

10. All italics are my own.

Suggested References

The number of possible references is vast and grows alarmingly. (The *Shakespeare Quarterly* devotes a substantial part of one issue each year to a list of the previous year's work, and *Shakespeare Survey*—an annual publication—includes a substantial review of recent scholarship, as well as an occasional essay surveying a few decades of scholarship on a chosen topic.) Russell Fraser, the editor of the Signet Classic *King Lear,* offers this warning: "These comments may be ventured, regarding the titles listed here, and the critical selections above. First, no work of criticism, however excellent in itself, is to be taken as rivaling in importance, much less as supplanting, the thing it criticizes. The play's the thing! and not the commentaries thereon. Second, any work of criticism, and particularly to the degree that it is excellent, ought to be scrutinized with a cold eye whenever it pretends to the making of a definitive judgment. In the interpretation of Shakespeare, no comment is sacrosanct or final. Let the reader beware, therefore; and let him also take heart. 'Judgment, like other faculties, is improved by practice, and its advancement hindered by submission to dictatorial decisions, as the memory grows torpid by the use of a table book.' Thus Dr. Johnson."

1. SHAKESPEARE'S TIMES

Byrne, M. St. Clare. *Elizabethan Life in Town and Country*. Rev. ed. New York: Barnes & Noble, Inc., 1961. Chapters on manners, beliefs, education, etc., with illustrations.

Craig, Hardin. *The Enchanted Glass: The Elizabethan Mind in Literature*. New York and London: Oxford University Press, 1936. The Elizabethan intellectual climate.

Nicoll, Allardyce (ed.). *The Elizabethans*. London: Cambridge University Press, 1957. An anthology of Elizabethan writings, especially valuable for its illustrations from paintings, title pages, etc.

Shakespeare's England. Oxford: Clarendon Press, 1916. 2 vols. A large collection of scholarly essays on a wide variety of topics (e.g., astrology, costume, gardening, horsemanship), with special attention to Shakespeare's references to these topics.

Tillyard, E. M. W. *The Elizabethan World Picture*. London: Chatto & Windus, Ltd., 1943; New York: The Macmillan Company, 1944. A brief account of some Elizabethan ideas of the universe.

Wilson, John Dover (ed.). *Life in Shakespeare's England*. 2nd ed. New York: The Macmillan Company, 1913. An anthology of Elizabethan writings on the countryside, superstition, education, the court, etc.

2. SHAKESPEARE

Bentley, Gerald E. *Shakespeare: A Biographical Handbook*. New Haven, Conn.: Yale University Press, 1961. The facts about Shakespeare, with virtually no conjecture intermingled.

Bradby, Anne (ed.). *Shakespeare Criticism, 1919–1935*. London: Oxford University Press, 1936. A small anthology of excellent essays on the plays.

Bush, Geoffrey Douglas. *Shakespeare and the Natural Condition*. Cambridge, Mass.: Harvard University Press, 1956; London: Oxford University Press, 1956. A short, sensitive account of Shakespeare's view of "Nature," touching most of the works.

Chambers, E. K. *William Shakespeare: A Study of Facts and Problems*. London: Oxford University Press, 1930. 2 vols. An invaluable, detailed reference work; not for the casual reader.

Chute, Marchette. *Shakespeare of London*. New York: E. P. Dutton & Co., Inc., 1949. A readable biography fused with portraits of Stratford and London life.

Clemen, Wolfgang H. *The Development of Shakespeare's Imagery*. Cambridge, Mass.: Harvard University Press, 1951. (Originally published in German, 1936.) A temperate account of a subject often abused.

Craig, Hardin. *An Interpretation of Shakespeare*. New York: Citadel Press, 1948. A scholar's book designed for the layman. Comments on all the works.

Dean, Leonard F. (ed.). *Shakespeare: Modern Essays in Criticism*. New York: Oxford University Press, 1957. Mostly mid-twentieth-century critical studies, covering Shakespeare's artistry.

Granville-Barker, Harley. *Prefaces to Shakespeare*. Princeton, N.J.: Princeton University Press, 1946–47. 2 vols. Essays on ten plays by a scholarly man of the theater.

Harbage, Alfred. *As They Liked It*. New York: The Macmillan Company, 1947. A sensitive, long essay on Shakespeare, morality, and the audience's expectations.

Smith, D. Nichol (ed.). *Shakespeare Criticism*. New York: Oxford University Press, 1916. A selection of criticism from 1623 to 1840, ranging from Ben Jonson to Thomas Carlyle.

Spencer, Theodore. *Shakespeare and the Nature of Man*. New York: The Macmillan Company, 1942. Shakespeare's plays in relation to Elizabethan thought.

Stoll, Elmer Edgar. *Shakespeare and Other Masters*. Cambridge, Mass.: Harvard University Press, 1940; London: Oxford University Press, 1940. Essays on tragedy, comedy, and aspects of dramaturgy, with special reference to some of Shakespeare's plays.

Traversi, Derek A. *An Approach to Shakespeare*. Rev. ed. New York: Doubleday & Co., Inc., 1956. An analysis of the plays, beginning with words, images, and themes, rather than with characters.

Van Doren, Mark. *Shakespeare*. New York: Henry Holt & Company, Inc., 1939. Brief, perceptive readings of all of the plays.

Whitaker, Virgil K. *Shakespeare's Use of Learning*. San Marino, Calif.: Huntington Library, 1953. A study of the relation of Shakespeare's reading to his development as a dramatist.

3. SHAKESPEARE'S THEATER

Adams, John Cranford. *The Globe Playhouse*. Rev. ed. New York: Barnes & Noble, Inc., 1961. A detailed conjecture about the physical characteristics of the theater Shakespeare often wrote for.

Beckerman, Bernard. *Shakespeare at the Globe, 1599–1609*. New York: The Macmillan Company, 1962. On the playhouse and on Elizabethan dramaturgy, acting, and staging.

Chambers, E. K. *The Elizabethan Stage*. New York: Oxford University Press, 1923. 4 vols. Reprinted with corrections, 1945. An indispensable reference work on theaters, theatrical companies, and staging at court.

Harbage, Alfred. *Shakespeare's Audience*. New York: Columbia University Press, 1941; London: Oxford University Press, 1941. A study of the size and nature of the theatrical public.

Hodges, C. Walter. *The Globe Restored*. London: Ernest Benn, Ltd., 1953; New York: Coward-McCann, Inc., 1954. A well-illustrated and readable attempt to reconstruct the Globe Theatre.

Nagler, A. M. *Shakespeare's Stage*. Tr. by Ralph Manheim. New Haven, Conn.: Yale University Press, 1958. An excellent brief introduction to the physical aspect of the playhouse.

Smith, Irwin. *Shakespeare's Globe Playhouse*. New York: Charles Scribner's Sons, 1957. Chiefly indebted to J. C. Adams' controversial book, with additional material and scale drawings for model-builders.

Venezky, Alice S. *Pageantry on the Shakespearean Stage*. New York: Twayne Publishers, Inc., 1951. An examination of spectacle in Elizabethan drama.

4. MISCELLANEOUS REFERENCE WORKS

Abbot, E. A. *A Shakespearean Grammar*. New edition. New York: The Macmillan Company, 1877. An examination of differences between Elizabethan and modern grammar.

Bartlett, John. *A New and Complete Concordance . . . to . . . Shakespeare*. New York: The Macmillan Company, 1894. An index to most of Shakespeare's words.

Bullough, Geoffrey. *Narrative and Dramatic Sources of Shakespeare*. New York: Columbia University Press, 1957–; London: Routledge & Kegan Paul, Ltd., 1957–. 4 vols. Vols. 5 and 6 in preparation. A collection of many of the books Shakespeare drew upon.

Greg, W. W. *The Shakespeare First Folio*. New York and London: Oxford University Press, 1955. A detailed yet readable history of the first collection (1623) of Shakespeare's plays.

Kökeritz, Helge. *Shakespeare's Names*. New Haven, Conn.: Yale University Press, 1959; London: Oxford University Press, 1960. A guide to the pronunciation of some 1,800 names appearing in Shakespeare.

————. *Shakespeare's Pronunciation*. New Haven, Conn.: Yale University Press, 1953; London: Oxford University Press, 1953. Contains much information about puns and rhymes.

Linthicum, Marie C. *Costume in the Drama of Shakespeare and His Contemporaries*. New York and London: Oxford University Press, 1936. On the fabrics and dress of the age, and references to them in the plays.

Muir, Kenneth. *Shakespeare's Sources*. London: Methuen & Co., Ltd., 1957. Vol. 2 in preparation. The first volume, on the comedies and tragedies, attempts to ascertain what books were Shakespeare's sources, and what use he made of them.

Onions, C. T. *A Shakespeare Glossary*. London: Oxford University Press, 1911; 2nd ed., rev., with enlarged addenda, 1953. Definitions of words (or senses of words) now obsolete.

Partridge, Eric. *Shakespeare's Bawdy*. Rev. ed. New York: E. P. Dutton & Co., Inc., 1955; London: Routledge & Kegan Paul, Ltd., 1955. A glossary of bawdy words and phrases.

Shakespeare Quarterly. See headnote to Suggested References.

Shakespeare Survey. See headnote to Suggested References.

5. OTHELLO

Bayley, John. *The Characters of Love*. New York: Basic Books, Inc.; London: Constable & Co., Ltd., 1961.

Bradley, A. C. *Shakespearean Tragedy*. London: Macmillan & Co., Ltd., 1904.

Clemen, Wolfgang H. *The Development of Shakespeare's Imagery*. Cambridge, Mass.: Harvard University Press, 1951. Originally published in German, 1936.

Eliot, T. S. "Shakespeare and the Stoicism of Seneca," *Selected Essays, 1917–1932*. New York: Harcourt, Brace & Company, Inc.; London: Faber & Faber, Ltd., 1932.

Elliott, G. R. *Flaming Minister: A Study of* Othello *as Tragedy of Love and Hate*. Durham, N. C.: Duke University Press; London: Cambridge University Press, 1953.

Granville-Barker, Harley. "Preface to *Othello*," *Prefaces to Shakespeare*. Vol. II. Princeton, N.J.: Princeton University Press, 1946–47. 2 vols.

Heilman, Robert B. *Magic in the Web, Action & Language in* Othello, Lexington, Ky.: University of Kentucky Press, 1956.

Kirschbaum, Leo. "The Modern *Othello*," *English Literary History, II* (1944), 283–96.

Knight, G. Wilson. "The *Othello* Music," *The Wheel of Fire*. 5th rev. ed. New York: Meridian Books, Inc., 1957, pp. 97–119.

Lawlor, John. *The Tragic Sense in Shakespeare*. New York: Harcourt, Brace & Company, Inc.; London: Chatto & Windus, Ltd., 1960, pp. 87–106.

Nowottny, Winifred M. T. "Justice and Love in *Othello*," *University of Toronto Quarterly, XXI* (1951–52), 330–44.

Rosenberg, Marvin. *The Masks of* Othello. Berkeley, Calif.: University of California Press, 1961.

Sedgewick, G. G. *Of Irony, Especially in Drama*. 2nd ed. Toronto: University of Toronto Press, 1948; London: Oxford University Press, 1949.

Sewell, William Arthur. *Character and Society in Shakespeare*. London and New York: Oxford University Press, 1951, 1952, pp. 91–121.

Stoll, E. E. "*Othello*, Tragedy of Effect," *From Shakespeare to Joyce*. New York: Doubleday & Company, Inc., 1944.

Seltzer, Daniel. "Elizabethan Acting in *Othello*," *Shakespeare Quarterly, X* (1959), 201–10.

Traversi, Derek. *An Approach to Shakespeare*. 2nd ed. New York: Doubleday & Co., Inc., 1956, pp. 128–49.

Wilson, Harold S. *On the Design of Shakespearian Tragedy*. Toronto: University of Toronto Press; London: Oxford University Press, 1957, pp. 52–67.

The SIGNET CLASSIC SHAKESPEARE

Superlatively edited paperbound volumes of the complete works of Shakespeare are now being added to the Signet Classic list. Under the general editorship of Sylvan Barnet, Chairman of the English Department of Tufts University, each volume features a general Introduction by Dr. Barnet; special Introduction and Notes by an eminent Shakespearean scholar; critical commentary from past and contemporary authorities, and when possible, the original source material, in its entirety or in excerpt, on which Shakespeare based his work. The first volumes, priced at 50¢ each, include:

MENTOR Books of Plays

EDITED BY SYLVAN BARNET,
MORTON BERMAN AND WILLIAM BURTO

Eight Great Tragedies
 The great dramatic literature of the ages, eight
 memorable tragedies by Aeschylus, Euripides, Soph-
 ocles, Shakespeare, Ibsen, Strindberg, Yeats, and
 O'Neill. With essays on tragedy by Aristotle, Emer-
 son and others.   (#MQ461—95¢)

Eight Great Comedies
 Complete text of eight masterpieces of comic drama
 by Aristophanes, Machiavelli, Shakespeare, Molière,
 John Gay, Wilde, and Chekhov. Includes essays on
 comedy by four distinguished critics and scholars.
                                          (#MQ343—95¢)

The Genius of the Early English Theater
 Complete plays including three anonymous plays—
 "Abraham and Isaac," "The Second Shepherd's
 Play," and "Everyman," and Marlowe's "Doctor
 Faustus," Shakespeare's "Macbeth," Jonson's "Vol-
 pone," and Milton's "Samson Agonistes," with cri-
 tical essays.   (#MQ438—95¢)

The Genius of the Later English Theater
 Complete plays, including Congreve's "The Way of
 the World," Goldsmith's "She Stoops to Conquer,"
 Byron's "Manfred," Wilde's "Importance of Being
 Earnest," Shaw's "Major Barbara," and Golding's
 "The Brass Butterfly." With critical essays.
                                          (#MQ448—95¢)

The Genius of the Irish Theater
 Complete texts of seven plays by Synge, Yeats,
 O'Connor, O'Casey, and others, and essays on the
 Irish dramatic renaissance.   (#MT315—75¢)